Charting Churches in a Changing Europe

CURRENTS OF ENCOUNTER

STUDIES ON THE CONTACT BETWEEN CHRISTIANITY AND OTHER RELIGIONS, BELIEFS, AND CULTURES

GENERAL EDITORS

JERALD D. GORT
HENRY JANSEN
LOURENS MINNEMA
HENDRIK M. VROOM
ANTON WESSELS

VOL. 28

Charting Churches in a Changing Europe

Charta Oecumenica and the Process of Ecumenical Encounter

Edited by
Tim and Ivana Noble
Martien E. Brinkman
Jochen Hilberath

Amsterdam - New York, NY 2006

BX
8.3
.C43
2006
c.2

Front cover:
"Saints Three Hierarchs" Monatery, Iasi, Romania.
Back cover:
Detail of Brancoveanu Monastery, Transylvania, Romania.
Both illustrations taken from "Monateries of Romania",
by prof.dr. Mircea Pacurariu.

Cover design: Pier Post

The paper on which this book is printed meets the requirements of
"ISO 9706:1994, Information and documentation - Paper for
documents - Requirements for permanence".

ISBN-10: 90-420-2009-1
ISBN-13: 978-90-420-2009-2
©Editions Rodopi B.V., Amsterdam - New York, NY 2006
Printed in the Netherlands

Table of Contents

General Introduction
En Route to *Koinonia*: Church Communion in Transition
MARTIEN E. BRINKMAN 1

Part I: Confessional Responses to the *Charta Oecumenica*

Introduction 7

The Significance of the *Charta Oecumenica* Today:
Critical Comments from a Protestant Perspective
KAJSA AHLSTRAND 9

An Assessment of the *Charta Oecumenica*
from a Roman Catholic Perspective
PETER DE MEY 17

Church Communion and the Reception of Ecumenical
Dialogues: An Orthodox Perspective
DORIN OANCEA 43

Enough is Enough? Preconditions for Church Communion
from a Lutheran Perspective
OLIVER SCHUEGRAF 63

Part II: Notions of Catholicity and Communion

Introduction 83

The Modern Inculturation Debate
and the Catholicity of the Church
MARTIEN E. BRINKMAN 85

The Catholicity of the Church:
A Matrix of Faith and Life in View of God's Final Kingdom
ANTON HOUTEPEN 95

Uniting Europe as a Challenge
to the Future of National Churches
EDDY VAN DER BORGHT 105

Gradual Church Communion as an Ecumenical Model?
Some Remarks from a Roman Catholic Perspective
JOHANNES OELDEMANN 127

Part III: The Sacramental Road to Unity

Introduction 143

The Roman Catholic Understanding of Sacramentality
and Its Potential for Church Unity
MARIA CLARA LUCCHETTI BINGEMER 145

From the Sacramentality of the Church
to the Sacramentality of the World
IVANA NOBLE 165

Epilogue
BERND JOCHEN HILBERATH 201

Appendix:
Text of *Charta Oecumenica* 205

Index 217

Contributors 221

General Introduction

En Route to *Koinonia*:
Church Communion in Transition

Martien E. Brinkman

This volume is dedicated to the theme of the 13th Academic Consultation of the European Society of Ecumenists (*Societas Oecumenica*) in Sibiu, the former Hermannstadt, in the region of Transylvania in Romania. *Societas Oecumenica* decided to relate its theme – On the Way to Koinonia: Church Communion in Transition – closely to one of the best current examples of cooperation between the churches of Western and Eastern Europe, namely the so-called *Charta Oecumenica*.[1] This charter was issued by the Conference of European Churches (CEC) and the Council of European Bishops' Conferences in 2001. It is an ecumenical consensus text of the main European Protestant, Orthodox and Roman Catholic Churches. It deals not only with the ecumenical relations among the churches but also with our common responsibility for the continent where we live: Europe. The text is printed as an appendix at the end of this volume.

The consultation was held from 24-28 August 2004 in an area with a long history of Lutheran-Orthodox relations. Apart from an Orthodox theology faculty, Sibiu also hosts a Lutheran Theological Seminary. So Sibiu itself is already a place of encounter.

The theme of the consultation emerges from that of *Societas Oecumenica*'s previous consultation in Salisbury, UK in 2002 on "Conversion and Identity in a Multicultural Europe." That opened up a whole raft of questions concerning who we are as Christians and what our roles are in the present social, cultural

---

[1] See for the text and the history of this document V. Ionita and S. Numico (eds), *Charta Oecumenica: A Text, a Process and a Dream of the Churches in Europe* (Geneva, 2003) and the appendix to this volume.

and political situation of a united/disunited Europe. Europe is uniting and yet struggling through various political and economic tensions, carrying wounds and divisions from the past, and searching with greater or lesser commitment to find some reconciliation, some vision shared by her fragmented identities. As Christians, we are part of this process and we have to examine our contribution, its possibilities and shortcomings. The changing situation of European society is also a challenge for churches to reconsider their divisions.

In this reflection the *Charta Oecumenica* could be of great help. It can be considered as a serious effort by the European churches to make fruitful use of the ecclesiological and societal insights of the different church traditions in Europe. The reflection upon the *Charta Oecumenica* and the regional bilateral dialogues will be embedded into theological reflections upon the question of what it is to be church in Europe and upon the question of which church concept could be of greatest help to us in our contemporary European plight.

So, the main text of reference is the *Charta Oecumenica*. The Charta forms part of a process which has moved forward since the first European Ecumenical Assembly at Basel (Switzerland) in 1989.[2] The preparations for the second European Ecumenical Assembly at Graz (Austria) in 1997 showed that the fall of the Iron Curtain in 1989 had made ecumenical relations more difficult rather than less.[3] The decision of the Conference of European Churches and the European Roman Catholic Bishops' Conference to draw up the *Charta Oecumenica* finds its origin in these apparent tensions.

In this regard it is highly significant that the *Charta* states that there is "no alternative to dialogue" (no. 6). Remarkable, also, is the link with the idea of baptism as a "bond of unity between Christians, as Vatican II had stated in the Decree on Ecumenism (No. 22) and the so-called *Lima Text* of the World

---

[2] Cf. *Final Document of the European Ecumenical Assembly Peace with Justice, 15-21 May 1989, Basel (Switzerland)* (Geneva, 1989).

[3] Cf. J. Kaufmann and M. Opis (eds.), *Reconciliation, Gift of God and Source of New Life: Second European Ecumenical Assembly 23-29 June 1997 Graz/Austria* (Graz, 1997).

Council of Churches repeated in its paragraphs on baptism.[4] Like the *Joint Declaration* between Lutherans and Roman Catholics on justification, the *Charta* distinguishes between main issues, basic truths and differing explications in particular statements. It thus clings to the concept of reconciled diversity. In its focus on the promotion of democratic processes, human rights, social justice, equal rights for women, concern for the environment and plea for hospitality towards foreigners and refugees the *Charta Oecumenica* integrates the typical church and society concerns into the classic Faith and Order concerns on the sacraments and the unity of the church. It would be easy to add many other interesting points regarding the *Charta Oecumenica*, but let us not anticipate the further discussion in this volume.

I would like to mention only one further hot issue with which the *Charta Oecumenica* deals, especially in no. 2,[5] namely, that of proselytism. In several Eastern or Southern European countries, such as Russia, Romania, Bulgaria and Greece, one church – the Orthodox Church – is the established church. This contextual situation has coloured the way many Orthodox theologians are inclined to speak about proselytism, sects and religious freedom, religious rights, etc. This situation will confront us in an intense and concrete way with the tension between identity and plurality. In a certain sense, this discussion will also confront us with the question of the relation of faith and ethnicity. Not only with regard to doctrinal questions but also with regard to social and political questions we shall experience that we have to cling to the idea of reconciled diversity.

Let me conclude these introductory remarks with a short anecdote. I began my academic career in the department of theology at the Vrije Universiteit (Amsterdam) in 1976 with research into the dogmatic aspects of the question of pluriformity

---

[4] Cf. *Baptism, Eucharist and Ministry*, Faith and Order Paper 111, (Geneva 1982), p. 3 (B.6). See for the full text of the Decree on Ecumenism of Vatican II www.vatican.va/archive/hist-councils/ etc.

[5] Cf. also the report "The Challenge of Proselytism and the Calling to Common Witness," issued as an appendix in: *Joint Working Group between the Roman Catholic Church and the World Council of Churches. Seventh Report* (Geneva 1998), pp. 43-52.

in the church. The question of the boundaries of pluriformity was central to that research. The heart of the matter was how much diversity the unity of the church could bear.[6] In 2003, however, I attended a conference in Bogor, Indonesia, on Faith and Ethnicity, sponsored by the International Reformed Theological Institute (IRTI), headquartered at the VU, and once again found myself impressed by the principles on which the independence of the state of Indonesia was declared in 1945. These were the five principles of what is termed *Pancasila* (divine omnipotence, humanity, national unity, democracy and social justice). With the aid of these five principles people in Indonesia have indeed made a serious attempt to give form to the motto of that new state, *Bhineka Tunggal Ika* (Diverse Yet One). Thus the central question in the founding of the state of Indonesia was not how much diversity unity can bear but how much diversity is necessary in order to be able to guarantee unity.[7]

These are two totally different approaches. The first, Reformed question is defensive and assumes that there is an existing unity that is threatened. This means that criteria must be developed for "legitimate variety." The image of a previously given unity still strongly defines the way Christians deal with their history. The schism between East and West in 1054 and the Reformation are seen as cracks in a previously unbroken unity. But such an image is an illusion. A high degree of diversity is already apparent in various contexts in the New Testament and this diversity has been with Christianity ever since.[8]

---

[6] Cf. M.E. Brinkman, "Kuyper's Concept of Pluriformity of the Church," in: C. van der Kooi and J. de Bruijn (eds.), *Kuyper Reconsidered: Aspects of His Life and Work*, Studies on Protestant History, Vol. III, (Amsterdam, 1999), pp. 111-22.

[7] At the IRTI conference in Princeton, NJ, USA, in 2001 J.A. Tituley presented a very extensive but extremely instructive exposition on the vicissitudes of the concept of *Pancasila* in the history of Indonesia under the title "The *Pancasila* of Indonesia: A Lost Ideal?" See E.A.J.G. van der Borght, D. van Keulen and M.E. Brinkman (eds.), *Faith and Ethnicity*, Vol. 1, Studies in Reformed Theology 6 (Zoetermeer, 2002), pp. 37-102.

[8] Cf. J.D.G. Dunn, *Jesus Remembered*, Christianity in the Making, Vol.1 (Grand Rapids/Cambridge, 2003).

This diversity is also necessary for a religion that claims universality. If every people are to confess Christ as their Lord, saviour, prophet, *Tuhan*, chief, ancestor, *bodhisattva* or *avatar*, then a far-reaching form of inculturation is necessary. Therefore, it is more sensible and inviting for contemporary Christianity to assume the motto of the Indonesian state, diverse yet one, than to be asking the question that once motivated our pluriformity project: "How much diversity can unity bear?"

However, one question remains: Who defends this unity in the midst of all the diversity? In Indonesia that is the job of the army. And in world Christianity? In part, it is the international ecumenical movement. There, all the remotest corners of Christianity remain in conversation with one another and a certain cross-fertilisation takes place. To some extent, it is also the task of academic theology, the international character of which is increasingly taking on institutional form. It was also the task, especially during this conference, of the *Societas Oecumenica* as well, I am inclined to add. That this volume may be a contribution to that task is my deepest desire at this moment.

Part I

Confessional Responses to the *Charta Oecumenica*

In this section four authors respond to the *Charta Oecumenica* from different confessional positions. Kajsa Ahlstrand, from the Church of Sweden, addresses the practical implications of the *Charta* from a Protestant perspective, even if she questions the applicability of the umbrella term "Protestant." Although she deems the document to have received a basically positive response from the Nordic Lutheran churches, she wonders if they may not bring a more individual-oriented response than other Christian traditions. To illustrate her point, she offers two not uncommon pastoral situations, where the demands of the *Charta* would seem to come into conflict with what could be considered to be good pastoral practice. She concludes with a reflection on the Church of Sweden's position on same-sex partnerships and the conflict this can lead to with other European churches. Is the *Charta* helpful in this situation or not?

Peter De Mey, a Roman Catholic theologian working in Louvain, Belgium, uses as his hermeneutical key for reading the document the question as to whether it helps or hinders further dialogue among churches on the nature of the church and church order. He begins by examining the process of revision of the *Charta* and how the final version was influenced by the input of different churches and Bishops' Conferences from around Europe. He divides these reactions into common Orthodox, Roman Catholic and Protestant ones, joint Roman Catholic and Protestant comments, and finally those points raised by each of the three groupings separately. The second part of his essay looks in more detail at Part II of the *Charta* to see in how far it allows for a discussion on the church. A joint proclamation of the Gospel should lead to churches' moving together and acting together, which is also to lead to their praying together. This section concludes with a discussion of further possibilities of dialogue emerging from the *Charta*. A key question in De Mey's work is whether the *Charta* did not miss a key opportunity to endorse the hermeneutical concept of differentiated consensus.

The third essay, by Romanian Orthodox theologian Dorin Oancea, considers the question from an Orthodox perspective. He concentrates on the issue of reception, starting with a look at the notion of reception in the Old Testament. Taking the notion of reception as including some form of confession of faith, he moves on to look at the way the Holy Tradition deals with the matter. There it is not simply a question of accepting verbal formulae but of accepting participation in the community which makes those confessions. Thirdly, Oancea considers reception in the Holy Liturgy. He starts by reflecting on the dynamic nature of the Orthodox liturgy, where all has its place. Within this dynamic comes the Liturgy of the Catechumens and the Liturgy of the Faithful. The distinction between these two parts of the liturgy lead him to spell out the reasons for this and the consequences for ecumenical dialogue. He concludes with some questions, asking whether the Orthodox need always to retain a maximalist position.

The final article in this series of confessional responses to the *Charta* is offered by the German theologian Oliver Schuegraf, resident in Coventry, England. He writes from a Lutheran perspective. Using recent documents from the United Evangelical Lutheran Churches of Germany, he considers the Lutheran understanding of ecumenism. In dialogue with the understanding of church communion as developed by the Leuenberg Church Fellowship he moves on to look at the dialogues into which Lutherans have entered with various other Christian churches and the successes and problems with these conversations. This is followed by a reflection on the meaning of church communion from a Lutheran perspective, based on unity in Word and Sacrament.

The Significance of the *Charta Oecumenica* Today

Critical Comments from a Protestant Perspective

Kajsa Ahlstrand

As a preamble, one may ask what a Protestant perspective is. Is there such a thing as *a* Protestant perspective? Indeed, what is Protestantism? The Porvoo communion churches are hesitant to label themselves "Protestant" and prefer designations such as "Evangelical Catholic" or the more neutral "Reformation churches." Given those provisos, I will nevertheless use the word "Protestant."

I will limit myself to some of the comments from the Nordic Lutheran churches. The main part of my essay will focus on some pastoral situations where the *Charta* is insufficient as a practical tool. I will finish with a look towards the future, considering an ecumenically bold step that the Church of Sweden is about to take and how that might relate to the *Charta*.

Responses from the Nordic Lutheran Churches

With a few exceptions the Protestant churches received the *Charta* with gratitude. A typical reaction is that made by a German Protestant church: "This is what we have already been doing for a long time." The *Charta* confirmed a practice that in many places was well established. This, however, gives rise to a different set of questions. If the *Charta* does not challenge the church, is there something in it that we have failed to see? To be blunt, the major churches of the Reformation have not as a rule been heavily involved in evangelising campaigns, aiming at stealing members from other churches, nor have they tried to prevent their members from leaving the church in order to join another Christian community. Our sins have been of a different kind; where we have been in the majority we have not always been sensitive to the needs and existence of minority churches. Historically, the situation has been very different, of course, but I take it that the *Charta* deals with current practice and experiences, not those of bygone eras.

The Nordic Lutheran churches, with the exception of the Danish church, did not find anything with which they could actually disagree. Certainly, there could have been stronger emphasis on certain issues (e.g., women, poverty, mission, or the world beyond the borders of Europe), but these are minor squabbles. The church representatives know that there is nothing in the *Charta* to prevent them from engaging in these aspects of the Christian life. The Nordic Lutheran churches have problems with the rhetoric of the *Charta*, which is perceived as being too pompous for the rather down-to-earth linguistic styles in the Nordic countries. The kind of rhetoric employed in the *Charta* makes it virtually impossible to use *verbatim* translations and thus the Nordic churches have produced their own short "guidelines for inter-church relations" regarding, for example, evangelising campaigns, "conversions" and contacts between churches.

The *Charta* has very rarely been referred to in Swedish ecumenical discussions, with one exception. The exception cannot even be labelled "ecumenical," as it took place within the Church of Sweden. A group of clerics who never accepted the decision to ordain women to the priesthood requested the synod to be treated as a minority in accordance with II.4 of the *Charta*: "We commit ourselves to defend the rights of minorities and to help reduce misunderstandings and prejudices between majority and minority churches in our countries." Their argument is as follows. If the Church of Sweden (henceforth CoSw) has agreed to defend minority churches, then minority groups within the church should also be protected under the same *Charta*. The counter-argument is twofold:

a) There is and should be a difference in attitude of the CoSw towards groups within the CoSw and those within other churches. The CoSw must defend the rights of Baptists within Swedish society, but that does not mean that pastors in the CoSw have the right to refuse to baptise infants as pastors in the CoSw.

b) Not all minorities are worthy of protection. A few people (that is, a minority) within the CoSw believe that God has so ordered the world that white people should rule over people with darker pigmentation. The mere fact that those who believe thus are few in number does not imply that they merit protection as a minority within the church.

In the Danish church the discussions have been livelier than in the other Nordic Lutheran churches. The Evangelical Lutheran Church in Denmark has chosen to remain sceptical in regard to several recent ecumenical inventions: the Porvoo agreement, the *Joint Declaration* and *Charta Oecumenica*. The main reason for this scepticism on the part of several bishops and church leaders can be summed up in the remarks of the chairman of the Council on International Relations of the Evangelical Lutheran Church in Denmark, Paul Verner Skærved:

> It is not in keeping with the tradition of the Danish Church, which separates religion and politics, and if the idea is to mix these two things, I cannot imagine a formulation I will vote for. But we must discuss it with the other churches and, perhaps, we can reply with some sensible comments. (*Kristeligt Dagblad*)

A representative of the Evangelical Lutheran Church in Denmark on the common working committee, the Revd. Steffen Ravn Jørgensen, declared that he "could not vote for a joint church document that mixes the spiritual and the secular fields and is, therefore, in its theology un-Lutheran." (He has since become Dean of Elsinore and resigned his seat on the Danish Ecumenical Council.) Some pastors have also questioned the relevance of the *Charta* for the Danish context.

The reaction, when I discussed the *Charta* with my colleagues in the Swedish Christian Council and the National Office of the Church of Sweden, was very much that there is not much to say because we wholeheartedly agree with it. And thus I could end here, but I will not. The problems I see "from a Protestant perspective" have less to do with what is stated in the *Charta* than with what is implied. And the most problematic implication is that interchurch relations may be seen as more important than respect for persons who approach a particular church with expectations that have not been foreseen by the ecclesiastical authorities.

The *Charta* deals with churches and structures, but in the life of the churches we encounter individuals. And, I think, this is where the Protestant ethos (if there actually is such a thing) may differ from Catholic and Orthodox central values.

I will give two examples from a pastoral context to show how difficult it can be when ecumenical agreements clash with people's lives as they live them.

Eucharistic Hospitality

Is there an obligation for some churches to enlighten members of other churches of the position of their respective churches or should every church have the right to speak for itself? A fairly common invitation to the Eucharist in Lutheran (and Anglican) churches is to say that everyone who is baptised is invited to receive communion. This invitation is sometimes followed by an explanation, such as "If you do not want to receive the elements, you can still proceed to the communion station, put your right hand on your left shoulder and receive a blessing." But not every Orthodox or Roman Catholic visitor to a Lutheran or Anglican service is aware of the position of his or her church. Should the inviting church take this into consideration and put the invitation thus: "This Church practices 'Eucharistic hospitality' and in as far as it is up to us, you are welcome to receive the sacrament. But if you are Orthodox or Roman Catholic you should know that your church does not allow their members to receive the sacrament in other churches and you might be excommunicated by your church if you do receive communion here." Of course, it could be put in ecumenically more acceptable wording ("we differ in our understandings of whether Eucharistic unity presupposes theological unity etc."), but the message will still be the same. Is the church that practices "hospitality" or an "open communion table" obliged to discourage communicants from more restrictive churches from receiving communion in order to maintain good relations with those other churches? Or is it more important that we treat every person who comes to church with respect for his or her own decisions?

Baptism across Ecclesiastical Borders

A somewhat similar situation arises when a family comes to the local Lutheran church seeking to have their child baptised. The family is living in Sweden for a limited period: they are citizens of an African country and intend to go back in a few years time. When asked about their church affiliation, they state that they are Roman Catholics. The pastor offers to help them to get in contact with the nearest Catholic church, but the parents decline. They say that they prefer to worship in their local church (which is Lutheran) and ask whether baptism in the Lutheran church would be recognised in the Catholic church. The pastor replies, "Yes, the baptism would be recognised, but isn't it a better idea to have your child baptised in the church to which you will return?" But the family insists that they want their child to be baptised in the church where they are currently part of the worshipping congregation. The ecumenical recommendations are clear – not to interfere with members of another church without consulting the relevant clergy – but what if the members know what they want? Are they not people who have come of age and can be trusted to make their own choices?

Different Understandings of Marriage and Family

The third example relates to same-sex relations, one of the most debated questions within and between the churches at this time. In the ecumenical world the CoSw is reputed to be one of the most inclusive/ liberal/radical churches in regard to this issue. In 1951 the bishops of the Church of Sweden issued a pastoral letter "On a question of the life of the people" in which they advocated vigilance in regard to homosexual people and expressed their hope that science would find a cure for what they regarded as an aberration in the human psyche.

In the autumn of 2004 the Synod of the Church of Sweden was to discuss the consequences of gender-neutral marriage legislation and a liturgy for the celebration of same-sex weddings. It is fair to say that the CoSw has not had any heated debate about the ordination of lesbian and gay persons who live in committed relationships. In the early 1980s the late Bishop of Stockholm, Lars Carlzon, stated, "Many of my best priests are homosexuals." At that time there were a few bishops that would not have ordained someone who lived in a same-sex relationship; the policy then was very much that of "don't ask, don't tell." Today no bishop would reject an ordinand on the basis of his or her living in a same-sex relationship (although, of course, not every person who lives in a same-sex relationship is suitable for the priesthood). A radical reorientation in these matters has thus taken place during the last fifty years.

There is a strong likelihood that the CoSw will soon adopt a liturgy for same-sex weddings to be included in our common Handbook. There is now a majority in the Swedish parliament in favour of gender-neutral marriage legislation. The developments within the CoSw will undoubtedly have ecumenical consequences. The CoSw has invited theologians and church leaders from other Christian traditions to a Hearing in order to "dialogue and discuss the issues together in the light of the Gospel" (*Charta* II.6). But whatever the outcome of these dialogues and discussions will be, the synodal and episcopal leadership of the CoSw are not going to abandon the lesbian and gay members of the CoSw for the sake of Christian unity.

As we (here I speak as a member of the CoSw) understand the Gospel, it is about God's unconditional love for every person and God's desire for every person to live in life-sustaining relationships. The consequence of this is that the majority in the CoSw see the increased acceptance of same-sex relationships as a way in which the Spirit is leading the church to a deeper understanding of God's abundant love. In order to proclaim the Gospel in our society and for the Gospel to be heard as good, liberating and life-sustaining news, we cannot but include committed same-sex relationships into our understanding of family. Thus, when we "insist on the reverence for life, the value of marriage and the family ..." (*Charta* 7) we do this wholeheartedly, but we do not want to limit the definition of marriage and family to heterosexual couples only.

Can the *Charta Oecumenica* be used against the CoSw in this matter? We feel that we cannot wait for the other churches to follow, because that would be to betray our understanding of the Gospel. Same-sex relationships are not "an issue" but lived experiences – not only of those who are directly involved but also of their parents, children, grandparents, friends and siblings.

There is no way that the churches can reach consensus or even an acceptable compromise here. This leads me to my concluding remarks. What would a critical Protestant perspective on the *Charta* be? There is general agreement in the major churches of the Reformation that the *Charta* is a fine and at times a useful tool for ecumenical relations and common responsibility in society, but it has its limits. There is always the provision that people matter more than church structures and even ecumenical relations. As Protestants, we cannot look to the hierarchy and expect them to define the truth and we cannot go to the sacred tradition and expect truth to be hidden there waiting to be found. We search the Scriptures, but it is not the written word that is the Word of God. It is when the Word is communicated and heard as a liberating and life-sustaining message in the lives of people and communities that it becomes the Gospel.

An Assessment of the *Charta Oecumenica* from a Roman Catholic Perspective

Peter De Mey

The process of reception of the *Charta Oecumenica* has already been going on for more than three years.[1] After a first gathering of ecumenical experts and young Christians in Strasbourg, on the occasion of the solemn proclamation of the *Charta*, the CEC-CCEE Joint Committee took the initiative of organising two more consultations in which representatives of all participating churches testified to the reception of the *Charta* in their countries. The publication, *Charta Oecumenica: A Text, a Process, and a Dream of the Churches in Europe*, has also contributed to the further dissemination of the message of the *Charta*.[2] In what follows, therefore, I presume that the history and the text of the *Charta* is already well known,[3] so in the first section of this

---

[1] An enumeration of several initiatives taken to promote the reception of the document is found in Sarah Numico, "Die Charta Oecumenica und die aktuelle ökumenische Situation," *Una Sancta* 58 (2003): 111-17.

[2] Viorel Ionita abd Sarah Numico (eds.), *Charta Oecumenica: A Text, a Process, and a Dream of the Churches in Europe* (Geneva, 2003). The English translation of the document is found on pp. 7-16. For a discussion on the reception of the *Charta* see the article by Sarah Numico, "Testimonies and Experiences from the Life of the Charta Oecumenica," in Ionita and Numico, *Charta Oecumenica*, pp 71-82.

[3] I will regularly refer both to the English translation of the draft version of the document (indicated by D, followed by the paragraph number) and to the English translation of the final version of the *Charta* with an indication of the paragraph number. The original German text and its translations have been co-edited by the secretariat of the CEC in Geneva and the secretariat of the CCEE in St. Gallen. A good overview of the document is given by Gerhard Voss, "Kommentierende Anmerkungen zur Charta Oecumenica der Kirchen in Europa," *Una Sancta* 56 (2001): 186-207. Reinhard Frieling, who was a

article I will restrict myself to a description of the dialogue process which culminated in the approval of the *Charta*.

I am aware, of course, that the ecumenical dialogue at a multilateral level is anything but an easy enterprise. In the 1998 draft of the Faith and Order document on *The Nature and Purpose of the Church* the material in the boxes appeared to be far more extensive than the body of the text, which reflects the common understanding on the nature and mission of the church.[4] We must wait and see whether the situation will be much different in the second version of this document, which will hopefully be presented during the WCC assembly in Porto Alegre in 2006. The endeavour to formulate guidelines for cooperation among the churches in Europe has not been an easy one either. I had the opportunity to consult the reactions by the episcopal conferences and member churches of the CEC on the draft which was made public in July 1999, as well as the subsequent drafts of the document during a study visit at the secretariat of the Council of European Bishops' Conferences.[5]

Therefore, in the second part of my presentation I will give an overview of the most important changes to the draft version as they were provoked by the reactions submitted by member churches of the CEC and episcopal conferences. In fact, in view of the difficulties and objections it seems almost a miracle that we have at our disposal an ecumenical charter on which the members of the CEC-CCEE Joint Committee could reach a con-

---

member of the drafting committee of the document, discusses the relevance of the document in the light of the current ecumenical situation in Europe in his article "The Ecumenical Movement in Europe: Challenges and Conflicts," *Concilium* (2004): 57-66.

[4] *The Nature and Purpose of the Church: A Stage on the Way towards a Common Statement*, Faith and Order Paper 181 (Geneva: 1998). A critical account of this document from a Roman Catholic perspective is given by Catherine Clifford, "Reflections on *The Nature and Purpose of the Church*," in *Ecumenical Trends* 32 (2003): 129-37 and Francis Sullivan, "*The Nature and Purpose of the Church*: Comments on the Material inside the Boxes," *Ecumenical Trends* 32 (2003): 145-53.

[5] My sincere thanks go to the Secretary General of the CCEE, Don Aldo Giordani and his cooperator, Sarah Numico, for their hospitality and help.

sensus during their meeting in Porto in January 2001. Both the drafting committee and the CEC-CCEE Joint Committee were involved in the final revision of the draft of the *Charta Oecumenica* and deserve our sincere thanks. I am of the opinion, however, that the input by the churches and episcopal conferences has been extremely helpful for the creation of a broad consensus on the *Charta Oecumenica*. Therefore, I wonder whether the outcome would not have been different if the revised text had been entrusted another time to the judgment of interested Christians in Europe before its final promulgation.

It was the intention of the churches that took the initiative for this document so that it would contain, as the subtitle puts it, "Guidelines for the Growing Cooperation among the Churches in Europe." Therefore, the preamble explicitly states that the document "has no magisterial or dogmatic character, nor is it legally binding under church law." However, I cannot help being a theologian who is particularly interested in the ecumenical dialogue on ecclesiological issues, be it at bilateral or multilateral levels. Thus, even if it is not the intention of the *Charta* to give an account of a doctrinal consensus between the churches in Europe, the question which guided my reading of it was whether it can be considered as a help or as an obstacle to further dialogue on the nature of the church and on issues of church order. In order to answer this question I will, therefore, in the final part of this contribution, focus especially on part II of the *Charta*: "On the Way towards the Visible Fellowship of the Churches in Europe."

An Overview of the Dialogue Process

The most striking feature of the collaboration between the CEC and the CCEE is the organisation of European ecumenical assemblies. The theme of the first assembly after the end of the Cold War, which took place in 1989 in Basel, was: "Peace and Justice for the Integrity of Creation." The theme of the second assembly, which took place in 1997 in Graz, was: "Reconciliation: Gift of God and Source of New Life."[6] At the end of this

---

[6] Council of European Bishops' Conferences (CCEE) and the Con-

assembly, a final communication and a reflection text were accepted, as well as recommendations for action.

In the second recommendation, under the heading "Looking for Visible Unity among the Churches," the churches were invited to prepare a joint document that would describe the basic ecumenical rights and duties of Christians in Europe. According to the Graz document, this would help Christians "to distinguish between proselytism and Christian witness, between fundamentalism and true faith, and to foster a better relationship between majority and minority churches."

During its annual meeting of 1998 the *Joint Committee* of CCEE-CEC established a working group of eight members, four from each institution, including their general secretaries,[7] which was given the task of drafting a text of about three pages. This text would not have any dogmatic or canonical pretensions, but, on the basis of the Holy Scriptures and the confessions of the various churches, it would consider the ecumenical tasks in Europe. Thus, the *Charta Oecumenica* has realised an important goal of the European Ecumenical Assembly in Graz. Moreover, it is obvious that the final documents of this assembly have inspired the *Charta* with respect to content.

During this meeting a precise timing was set up, which has been respected. It was decided to present a first draft to a larger group of experts, delegated by CEC and CEC, in the spring of 1999. This consultation was necessary because, apart from the production of a common text, an ecumenical process had also been envisaged. The second draft was then to be handed to the

---

ference of European Churches (CEC), *Reconciliation. Gift of God and Source of New Life* (Graz, 1998). The Third European Ecumenical Assembly will be held from 4-8 September 2007 in Sibiu, Romania. The theme of this meeting will be: "The Light of Christ Shines upon All: Hope for Renewal and Unity in Europe."

[7] On behalf of CCEE: Prof. dr. Ilona Riedel-Sprangenberger (Germany), Prof. dr. Waclaw Hryniewicz (Poland), Remi Hoeckman (PCPU) and General Secretary Don Aldo Giordano. On behalf of CEC: Prof. Reinhard Frieling (Germany) of the Evangelische Kirche Deutschlands, Gianna Sciclone, pastor in the Waldensian Church of Italy, Vladimir Shmaly of the Russian Orthodox Church and General Secretary Dr. Keith Clements.

various member churches of the CEC and to the national bishops' conferences between June 1999 and June 2000. Their reactions were to be integrated in a new version of the text, which was to be prepared in the autumn of 2000. At its meeting of January 2001 the *Joint Committee* of CCEE-CEC would then finalise the document which, during an ecumenical assembly, would be signed by the presidents of CCEE and CEC in spring, 2001.

During their first meeting the drafters coined the term *Charta Oecumenica*. The term indicates well that this ecumenical text does not aim at describing a doctrinal consensus. This does not, of course, imply that it would be a text without any theological content. By analogy with a political charter, which is explicitly binding for the subscribing nations, the *Charta* is binding for the Christian churches in Europe and for all Christians. The drafters were partly inspired by the *Barmen Erklärung*. During this meeting it was also agreed that the charter would be signed by the presidents of CCEE and CEC, so as to show that the subjects of the document, which was formulated in the first person plural, are the various European churches. Later on, in some reactions of churches and Bishops' Conferences the title was questioned, but the designation *Charta* stood firm, which, in my opinion, was very fortunate.

The first draft consisted of four parts. The first part indicated that it is God who calls the churches to unity. The second part contained more general obligations – the obligation to take care of communion, ecumenical spirituality, dialogue and cooperation. The third part discussed points of concrete interest for the churches. Among them, the following points were mentioned in the recommendation of the European ecumenical assembly of Graz: the relationship between majority and minority churches, proselytism and fundamentalism. The final part on living together in Europe spoke of basic rights, peace and security, and the relation of Christians in Europe to other religions. Differently from part one, in parts two to four the subtitle was immediately followed by some points of action, introduced by the words: "We Christians and churches commit ourselves."[8]

---

[8] My translation. The original German text reads: "Wir Christen

The draft that was released in July 1999, i.e. after the discussion of the initial draft by a larger group and the editing work by the drafting committee, consisted of three parts: "It is God who calls us to unity," "On the way to visible fellowship among the churches in Europe," "The ecumenical community in service to Europe."[9] Parts two and three were each divided into four subsections. Each of the now nine subsections of the document – the final text would have twelve subsections – showed the same structure. A descriptive introduction is followed by a number of obligations introduced by the words: "We commit ourselves" (German: "Wir verpflichten uns"). From this draft onwards it would become usual to have the three major parts preceded by a Bible quotation – this was the explicit request of the experts who had been consulted – and the introduction by a trinitarian doxology.[10] The opening paragraph describes the foundation of the cooperation of the churches in Europe much more explicitly than had been the case in the initial draft. This foundation is the faith in the Triune God, as formulated in the creed of Nicaea-Constantinople (381). From this version onwards the drafters also agreed to condemn the idea of proselytism but not to maintain the term, in spite of intense pressure from the Orthodox churches. One of the sub-themes of the third part was given as its title the famous line of Jacques Delors, "Donner une âme à l'Europe." Many respondents, however, believed that this title could be misunderstood. The Orthodox, for

---

und Kirchen verpflichten uns."

[9] In the official version, the German one, the titles read as follows: "Gott selbst ruft uns zur Einheit," "Auf dem Weg zur sichtbaren Gemeinschaft der Kirchen in Europa" and "Der Dienst der Ökumene für Europa."

[10] The drafters opted for the following doxology: "Glory be to the Father, and to the Son, and to the Holy Spirit." The biblical foundation for God's call to unity is understandably John 17:21: "… that they may all be one. As you, Father, are in me and I am in you, may they also be in us, so that the world may believe that you have sent me." Another text from the fourth Gospel, John 13:35, serves as the epigram to part II: "By this everyone will know that you are my disciples, if you have love for one another." Matt 5:9 serves as introduction to part III: "Blessed are the peacemakers, for they will be called children of God."

instance, criticised the fact that under such a point one should do as promised instead of reducing the soul of Europe to a reflection on social and cultural values. In the final text, "A soul for Europe" would be replaced by "participating in the building of Europe."

While the draft, which had been translated into sixteen European languages, was discussed by the member churches of CEC and the European Bishops' Conferences, the annual gathering of the *Joint Committee* in principle approved the document. The *Joint Committee* even explicitly asked the editors that after considering the suggestions the text would not be completely rewritten and would not be made much longer. At the CEC secretariat in Geneva 75 reactions were received; the secretariat of the Council of European Bishops' Conferences in Sankt-Gallen received twenty reactions from Bishops' Conferences, and about fifty others. During the meeting of the editing committee at the end of September 2000, the secretaries general of CCEE and CEC presented a summary of the contributions, but the members of the editorial staff had access to the whole material.[11]

The drafting committee reworked the text during their meeting in November 2000 on the basis of the reactions of Bishops' Conferences and churches. They especially tried to take into account as much as possible the sensitivities and objections of the Orthodox churches, so as not to end up with a kind of "bilateral" declaration. There were only a few of their desiderata, like the request for a stronger rejection of proselytism and the defence of the rights of majorities or the Orthodox difficulty with the term ecumenism as such, with which they did not agree. Happily, the observations from the side of the Orthodox

---

[11] The drafting committee had in the meanwhile been changed slightly. Besides the general secretaries, the study secretaries, Sarah Numico (CCEE) and Prof. Dr. Viorel Ionita (CEC), were now also invited. The other members on behalf of CCEE were now Prof. Dr. Waclaw Hryniewicz, Jozef Maj (PCPU) and Norbert Witsch, who replaced Ilona Riedel-Spangenberger. On behalf of CEC the former representatives were present, as well as Prof. Dr. Grigorios Larentzakis, representative of the Ecumenical Patriarchate.

churches were not only critical but oftentimes also constructive. For instance, the following paragraph of the preamble has almost literally been borrowed from the conclusions of an Orthodox consultation in Crete:

> Europe – from the Atlantic to the Urals, from the North Cape to the Mediterranean – is today more pluralist in culture than ever before. With the Gospel, we want to stand up for the dignity of the human person created in God's image and, as churches together, contribute towards reconciling peoples and cultures.

During the meeting of the Joint Committee in Porto in January 2001 the text was revised for the last time. The declaration *Dominus Iesus* of the Congregation for the Doctrine of the Faith received much attention. The vice-president of CCEE, Karl Lehmann, who during this meeting received the news that he had become a cardinal, was successful in assuring the representatives of the other churches of the Catholic Church's commitment to the ecumenical process. The Orthodox members of this commission were highly cooperative in the process of finding a consensus. Fully understanding that a charter of this sort is always open to improvement, the text was deemed ready for signing. This happened in the Easter week of 2001 in the context of a European ecumenical assembly in Strasbourg. Together with the final text of the *Charta* a protocol was promulgated, in which CCEE and CEC announced that further revisions of the text were not envisaged. If this is thought desirable, the churches and the Bishops' Conferences can make additions to the text that are relevant for their local or national context. By inviting a considerable group of young people to discuss the *Charta* intensively, the reception process started officially. On Sunday, 22 April 2001, the *Charta* was solemnly signed by the presidents of CEC and CCEE, respectively Metropolitan Jérémie and Cardinal Vlk.

The Charta: *A Text, a Process, and a Miracle*

The Outcome of the Public Discussion on the Draft Version

I have chosen to present my study of the different reactions submitted to the CEC and the CCEE as follows. First, I will treat the difficulties with the draft version that were mentioned in

Orthodox, Protestant and Roman Catholic reactions. Thereafter I will discuss the specific difficulties which the Orthodox churches experienced with the document. Before dealing with objections that are exclusively found in responses by Protestant churches and by Roman Catholic episcopal conferences, I will pay attention to the observations that are found in reactions from both sides. I believe I join the available literature on the redaction process of the *Charta Oecumenica* by making a distinction between the Orthodox reactions and the other reactions by member churches of the CEC, but I realise that the indication "Protestant churches" perhaps does not fully do justice to the self-understanding of the churches involved.

a) Orthodox, Protestant and Roman Catholic Reactions
In many reactions it was argued that the term "Charta" presupposes that the text has a juridical status which it does not possess. I am happy, though, that the term survived the discussions, because it indicates that Christians in Europe are morally bound to apply the ecumenical commitments in their lives. It was also not clear to many readers of the draft who the "we" in the introduction to the commitments are. Later on it was agreed that the respective chairs of the CEC and the CCEE would sign the document in the name of the churches they represent. The drafting committee was also asked to reduce the number of commitments and to make sure that the commitments correspond to the content of the body of each paragraph.

There are also a number of objections of content that return in the responses by Orthodox, Protestant and Roman Catholic church bodies. Three of them deal with the commitments in the paragraph on "Witnessing Together to our Faith" (D, 4; *Charta* 2). (1) The drafting committee had made the decision to condemn the reality of proselytism, without mentioning the term. "We commit ourselves," the text read, "not to induce people to change their church membership, and never to use physical force, moral constraint, psychological pressure or material incentives to motivate people to conversion." The Orthodox churches held that the evil of proselytism deserved a more explicit condemnation. Both Protestant and Roman Catholic responses insisted that the freedom of the churches to evangelise as well as the freedom of individual Christians to change their religion, when urged by their conscience, should appear in the text as well. (2) Most reactions experienced difficulties with the statement in the draft version that "it is important to distinguish between church communities and sects" (D, 4), especially because such a statement does not make sense without mentioning the criteria for doing so. (3) To me, it was strange to read so many reactions that were opposed to the commitment "to support the conversion of the churches" (D, 4). Apparently, despite the wonderful study by the Groupe des Dombes on this theme,[12] this idea has not been received by many churches and Christians in Europe.

In part III the virtues that were mentioned to preserve "Europe's soul" seemed to be borrowed more from the Universal Declaration on Human Rights, whereas typically Christian values like "peace, reverence for life, the value of marriage and the family, the preferential option for the poor, the readiness to forgive, and in all things compasssion" (*Charta* 7) were not mentioned.

b) Objections from the Orthodox Churches

The critical reactions from the Orthodox churches constituted a major obstacle for the future of the *Charta Oecumenica*. The Department for External Church Relations of the Moscow Patriarchate submitted their criticism together with a letter of their chairman, Metropolitan Kirill, in which he stated that the *Charta* in its current form was fully unacceptable to the Russian Orthodox Church because of the predominantly liberal position which it defended. It was even doubted whether the Russian Orthodox Church could further participate in ecumenical meetings at the European level. A more nuanced criticism was of-

---

[12] See Groupe des Dombes, *For the Conversion of the Churches* (Geneva, 1991). Jean-Marc Prieur, "La charte œcuménique européenne: aspects théologiques," *Positions Luthériennes* 50 (2002) : 227-36, esp. p. 234, is less concerned about this omission: "La Charte ne mentionne, il est vrai, pas la distinction entre conversion ecclésiale et conversion individuelle, mais il est clair que ces deux aspects sont sous-entendus."

fered in the conclusions of the Working Meeting of Orthodox Churches, which took place in July 2002 in Crete.

The Orthodox churches refused to consider it as a commitment for them "to pray with one another" or "to hold ecumenical worship services regularly"[13] (D, 3). In their opinion, in the draft version praying together was seen as an instrument to bring about unity whereas in fact it belongs to the life of the churches after their unification. As I already indicated, the Orthodox churches also expected the churches in Europe to condemn proselytism in a stronger way. More at the level of principles were their reactions against what they believed to be expressions of a Protestant view on church unity. Especially the preamble was believed to be full of unacceptable statements like "confessing our common faith in worship," "we are striving for a clearer and fuller unity of the church of Jesus Christ in this world," "we commit ourselves to preserve and continue to develop the ecumenical fellowship which has grown up among us." The reference to our common affirmation of the ecumenical creed in the first paragraph must be accompanied by the realistic affirmation of the presence of important doctrinal differences among the churches (D, 1). The second commitment can no longer pretend that the one faith has only to be made more visible.

The paragraph on "Coming to Meet One Another" incorrectly states that "because of differences over questions of faith, but also because of human weakness and sin, the fellowship of the one church of Jesus Christ has been broken" (D, 2). Whereas it is obvious to Orthodox ecclesiology that the communion among the churches is broken, the unity of the church is not. "The spiritual riches of the different Christian traditions" have to be studied first before Christians can be encouraged "to recognise" them. The common proclamation of the Christian faith

---

[13] In the same period, a special commission was discussing the conditions for further participation of the Orthodox churches in the WCC. An appendix in the 2002 Final Report offers "A Framework for Common Prayer at WCC Gatherings." See "Final Report of the Special Commission on Orthodox Participation in the WCC," *The Ecumenical Review* 55 (2003): 4-38, esp. pp.18-26.

presupposes the restoration of unity (D, 4). It is also difficult for the Orthodox churches to accept that they should already experience that they "belong together in Christ" (D, 5), as the opening line of the paragraph on dialogue suggests.

The Orthodox churches, furthermore, make no distinction between fundamental and secondary doctrinal points, rendering it unacceptable for them to accept the statement that "communion among churches can have its theological basis only in agreement with the fundamental truths of our faith" (D, 5). The commitment about the reception of "the results of theological conversations among our churches" (D, 5) sounds equally too strong.

In general, the Orthodox churches were very pleased with the third part of the document. One of their suggestions was to complement the commitment "to defend the rights of minorities" (D, 6) with the protection of majorities. The addition "in all areas of life" in the commitment "to strengthen the position and equal rights of women" (D, 8) was not deemed necessary. Finally, the Orthodox churches are in favour of the establishment of a common day of prayer for the preservation of creation.

c) Common Protestant and Roman Catholic Desiderata

The episcopal conferences did not raise the same objections as the Orthodox churches against the understanding of the way to unity as reflected in the *Charta*. On the contrary, their observations were mostly of the same kind as those found in reactions sent to the CEC. Let it be clear, however, that it was in the first instance a strong desideratum from the side of the Protestant churches to give the task of "Witnessing Together to our Faith" (D, 4) a more central place in the document. However, it was also obvious to a number of episcopal conferences that this paragraph sounded too negative in the draft version. The common mission of the churches is not only necessary "in the face of the advancing secularisation and ebbing of Christianity in Europe" but belongs to the heart of our Christian faith.

Mostly in reactions by Protestant churches but also in reactions by a number of episcopal conferences, there was much indignation about the fact that nowhere in the draft version was it mentioned that visible unity also includes Eucharistic fellowship.

Many Protestant churches and Roman Catholic episcopal conferences were of the opinion that part III almost sounded like a political plea in favour of the European Union, especially through statements like: "The churches are in favour of European unity." Furthermore, it was mentioned in reactions that were sent to both CEC and CCEE that forgiveness should be asked for the suffering inflicted by Europeans in other parts of the world.

There was also a strong awareness that the paragraph on "Reconciling Peoples and Cultures, Preserving Creation" (D, 8) would be better split up into two paragraphs (*Charta* 8, 9). It was also mentioned in almost every contribution that three separate paragraphs should be made out of the one paragraph on "Fostering Relations with Other Religions" (D, 9). These paragraphs would deal subsequently with "Strengthening community with Judaism" (*Charta* 10), "Cultivating relations with Islam" (*Charta* 11) and "Encountering other religions and world views" (*Charta* 12). This is not to deny, however, that, for proper theological or contextual reasons, a small number of Protestant churches and episcopal conferences expressed their reservations about the dialogue with Judaism, Islam or other religions and worldviews.

d) Requests from Protestant Churches

For some churches the following line in the preamble is in contradicttion with Protestant soteriology: "We are aware that it is only through our own inner conversion that we can reach the unity which God is working to bring about." Reservations were also formulated against the idea that churches would have to "search together for God's truth," since God's truth has been revealed in Christ. Churches practising re-baptism also experienced difficulties with the idea that the churches in Europe have "to make visible the unity of the one faith and the one baptism." From the side of the Free Churches it was mentioned that the Nicene-Constantinopolitan Creed does not occupy the same position in their church as in other Christian churches. In their opinion, the draft version of the *Charta* also focussed too much on "liturgical prayers and hymns" (D, 3), to the neglect of free liturgical prayer. It also appears to some Protestant churches that the heart of ecumenism is the Gospel, not "praying together." It is a pity, another reaction states, that the Lord's Prayer has not been referred to as of great ecumenical significance. Objections were also made against the goal of new evangelisation, which was mentioned only in the original German version of the draft (D, 4) but which sounded much too Catholic in Protestant ears.[14]

It was also asked whether it was necessary to insert the Lund principle in a text like this (D, 6).[15] Another remark dealt with the responsibility of Christians in Europe for "the poor in the countries of the so-called Third World" (D, 7) which would be better reformulated as their responsibility for "the poor in the rest of the world." "Reconciling peoples and cultures" is also said to imply efforts to "overcome unemployment" (*Charta* 8), an aspect which was not mentioned in the draft text. This would also be the appropriate paragraph, according to another church, to make reference to the recommendation of the European Ecumenical Assembly in Graz that the CEC and the CCEE should establish their own institute for conflict resolution. Other Protestant churches, however, precisely deplore the confusion between the Gospel and the Law which is reflected in a statement like this one: "We direct our common efforts towards evaluating and resolving political and social issues in the spirit of the Gospel" (D, 8).

---

[14] D, 4 (German): "Angesichts der fortschreitenden Säkularisierung und Entchristlichung in Europa bestärken wir uns im gemeinsamen christlichen Zeugnis unseres Glaubens zur gemeinsamen Neu-Evangelisierung und Mission in Europa." The English translation reads: "In the face of the advancing secularisation and ebbing of Christianity in Europe, we resolve to strengthen one another in a common Christian witness to our faith, to a common evangelisation and mission in Europe."

[15] D, 6: "Until we reach the goal of full church communion, we intend to act together in all matters in which no deep differences of conviction compel us to act separately. This principle shall be valid for all levels of the life of the churches in Europe."

e) Requests from Roman Catholic Episcopal Conferences
Sometimes episcopal conferences find the formulation of the commitments too strong. In the paragraph on "Praying Together is the Heart of Ecumenism" (D, 3), e.g., it is believed to be sufficient if Christians in Europe "learn to know and appreciate the worship and other forms of spirituality of one another's churches," but it is not deemed necessary to "search for a common ecumenical spirituality." The commitment "to hold ecumenical worship services regularly" must not become a substitute of the obligation for Catholics to celebrate the Eucharist on Sunday. Therefore, one episcopal conference even asks for the removal of this expectation. With regard to the paragraph on "There is no alternative to dialogue" (D, 5) there is no objection to the need for a better reception of the results of the ecumenical dialogue as such, but "to take the consequences of such results" is one bridge too far.

One episcopal conference was of the opinion that the terminology of "ecumenical fellowship" (D, 5) was in contradiction with the Roman Catholic tradition of speaking about "full ecclesial communion." In the same sense it was observed that Catholic ecclesiology speaks about the hierarchy of truths, not about a distinction between fundamental and non-fundamental truths. Another voice wondered, with regard to the same paragraph, whether the statement that "the belonging together in Christ which we already experience is of fundamental importance in relation to our differing theological and ethical positions" (D, 5) could not lead to theological and ethical relativism.

One of the commitments in the paragraph on "Reconciling Peoples and Cultures, Preserving Creation" (D, 8) asks the churches to be open to "foreign persons." According to one episcopal conference, one can better speak about "migrants" (*Charta* 8) here. Finally, attention to the problems of mixed marriages was seen to be missing in the draft text.

The Revision at the Level of the Drafting Committee
and of the CEC-CCEE Joint Committee

First of all, a close reading of the final text of the *Charta Oecumenica* makes it clear that the observations made during the period of critical reception of the first draft have been taken seriously. In light of the amount of critical remarks it almost seems a miracle that, in the first instance, the drafting committee, and, in the second instance, the CEC-CCEE Joint Committee, have been able to provide a final version of the *Charta Oecumenica* which now seems acceptable to most churches and episcopal conferences that have participated in this process. They have especially tried to take into account as much as possible the sensitivities and objections of the Orthodox churches, so as not to end up with a kind of "bilateral" declaration. As was seen above, whereas some points could not be brought into the final document, there were also positive contributions from the Orthodox world that are reflected in the *Charta*.

The revision of the *Charta Oecumenica* came to an end during the meeting of the Joint Committee in January 2001. Especially the preamble and the body of the paragraph on "Strengthening Community with Judaism" (*Charta* 10) were still intensively revised during this last meeting. As I promised in the introduction, I will now offer a more detailed analysis of part II of the *Charta Oecumenica*: "Towards the Visible Fellowship of the Churches in Europe," realising, however, that the second commitment of paragraph 1 anticipates it already. "We commit ourselves in the power of the Holy Spirit, to work towards the visible unity of the Church of Jesus Christ in the one faith, expressed in the mutual recognition of baptism and in eucharistic fellowship, as well as in common witness and service."

Towards the Visible Fellowship of the Churches in Europe

Proclaiming the Gospel Together

In the draft version part II opened with a paragraph on "Coming to Meet One Another" (D, 2) That the first paragraph of the final version deals with "Proclaiming the Gospel together" (*Charta* 2) has surely been provoked by the strong wish in many Protestant reactions to give the task of a common mission a more dominant place in the document. Therefore, the opening line of paragraph 2 now makes it clear that there is a hierarchy among all the elements which contribute "towards the visible fellowship of the churches in Europe": "The most important task of the churches in Europe is the common proclamation of the Gospel, in both word and deed, for the salvation of all."

The commitments are an attempt to make this ideal more concrete. The first commitment states that the churches have to discuss their "plans for evangelisation with other churches, entering into agreements with them and thus avoiding harmful competition and the risk of fresh divisions." (*Charta* 2) It is to be appreciated that the text employs the term "churches." In the accompanying letter to the final version of the *Charta* it is stated that the concept of "Church "has been used in the sense in which it is understood by all instances that participate in this initiative."[16]

In the second commitment the prohibition against proselytism has been maintained but complemented by two statements about the freedom of conscience. It is remarkable that the second statement, the one following the reflection on proselytism, was only added to the text during the final meeting of the CEC-CCEE Joint Committee. The commitment reads as follows:

> We commit ourselves to recognise that every person can freely choose his or her religious and church affiliation as a matter of conscience, which means not inducing anyone to convert through moral pressure or material incentive but also not hindering anyone from entering into conversion of his or her own free will.

---

[16] This is the text of the original German letter of which I have translated the relevant lines into English: "Es ist auch wichtig, an den Status der Charta zu erinnern, und deshalb bitten wir Sie, das Vorwort aufmerksam zu lessen. Da sie keinen lehramtlich-dogmatischen oder kirchenrechtlich-gesetzlichen Charakter hat, befasst sich der Text nicht mit ekklesiologischen Fragen und benutzt den Begriff 'Kirche' so, wie er von jedem er dan der Initiative beteiligten Subjekten verstanden wird. Ausserdem wird ersichtlich, dass in dem dem Dokument beigefügten Protokoll die Charta den Kirchen von KEK und CCEE als Basistext empfohlen wird. Es ist nicht beabsichtigt, diesen Text weiter zu revidieren. Es besteht jedoch die Hoffnung, dass Kirchen und ökumenische Gremien in Europa die Charta annehmen, studieren und weiter diskutieren sowie konkrete Schritte zu ihrer Umsetzung unternehmen, und, wenn nötig, darauf aufbauren und sie an ihre jeweiligen örtlichen und nationale Kontexte anpassen werden."

It remains a challenge for the churches in Europe to make this "most important task" more concrete. During my visit to the secretariat of the Council of European Bishops' Conferences, the secretary general Don Aldo Giordano admitted that their relatively small secretariat cannot play an active role in everything. "Our Common Mission in Europe" is from 2004-2009 one of the working priorities for the CEC Commission "Churches in Dialogue." The CCEE secretariat is certainly willing to send representatives to the initiatives developed by them.

Moving towards One Another

The churches in Europe have to enter a learning process of "moving towards one another." We have to become appreciative of the rich tradition of other churches. This learning process also involves an element of conversion and of the reconciliation of memories. The reality of the divisions and schisms of the past have an implication for the proclamation of the faith in the present. In my opinion the formulation of this implication in the draft version, speaking about "the lack of credibility which this has caused for the Christian witness" sounded stronger than the formulation in the final text. However, respondents were of the opinion that the draft version was much too optimistic in its judgement that this damage now belongs to the past. According to the draft version, "the lack of credibility which this has caused for the Christian witness has been reduced in this century by the ecumenical movement, and has given way to reconciliation among Christians." The final version prefers a realist attitude. "Human guilt, lack of love and the frequent abuse of faith and the church for political interests have severely damaged the credibility of the Christian witness." This insight has been repeated in many ecumenical dialogues. It reminds me, as a Roman Catholic theologian, also of paragraph 98 of the encyclical *Ut Unum Sint* by Pope John Paul II: "At the same time it is obvious that the lack of unity among Christians contradicts the truth which Christians have the mission to spread, and, consequently, it gravely damages their witness."[17]

---

[17] See also the CCEE-CEC final report of the Graz assembly *Reconciliation. Gift of God and Source of New Life*, A 14: "In this way the credibility of our common Christian witness has been weakened." Another

Acting Together

The paragraph on "Acting together" contains in the body of the text a number of recommendations which in the draft version were located in the first paragraph of part III:

> We recommend that bilateral and multilateral ecumenical bodies be set up and maintained for cooperation at local, regional, national and international levels. At the European level it is necessary to strengthen cooperation between the Conference of European Churches and the Council of European Bishops' Conferences (CCEE) and to hold further European Ecumenical Assemblies. (*Charta* 4)

These recommendations have certainly found a better place in part II, since they clearly contribute to "the visible fellowship of the churches in Europe." I deplore, however, very strongly that a line has been removed from the draft version which would have implied the common recognition by the churches in Europe of the hermeneutical method of the differentiated consensus. The original commitment, namely, read as follows:

> to clarify, at local, regional, national and international levels, in bilateral and multilateral conversations, on which statements of principles agreement is indispensable, and in which issues difference need not lead to division and can be mutually tolerated. (D, 6)

To my knowledge it was requested in only one reaction submitted by one of the member churches of the CEC that this dense formulation be further unpacked.

---

example can be found in the document *The Challenge of Proselytism and the Calling to Common Witness* of the Joint Working Group of the WCC and the Roman Catholic Church, par 9: "Divisions among Christians are a counter-witness to Christ and contradict their witness to reconciliation in Christ" (*Growth in Agreement II. Reports and Agreed Statements of Ecumenical Conversations on a World Level, 1982-1998* [Geneva], p. 893).

Praying Together

My account of the reactions to the draft version has already made it clear that the discussion on this paragraph was not easy. Even if it sounds like a contradiction in view of the first commitment, I am happy that the final version has maintained the title "Praying together." It is also to be appreciated that the drafting committee has decided to add to this paragraph an observation that filled what was believed to be an important lacuna by many respondents. "A particularly painful sign of the divisions among many Christian churches is the lack of Eucharistic fellowship." (*Charta* 5) A new commitment also speaks about the necessity "to move towards the goal of Eucharistic fellowship."

The final version does not hide the fact that the discussion on this paragraph has not led to a consensus. "In some churches reservations subsist regarding praying together in an ecumenical context." The final text, however, continues to mention what is happening already in many places to realise the goal of praying together: "But we have many hymns and liturgical prayers in common, notably the Lord's Prayer, and ecumenical services have become a widespread practice: all of these are features of our Christian spirituality."

Continuing in Dialogue

The *Charta Oecumenica* does not deal with the content of the ecumenical dialogue but offers a formal plea to pursue it. It is admitted that there exist "differing theological and ethical positions" between the churches and that the current "separations between churches" are the consequence of "differences of opinion on doctrine, ethics and church law." These observations, however, are only the second part of the first and second line of paragraph 6. The first idea in each sentence draws attention to what is more important than the divisions between the churches. The first line reports the fact that we "belong together in Christ." On the basis of the English translation it is not clear that the final version has somehow taken into account the critique from the Orthodox churches that they do not experience this. The German text no longer speaks about "unsere tatsächlich vorhandene Zusammengehörigkeit in Christus" but about "unsere in Christus begründete Zusammengehörigkeit." The second line opens with the idea that there is a plurality of theological, ethical and canonical opinions that does not lead to church divisions but which constitutes a legitimate diversity. Just as it was said that our communion is based on our belief in Jesus Christ, the *Charta* sees our diversity as "a gift."

The immediate source of inspiration of the first line – "We belong together in Christ, and this is of fundamental significance in the face of our differing theological and ethical positions" – is the document of the Joint Working Group on *The Ecumenical Dialogue on Moral Issues* (1995) which formulated ten guidelines. I quote the last one in full:

> When the dialogue continues to reveal sincere but apparently irreconcilable moral positions, we affirm in faith that the fact of our belonging together in Christ is more fundamental than the fact of our moral differences. The deep desire to find an honest and faithful resolution of our disagreements is itself evidence that God continues to grace the *koinonia* among disciples of Christ. [18]

Both texts, however, reflect a different dynamic. In *The Ecumenical Dialogue on Moral Issues* it is the existence of "irreconcilable moral positions" at the end of the dialogue process which is addressed. Still, this is not believed to be threatening to the basic communion between the churches in Christ. In the *Charta Oecumenica* the differences between the churches are not believed to be irreconcilable. On the contrary, the more important fact of their communion in Christ should encourage the churches to continue the dialogue.

The opening part of the second line – "Rather than seeing our diversity as a gift which enriches us" – was added during the meeting of the CEC-CCEE Joint Committee. Of the ecumenical texts which may have inspired this formulation, the following paragraph on catholicity in the ARCIC II document on *The Gift of Authority*[19] seems to be a good candidate.

---

[18] *Growth in Agreement II*, p. 910.

[19] See *The Gift of Authority: Authority in the Church III*, in *The Pontifical Council forPromoting Christian Unity. Information Service* (1999) 17-29.

> This diversity of traditions is the practical manifestation of catholicity and confirms rather than contradicts the vigour of Tradition. As God has created diversity among humans, so the Church's fidelity and identity require not uniformity of expression and formulation at all levels in all situations, but rather catholic diversity within the unity of communion. The richness of traditions is a vital resource for a reconciled humanity. (27)

It is likely that the members of the CEC-CCEE Joint Committee also had the following passage from the section on "The diverse expressions of the one apostolic faith" of the discussion paper of the Fifth World Conference on Faith and Order in mind:[20]

> The need to interpret, live, confess and celebrate the one faith in many contexts and accordingly in diverse forms of expression is not to be regarded as a threat to unity, but as the necessary consequence of the incarnational character of the Christian faith. Such diversity is integral to the emergence of true and full unity and has its deepest foundation in the diversity in unity of the Triune God. Yet what has the potential of manifesting the rich diversity of the expressions of the apostolic faith often leads to conflicts which threaten existing unity. (55-56)

The text of the *Charta Oecumenica* continues by insisting that the dialogue between the churches should be oriented towards a consensus. Churches that enter in dialogue are already in communion with one another. This communion is deepened by the dialogue process. The goal of full ecclesial communion between churches, however, presupposes "unity in faith," as the revised text of the *Charta* reads. The official English translation, "Only in this way can church communion be given a theological foundation" (*Charta* 6), is at this point completely unreliable. The original German text of this phrase, which has been added to the *Charta* during the last meeting of the CEC-CCEE Joint Committee, reads as follows: "Ohne Einheit im Glauben gibt es keine volle Kirchengemeinschaft." It can be asked whether this line is not an implicit rejection of the tradition which has been developed among some Protestant churches to restore or realise

---

[20] See *On the Way to Fuller Koinonia*, Faith and Order Paper 166, (Geneva, 1994).

church communion on the basis of a differentiated consensus. This question is legitimate, especially if one pays attention to a line which has been omitted because of the critique of the Orthodox churches: "Communion among churches can have its theological basis only in agreement with the fundamental truths of our faith" (D, 5).

Professor Hryniewicz, one of the co-authors of the draft version, expressed the following warning in a lecture he gave during a consultation on one of the *Charta*'s earliest versions.

> The model of unity which the Orthodox churches adhere to consists in the complete identity of faith of all local churches and in the eucharistic assembly. Western models of unity, which are based on a gradual consensus, are difficult for the Orthodox churches to accept. The idea that the recognition of a communion between churches can happen in several stages is, in their perspective, impossible.[21]

In view of the two important omissions in paragraphs 4 and 6, I regret that the Protestant and Catholic members of the CCEE-CEC Joint Committee have not been able to convince their Orthodox colleagues to subscribe to the hermeneutical method of the differentiated consensus, because this approach is, in my opinion, indispensable to ecumenical progress.[22]

---

[21] Original version: "Die Orthodoxie findet ihr Einheitsmodell in der vollständigen Identität der einzelnen Ortskirchen im Glauben und in der eucharistischen Versammlung. Die westlichen Modelle von abgestuften Konsensen sind für die Orthodoxen kaum annehmbar. Der Weg einer schrittweise realisierbaren Anerkennung von Kommunionsgemeinschaft ist in dieser Perspektive nicht möglich."

[22] Jean-Marc Prieur makes a similar observation on p. 233 of his article on the *Charta Oecumenica* (see the reference in n. 6): "Le texte prend ici indirectement position dans un débat qui implique notamment les orthodoxes et les catholiques d'une part, les protestants de l'autre, et qui consiste à se demander si l'unité dans la foi doit précéder la communion pratique ou si elle en est une conséquence. Pour la Charte, l'unité dans la foi conditionne la pleine communion ecclésiale. Une affirmation que nul ne conteste fondamentalement, mais que les uns et les autres ne comprennent pas de la même manière. Car tout dépend de l'étendue du consensus de foi requis pour parvenir à la

Fortunately, the commitment to promote the reception of the results of the ecumenical dialogue is still to be found in the final version of the *Charta Oecumenica*.²³ But, whereas this text exhorts the churches "to examine the question of how official church bodies can receive and implement the findings gained in dialogue" (*Charta* 6), the draft version sounded stronger. There the commitment read: "to make sure the results of theological conversations among our churches are received at all levels of church life, and to take the consequences of such results" (D, 5). I believe it makes sense to refer one more time to the public lecture by Professor Hryniewicz:

> The ecumenical experts have not been successful in mediating the results of interconfessional dialogues to the authorities, theologians and believers of their churches. The results and insights that were looked for in the ecumenical dialogue have, generally speaking, not been received by the authorities of the churches, and remained, therefore, unsuccessful. A convergence text is not satisfactory to everyone. One reads such a text usually with confessional eyes and requires that it reflect our own position. A true learning process seems to be for many a much too difficult challenge. When a Church elevates her own theological insights as criterion for evaluation, then one can

---

communion ecclésiale. Or on sait que cette exigence est beaucoup plus étendue du côté des orthodoxes et des catholiques que du côté des protestants." I do not agree with the interpretation given in Wolfgang W. Müller, "Die Charta Oecumenica als Chance für die Christen und Christinnen in Europa ?" in *Catholica* 57 (2003): 1-12, p. 3: "Die Einheit als geglaubte theologale Größe wird im Sinne einer 'versöhnten Verschiedenheit' oder eines 'differenzierten Grundkonsenses' gedacht, welche den zu beschreibenden Weg zur Einheit darstellen."

²³ Compare UUS 80: "While dialogue continues on new subjects or develops at deeper levels, a new task lies before us: that of receiving the results already achieved. These cannot remain the statements of bilateral commissions but must become a common heritage. For this to come about and for the bonds of communion to be thus strengthened, a serious examination needs to be made, which by different ways and means and at various levels of responsibility must involve the whole people of God."

speak only with difficulty about a legitimate plurality and diversity.[24]

Conclusion

After having carefully studied the reactions by episcopal conferences and member churches of the CEC I have become very appreciative of the patient attempts of the drafting committee and of the CCEE-CEC Joint Committee to achieve a consensus on the *Charta Oecumenica*. It can be demonstrated that the objections that were raised against the draft version of the *Charta* by Orthodox, Protestant and Roman Catholic readers have been taken seriously. In my opinion, however, the draft version sounded stronger on some occasions. I also wonder whether it is sufficient, in view of pursuing the dialogue between the churches in Europe on doctrinal themes, to state that "there is no alternative to dialogue" (*Charta* 6). The final version of the *Charta* is, in my opinion, a missed opportunity to make the hermeneutics of the differentiated consensus acceptable for all churches in Europe.

Therefore, I will end my presentation by subscribing to an important observation which was made by the Evangelical-Lutheran Church in Thüringen:

> The draft for a *Charta Oecumenica* does not deal with doctrinal questions but with the practical living together of the churches in Europe. This is the strength but, at the same time, the weak-

---

[24] "Es ist den Ökumenikern nicht gelungen, die Ergebnisse der interkonfessionellen Dialoge den Kirchenleitungen, den Theologen und der Gläubigen ihrer eigenen Kirchen zu vermitteln. Die im ökumenischen Gespräch erzielten Ergebnisse und Einsichten sind weithin kirchenamtlich kaum rezipiert worden und deshalb folgenlos geblieben. Kein Konvergenz-Text kann alle befriedigen. Man liest ihn gewöhnlich mit den konfessionellen Augen und verlangt, dass er unsere eigene Position widerspiegelt. Ein wirklicher Lernprozess scheint noch für viele eine zu schwierige Herausforderung zu sein. Wenn eine Kirche ihre theologischen Einsichten zum Masstab der Beurteilung erhebt, dann kann man kaum von einer legitimen Vielfalt und Verschiedenheit sprechen."

ness of this draft. The question arises as to whether such a separation of doctrine and life can be carried through and whether it ultimately makes sense, or whether doctrine and life are not inseparably connected to each other, so that one has to strive for a differentiated consensus in theological matters.[25]

---

[25] Original version: "Der Entwurf für eine '*Charta Oecumenica*' bezieht sich nicht auf theologische Lehrfragen, sondern auf das praktische Miteinander der Kirchen in Europa. Das ist die Stärke, aber auch zugleich die Schwäche dieses Entwurfes. Es stellt sich die Frage, ob diese Trennung von Lehre und Leben so durchhaltbar und auf Dauer auch sinnvoll ist, oder ob nicht doch Lehre und Leben untrennbar miteinander verbunden sind und man um einen differenzierten Konsens in theologischen Fragen ringen muss."

Church Communion
and the Reception of Ecumenical Dialogues

An Orthodox Perspective

Dorin Oancea

Introductory Remarks

One of those facts so familiar to Christian history that we tend not to notice them anymore is related to the doctrinal differences between the historical denominations and the many others which have appeared in the last two centuries, on the one hand, and the lack of intercommunion between them, on the other. There are a lot of historical arguments to explain this reality, familiar enough to need no rehearsing here.

Yet the fact has been one of the difficult realities in Christian life for many centuries. Our times have obviously brought a certain difference, because if in the past, for a long time, people did not seem to be very much concerned about these realities, nowadays – and I mean by that from the last century onwards – people are very much concerned by the lack of intercommunion based on doctrinal differences and have tried to overcome the different obstacles they meet on this road.

Therefore, today, when people speak so much about intercommunion, a word which expresses the highest goal of the ecumenical movement, we are certainly confronted with a paradox: on the one hand, we can notice a real longing for communion amongst members of different denominations on several levels, and, on the other hand, we also notice serious reservations against it. Most theologians and members of the higher church hierarchy, especially Orthodox and Roman Catholic, would argue that intercommunion must be preceded by a doctrinal consensus. In order to overcome the existing differences and to meet this exigency of consensus, the different churches have developed different methods; one of them is that of ecumenical dialogue.

Ecumenical dialogues have been organised for some decades now, both on a bilateral and a multilateral level, and in some cases have led to significant agreements. I mention in this respect first of all that between the EKD and the Romanian Orthodox Church, highly valued by our Lutheran partners and us. Despite these good results, it is very difficult to speak of convergences between the churches in this respect: on the contrary, we are confronted with many setbacks that urge us to reflect on the significance of such dialogues. Whereas nobody can really deny their necessity, one must wonder whether their results are properly understood by the different churches and included in their own identity.

It is my conviction that this lack of reception is the main cause for the backward steps just mentioned, because without the completion of this process, we cannot expect Eucharistic communion between the different denominations to become a reality of our Christian existence.

In this paper I want to relate the reception of ecumenical dialogues to the fundamental realities of Christian life, as an argument for their present necessity. In order to show the present connection between intercommunion and the reception of ecumenical dialogues, I shall mention some meanings of reception in the Holy Scripture, concentrating upon the Old Testament, as the place where one can find the first patterns of reception. There are many similar and highly significant instances in the New Testament too, but I will leave them aside, since they are implicitly present in the arguments put forward by the Holy Tradition, which will be dealt with in the same context.

My main focus will be directed towards the Holy Liturgy as the special place, time, event, process where reception and full communion of the faithful with Christ meet in an unique way. At the same time I hope to make clear why the Orthodox experience huge difficulties with intercommunion, unless those interested in it reach a full doctrinal agreement during and after a process of mutual doctrinal reception.

Patterns of Reception in the Old Testament and in the Orthodox Tradition

Reception in the Old Testament

a. The basic pattern of reception as a communicatory and at the same time existential reality can be found in the Genesis stories of creation. God gives a certain identity to his human creation – man and woman – and starts a permanent communicatory process between himself and them, on the basis of certain criteria of accomplishment with a nominal value of truth, which are compared with the actually achieved performances, which have a truth value of their own. One could say that he verifies human actions to see whether they do or do not correspond to the identity fixed by him and continues his communication with humans in the first case or modifies its conditions in the second, in order to equalise the actual value of truth with the nominal one. If humans do not fit into this scheme of reception they die and stay dead until they function properly, as is the case with Jesus Christ. Globally speaking, reception means life and its absence, death.

Under these circumstances reception means the complex process of noticing the actual values of truth specific to certain human actions, of comparing them with the already known values, of continuing communion when the two sets of value are identical or to modify its conditions if the values are different, so that they might become equal again. One could say that reception implies here a nominal value agreed upon by God and humanity, an existential decision of humanity with respect to this value, and then a decision made by God with consequences not merely for the moment but also for the future of humanity.

b. More or less similar, but with a different orientation, is God's reception by humanity. I have in mind his conversation with Moses on Mount Horeb, as related in Exodus 3. He gives certain commandments of vital importance for the future of the people, opens up far-reaching perspectives and expects everybody to act accordingly. Moses is willing to do so for himself but knows that such a commitment on the side of the people requires a certain identity. Therefore his question: "If ... they ask me: 'What is his name?' what shall I say to them?" God gives an answer which, as far as he is concerned, covers this identity perfectly well. He says: "I am who I am." But he also knows that Moses cannot go to the people with this name only, because they would have no reference point and therefore he adds: "Say: The Lord, the God of your fathers, the God of Abraham and Isaac, and the God of Jacob, has sent me to you. This is my name for ever, and thus I am to be remembered throughout all generations." One might think that he wants to be remembered only as "I am who I am," but it is obvious that the description of his acting in history is part of this definition too. He introduces these elements as a mutually accepted value. He can ask for obedience now because his past actions and their specific truth value have been acknowledged by the people during a past process of reception. This is the starting point of a new process of reception, by which the whole event of communication taking place on Mount Sinai can be initiated. It is quite clear that he wants to be identified by means of these already acknowledged qualifications, in order to enjoy a new reception by the people. Reception is in this case both a problem of accepted identity and of existential integration, because on the ground of this identity Israel will follow the path he opens, which leads to the covenant on Mount Sinai.

c. Very similar to this pattern of reception is that of Abraham, again by God. I refer here to the whole process initiated by God with Abraham's election in Genesis 12 and continued with the well-known episode of Abraham's confession of faith, i.e. the promise made to him in Genesis 15:5 and his faith in it, as expressed in the next verse. This is a communicatory event with three elements: God's initiative: "Look toward heaven, and number the stars, if you are able to number them ... So shall your descendants be"; Abraham's faith: "And he believed the Lord"; and God's answer to this faith: "... and He reckoned it to him as righteousness." The first step is a communicatory reality, followed by a certain statement with an absolute value of truth and then the reception itself that is at the same time a higher form of communication.

It is also important to notice that this is only the first step of reception, very important but nevertheless waiting for confirmation, which comes during the episode of Isaac's anticipated sacrifice, as related in Genesis 22. This is the moment when Abraham acts according to the standards of communion stated by his being received by God the first time, giving up any presumption of false autonomy in his relation with his Creator. His acting is a statement itself, a confession of faith made without words and this is recognised by God (22:16-17), who establishes a final pattern of existential communication, of communion between him and Abraham's offspring: "... because you have done this ... I will indeed bless you ... because you have obeyed my voice."

In this third case it becomes more obvious that final reception, or the reception of one's whole being by God, includes as a central part a statement that one may call "a confession of faith," consisting of words and/or works, of a certain truth regarding the two partners and the act of communication between them.

Reception in the Holy Tradition

When we look at the experience of the early church and then at the development during the period of the ecumenical councils we are really impressed by the unity in doctrine, especially by the institution, the proceedings and results of local councils and then of the ecumenical councils. One might almost say that the whole history of the church up to the eigth century is dominated by doctrinal controversies and by the attempts to safeguard unity despite all of them, using as the criterion a dogmatic formula. In this context reception seams to have meant first of all the acceptance of certain propositions with an absolute value of truth, of certain dogmatic sentences by all Christians and by the whole of the church with its structures. The dogmatic articulation of the faith, as revealed in the Scriptures, and its reception are, in the understanding of the Fathers, an essential part of Christian life.

I think it is very important to keep in mind the significance of this reception of certain items of doctrine by the whole body of the church. This is possible if we consider its deep-rooted origin and its purpose.

This long history of asserting certain items and of rejecting others, not accepted and condemned as being heretical, might suggest that reception is related to those doctrinal items only, which address some levels of Christian understanding necessary for the whole of the church but really intelligible only to a small group of specialists, whom today we call theologians. It would be definitely wrong to limit the meaning of reception this way. It would be wrong because the Fathers of the councils did not invent certain doctrines and consequent dogmatic sentences out of nothing just for the sake of reflection, afterwards imposing them upon the faithful, but expressed in their theology and especially in the doctrine of the councils and in the dogmatic formulas a vivid reality, experienced by the community they came from and by the whole body of Christ in an unspoken way, at least at some point. This means that between the life of the community and those doctrinal items there was no distance at all but a perfect correspondence: not separation but organic unity. The source of the dogmatic sentence was the life of the church in the Holy Spirit, where the communion with God in Christ had been experienced from the very beginning. An essential part of this experience consisted of the vivid tradition of the church, including the revealed, accepted and confessed truth. The ecumenical council, and all the endeavours preceding it, gave a final form to these confessed formulas only when communion with Christ in the Holy Spirit was jeopardised and aimed at healing those wounds and restoring broken communion.

One must understand reception in the context of the early church and of the ecumenical councils as a means to accept not certain sentences but a community willing to confess them. The dogmatic formulas have no significance in themselves but always aim at communion. They come from a community with a vivid communion and aim at restoring communion which is lacking with another part of the body of Christ and at experiencing communion with it by means of these formula. Once formulated, this articulated dogmatic truth becomes part of the actual experience of the community, of all communities. It is possible to say that this noetic dimension referring to truth has always been present in the life of the Christians: at the beginning in an unarticulated form and, after a certain while, in an articulated form.

We can conclude these short reflections about the Fathers by pointing out the connection between the confession of a certain item of doctrine and the living communion between Christ and his followers, amongst all members of the church, of those who are the body of Christ. The link between these two aspects in the process of reception has been existentially expressed from then till now in the liturgical life of the church, most of all in the Holy Liturgy. This will be the focus of my following considerations.

Reception in the Holy Liturgy

The Dynamics of the Holy Liturgy

The first thing an Orthodox normally notices about everything happening during the Holy Liturgy is that it is not an event in which the believer simply participates without being changed, but that it is a process during which he or she experiences a development: there is an important difference between his or her own identity at the beginning of the Liturgy and at its end. This process, specific not only to Liturgy but also to the whole life of the believer, is usually known as *theosis*. This idea of development helps people, especially those coming from outside, understand the structure of the Holy Liturgy, including those parts which seem to be redundant. There are certain litanies with similar content, but each time they are uttered under different spiritual and ontological circumstances, according to the internal dynamics of the service. So, redundancy would be real, if we had in front of us a singular event only, unable to change the participants. But as long as in Orthodox understanding a person is being changed during the Liturgy, all redundancy disappears.

We should also notice that, as regards this dynamics, it includes all those present, both the priest and the faithful. But in the case of the priest it is less obvious, because he is supposed to have achieved a higher level of communion already, so that his own development, as imperative as it is, can be read only in the subtext of the different prayers he says in a low voice. It is the community of the participating faithful which expresses in a more clear way the process, together with its different steps, rests and goings.

The process nature of the Liturgy is revealed especially by its two parts. We normally speak about the Liturgy of the Catechumens and that of the Faithful.

a) The Liturgy of the Catechumens
This includes prayers for the universe, for the whole of the church, for different events in daily life, for the particular community. One could say that it is primarily a devotional experience, which relates the faithful directly to God by addressing him – the "Lord, have mercy" reveals the real content of each intercession – on the one hand and, on the other, meets him in the midst of all mundane facts, enumerated in a synthetic way in the text of the intercession. Here we have actual communion in the Holy Spirit, we feel the Spirit dwelling and acting everywhere and concentrating the whole energy, the whole dynamics of this process in the communion between God and humanity in the microcosmos which is the holy place, the church.[1]

The reference to the church as a microcosmos keeps us from limiting communion to the psychological level of personal encounter. The Liturgy of the Catechumens brings into the circuit some elements of Christian knowledge complementary to the psychological dimension just mentioned. I mean here, first of all, the direct message of the Lord as expressed in the Blessings and readings from the epistle and from the Gospel, by which the believer becomes a contemporary of the Lord, a listener to his word. It is well known that the Orthodox perceive several levels of understanding of the words and acts of the liturgical reality. In this case we are reminded first of all of the teaching of Christ, as an essential part of His activity. The second level of understanding is concentrated on the doctrinal content of the

---

[1] The Liturgy of the Catechumens is the first part of the service, starting with the first blessing – "Blessed is the kingdom of the Father and the Son and the Holy Spirit, now and forever and to the ages of ages" – and ending with the dismissal of the catechumens. In the Old Church the catechumens participated in it together with the baptised faithful, who continued their prayers after the former's dismissal. This whole part has been preserved in the structure of the Holy Liturgy, even after the institution of the catechumens had ceased to exist, because of its significance for the whole process of liturgical *theosis*.

teaching, because it reveals essential things about God, about humanity, about communion between them, about the communion between humanity and the rest of the world and its relatedness to God. The Blessings and the readings stand here for the whole of doctrinal truth, as revealed in the Holy Scriptures. The third level includes the preceding two and is more difficult to be perceived. Here the believer is invited to become a real contemporary of Christ, as I said before, a person listening to him, being moved by him, becoming willing to follow him. Remembering Christ, hearing and understanding his words become the unavoidable premises of experiencing communion with him.

Of equal importance is to share the same understanding of the universe, of God's action for humanity and his salvation. This is why the priest appeals in his prayers to God by making reference to promises made in the past or to God's revelation and its significance for the life of the faithful. I quote only one example from many, to show how certain items of doctrine are premises for an act of communion; a prayer the priest says in a low voice during the Trisagion Hymn:

> Holy God, You dwell among Your saints. You are praised by the Seraphim .... You have brought all things out of nothing into being. You have created man and woman in Your image and likeness .... You give wisdom and understanding to the supplicant and do not overlook the sinner but have established repentance as a way of salvation ....

We recognise here some important elements of Christian teaching, such as the doctrine about God – the relation between his uniqueness and threefoldness appears in the ecphonisions after each intercession – about the angels, the saints, about creation.

The participants also include in their intercession another important element of the confession of faith, the relation with the Blessed Mother and all the saints, and its significance for communion with Christ: "Remembering our most holy, pure, blessed and glorious Lady, the Theotokos and ever virgin Mary, with all the saints, let us commit ourselves and one another and our whole life to Christ our Lord." They also refer directly to the understanding of God's threefoldness as expressed in the ecphonisions of the priest and accept it without restraint: the announcement of the priest "For to You belong all glory, honour, and worship, to the Father and the Son and the Holy Spirit …" is met by them with an "Amen," which means that it becomes their own confession of faith as a part of their own communion with God.

Thus we are led back to the direct and indirect communion of the intercessions, with their "Lord, have mercy" and can understand the deep connection between the devotional life of the community and the content of its faith, as expressed in the good news proclaimed by the Lord, his apostles and their successors. The two are never separated, not even for a moment, but are complementary elements of one and the same reality.

b) The Liturgy of the Faithful[2]

As rich as it is, the first part of the Liturgy comes to an end and is concluded with a call, addressed to the catechumens to leave the church and the Great Entrance, symbolising Jesus Christ's entrance into Jerusalem. After a new series of petitions, immediately before the Creed, there follows a second call, addressed to the faithful, to have the doors shut: "Guard the doors. Wisdom." "Let us be attentive!" Why is this so? Is this discrimination against the catechumens? Certainly not. It is a way to protect them, because the faithful are now going onto a path that could be dangerous for those who are not prepared for it, not prepared in different ways, which would include a deep knowledge of the doctrine of the church.

The hitherto almost unknown reality with which we are confronted is expressed not only by the call to close the door. There are some elements at the beginning of this Liturgy of the Faithful, which fill us with a sense of perplexity. There is, first of all, the self-description of the faithful before the Great Entrance: "We who mystically represent the Cherubim sing the thrice holy hymn to the life giving Trinity." This is the place where the faithful stand, together with the Cherubim and at a

---

[2] This starts with the Great Entrance and ends with the Dismissal of the Faithful.

clear distance from the catechumens. They are able to do everything required, first of all to leave aside not the world but the ordinary egoistical problems of the word: "Let us set aside all the cares of life, that we may receive the King ...."

Another sign, equally significant, of this new quality, comes with the litany following the Entrance. Its first petition reads: "Let us complete our prayer to the Lord." There is no doubt here, no possible misunderstanding: as rich as the former litanies might have been, they did not satisfy the expectations of a real communion with God. Something more is needed, to make the prayer complete, in order to achieve a full communion. And this is given by uttering the different petitions of this litany. Up to now the litanies have made frequent reference to different instances of the world, to the welfare of the world. This litany of petition after the Great Entrance, includes them all, but refers directly to different aspects regarding the spiritual welfare of the faithful and of the community: "For our deliverance from all affliction, wrath, danger, and distress; for a perfect, holy, peaceful and sinless day, for forgiveness and remission of our sins and transgressions ... let us ask the Lord." And there are several more. Each one and all of them together speak about a living communion with God, in which He has the initiative and for which humanity can only ask. One might think that this is the real climax of the whole process. The Orthodox know well enough, however, that this is not the case. On the contrary! For an outsider what follows must be a total surprise, for neither the petition for a Christian end, nor the remembrance of the Theotokos, nor the mutual self-giving to the Lord are meant to set a final point to this crescendo of petitions, each of which are a step on this ladder of vivid dialogical communion. They conclude with the Creed, i.e. a succession of statements concerning doctrine, as formulated in Nicea and Constantinople. It is important for the line of my argument to pay full attention to this succession: the experience of the dialogical communion leads to the confession of faith. The process has the same structure as in the case of the formulated dogma: it comes out of an experienced communion and aims at communion, as we shall see.

As important as this conclusion seems to be, we are confused once again, because it is difficult to understand the significance of such a reference to the content of the faith in a process which continues with more important events, one might say, such as the consecration of the gifts. One might almost think that the Creed is a mere introduction to them. But looking at the structure of the whole Eucharistic Anaphora we understand that it is much more. One could almost say that it is the foundation of a new level of communion. Everything said in the Creed is basic for the whole process, for this happening, and one can find here the whole of revelation in a concentrated form. I think it is important to be fully aware of the fact, that, according to its basic meaning, the confession of faith made here does not include only the articles formulated in Nicea and Constantinople, but all the other elements of the faith agreed upon in a spoken or unspoken form by the whole of the church, from its beginnings until now. At the same time it includes all the doctrinal controversies of the early church, the readiness to overcome separation and to experience a new communion with those who are separated and the necessity to exclude from this experience those who are not willing to share the same truth. For them the gates are closed.

Here we notice an important difference between the Liturgy of the Catechumens, with its explicit references to God as creator and general saviour of sinful humanity, and that of the Faithful, where the doctrine on God is fully elaborated, together with that of salvation, in connection with that of the church. Only those who share the fullness of the doctrine are able to continue, only they can dare to make the next steps during the process.

Another important difference between the two levels of truth comes from their sources. In the first case we are confronted mainly with the revelation of the Holy Scripture, as mentioned before, and with implicit elements of the Holy Tradition, in the ecphonisions, for example. In the Liturgy of the Faithful the Holy Scriptures preserve their significance untouched, but the attention of the faithful is concentrated towards the Holy Tradition, the second complementary branch of Revelation. But in Orthodoxy the Holy Tradition is regarded as an expression of the vivid communion with Christ of the whole community and in this sense the Creed simultaneously comes out of communion and is its foundation.

We can conclude the argument by referring back to the formula preceding the Creed: "Guard the doors, Wisdom." "Let us be attentive!" which makes it perfectly clear that there is a clear distinction between the catechumens and the faithful, pointing out the difference between the two levels of doctrine/communion and the necessity of a full confession of faith for the experience of a full communion. This should be always kept in mind, for it points to the significance of ecumenical dialogues, which have everything to do with the full content of doctrine, with the confession of faith.

Having understood the new doctrinal starting point for the Liturgy of the Faithful, it is possible to concentrate upon the next step towards communion. According to our human wisdom, this should lead first of all to the consecration of the gifts and then immediately to the Eucharistic communion of the Faithful. But just before the moment of communion, when God is addressed by the words of the Lord's Prayer, the faithful ask God permission to call him "Father." Note the significance of this moment. Normally we say this prayer quite often in our religious life, but here we understand its real significance. We do not address him in a casual way but ask for permission to speak to him and only after being certain that this permission is granted are we able to address him by these well-known words. Only after that, only after realising one's existence at different levels of faith and the real meaning of the relation between God and oneself, and of the whole history of salvation also, as revealed in the Scriptures and in the Holy Tradition, with the Creed as its highest expression present at the very beginning of the Liturgy of the faithful, only then is the believer allowed to receive the Holy Eucharist, to share it with the other members of the body of Christ which takes shape in these moments.

Having remembered the saints and the departed, experiencing a different type of communion with God and then his or her own life in the midst of the community and at a personal level, the believer is able to realise the actual meaning of what has happened: "We have seen the true light; we have received the heavenly Spirit; we have found the true faith, worshipping the undivided Trinity." One might think that "the true faith" is either fully intellectual or totally non-intellectual. But a deeper insight makes it clear, that this "either/or" is inappropriate here, that we stand here before an emergent reality: doctrinal truth springs out of communion, leads to communion and is understood profoundly by communion. It is obvious that the true faith the believer confesses here is more then an item of doctrine, it is a fact which embraces all levels of one's personality. At the same time now, when confronted with this concluding part of the Liturgy, one might forget what stands at its beginning, namely the Creed and together with it the whole body of doctrine. But actually this is not possible. The structure of the Liturgy makes it definitely clear that between this end and the beginning there is an organic unity. It is not possible to experience communion with Christ himself, communion with the other members of his body belonging to that specific Eucharistic community, without doctrinal knowledge, the essential part of the confession of faith.

If one remembers that in the Creed, in the confession of faith, we do not confess only two dogmas but the whole reality of revelation, it becomes obvious that only the whole of revelation, as it stands here, expressed in the canonical way by the church, is the basis for experiencing communion with Christ, Eucharistic communion. We see once again the organic relation between the two of them, but now we may understand better the significance of this doctrinal commitment and the agreement of the faithful in order for them to be able to experience communion with Christ. I say doctrinal agreement because the Creed is such an agreement and it includes almost automatically all other agreements, past, present or still to come. This is the place where, almost automatically, we feel like remembering the ecumenical dialogues — if not all their proceedings, then at least their positive results. They should be included in the Creed too, in order to make intercommunion possible, provided they have been previously received by the church, by the churches.

I cannot conclude this part of my paper without saying something about the consequences of a wrong approach to Eucharistic communion, with its basic elements as mentioned here. They were already suggested in the context of the Lord's Prayer. But even before, immediately after the consecration of the gifts, the priest utters several words in a low voice, which makes us see the whole process in a dramatic perspective:

> So that they (the body and blood of Christ, as it stands there as bread and wine) may be to those who partake of them for vigilance of the soul, forgiveness of sins, communion of Your Holy Spirit, fulfillment of the kingdom of heaven, confidence before You, and not in judgment or condemnation.

One will have certainly noticed the dramatic turn, the alternative opened at an unexpected moment, when everything seems to be related only to saintly communion. The alternative is condemnation, lack of communion, what we also call hell. Exactly the same idea is repeated in the same low voice before speaking it out loudly before the Lord's Prayer, as we already know. But the clearest expression of this alternative comes just before taking the communion. It is spoken out loudly, so that no confusion is possible: "Let not these holy gifts be to my condemnation because of my unworthiness, but for the cleansing and sanctification of soul and body and the pledge of the future life and kingdom." In terms of reception we return to the Old Testament instances dealt with, when we concluded that its absence is equal to a lack of communion between God and humanity, with the latter's death. By corroborating the two instances and relating them to the significance of the Creed, i.e. of doctrinal agreement, for the communion of the faithful with God, one can conclude that communion without this agreement means death. At least, it does so in the logic of the Orthodox liturgy.

This is the right perspective, which makes us understand the purpose of the dynamics I spoke of from the very beginning, called *theosis* by the Orthodox, which shows what significance the connection between knowledge and experience has and which shows that both of them must reach a certain level, in order to lead to salvation and not to condemnation.

We have already made it clear that the confession of faith stands not only for itself, but also for the whole revealed and accepted doctrine of the church. Having remembered this, we can better understand the necessity of unity in truth between the different parts of Christ's body. And only now can we understand the significance of efforts made in order to reach agreements between the different Christian denominations in our time. The ecumenical dialogues are such efforts. This leads to the third and last part of this paper.

Ecumenical Dialogue and Orthodox (Christian) Self-Understanding

It is the natural consequence of this understanding of the Holy Liturgy that it leads to Eucharistic communion with Christ and at the same time to communion with all members of the ecclesial community, who participate in the same Eucharistic communion. One could say that for those present communion is *an absolute imperative,* so that all the faithful present must take Christ's body and blood, provided they are ready for it.

Exactly the same is true for the communion of the larger body of Christ, between those who do not belong to the Orthodox Church and its faithful. The Orthodox and the non-Orthodox are called to participate in the body of Christ in the same way as the members of a certain local Eucharistic community do and it is important to know that intercommunion is not an option: it is an imperative, and all Christians should be aware of that.

On the other hand, this liturgical meaning of the Creed underscores the impossibility of experiencing intercommunion without unity in faith. In the Orthodox understanding, at least in this understanding, this would lead to spiritual death for everybody concerned, Orthodox or non-Orthodox. Without unity in faith a noble intention would have a disastrous end. This is the deeper reason for the Orthodox not accepting intercommunion unless the agreement in doctrine is given.

Knowing that communion is an imperative nobody can overlook, we are suddenly confronted with a second imperative, i.e. the necessity to seek the unity of faith and this we do by means of the theological dialogue between different denominations, by means of ecumenical dialogue. In this case too, there are no alternatives. Ecumenical dialogue must be regarded as an imperative expression of our self-understanding and in that case we can truly underscore only the significance of its reception. We are bound to do everything possible to have the results of these dialogues accepted by our own ecclesial bodies. Why? Because only after this acceptance are we able to confess that common faith that makes the communion possible between those belonging to different Christian denominations. Only after that are we able to accept and receive one another as communities, exactly as the Fathers did, when they gathered in Ecumenical Councils to accept other communities by means of dogmatic formulas, in order to share the same cup without fearing judgment and condemnation.

This would mean that the reception of dialogues becomes a part of one's own ecclesial experience, that it is not possible to be an Orthodox Christian anymore without trying to do one's best to listen to the imperative of dialogue and without trying to receive its results into one's own identity. Certainly this is not a selfish desire but aims at receiving the other denomination as an equal part of the same body of Christ. Trying to deepen this process of reception one can notice a development in the understanding of the other's faith, for example, with respect to items concerning subjective salvation, to use a traditional concept, but this would actually mean a progress in communion with that person, by which a new reality emerges, which is different from what existed before. There does not exist just an Orthodox, a Roman Catholic or a Lutheran anymore, as it was at the beginning of this process, but we now have Orthodox, Roman Catholic and Lutheran people and communities who accept one another in a process which brings them closer and closer, until they are ready for intercommunion, until they are ready to say together that they have experienced the same truth.

This is a long process for the whole community and in certain cases some people might be much quicker than others, i.e. some people might make greater progress during this process of mutual understanding and communication of communion on different levels. One might say that they are better prepared for intercommunion than others, that they have already reached those standards required for intercommunion we tried to suggest when referring to the Holy Liturgy. On the other hand, it is not possible to forget the unity between one member of an ecclesial community and all its other members. Therefore, one wonders whether this individual is allowed to do anything against the understanding of the body in which he or she was put by God himself, when he or she was born into a certain community, socialised into it or entered it by conversion. This is where we stand now. Many of us would think that in certain cases or under certain circumstances we could make the final step to intercommunion, but would nevertheless feel like showing solidarity with the other members of our own community. It is another paradox of this whole situation: I am already there and, at the same time, I am not and I do not complain about it.

I will conclude these considerations with some questions:
1. To what extent are Christians truly conscious of the necessity of intercommunion for the very essence of Christian identity?
2. To what extent are they convinced that ecumenical dialogues are an imperative without which the unity of faith and thus the experience of a real Christian identity are not possible?
3. To what extent do we promote a real process of reception of these dialogues, so that all parts of the ecclesial body are integrated into it?
To these questions I might, as an Orthodox looking at his own tradition, add another one:
4. Is our liturgical argument the only possible Orthodox way to answer the longing for intercommunion?

I do not think so! My approach in this paper corresponds to the past and present standards set up by the Orthodox when meeting people from another Christian tradition and facing the problem of intercommunion. They are perfectly legitimate maximal standards, as I have demonstrated by showing their internal liturgical logics. No Orthodox and, I think, no conscious Christian could ever doubt them seriously.

At the same time we should consider the possibility of a real communion with God that does not match those maximal standards. I think of God's willingness to save Sodom and Gomorrah, provided a single righteous person still lived there, or of the thief on the right hand of Jesus, crucified together with him, who was assured of meeting him in heaven – it is most certain that his communion with Christ did not equal that of the apostles, but he was accepted too. These are minimal standards of communion, nevertheless legitimated by revelation and effective in Orthodox everyday life, when believers of different spiritual levels share the same body of Christ in the Holy Eucharist.

It is my conviction that a solution of this problem of church communion will emerge from the tension between the maximal and the minimal standards considered here. For the moment Orthodoxy refers mainly to the maximal standards the logic of which I tried to explain in terms of a liturgical approach. But on another occasion we should also look at the minimal standards.

Enough is Enough?

Preconditions for Church Communion from a Lutheran Perspective

Oliver Schuegraf

Church Communion: A German Point of View

In February 2004 the United Evangelical Lutheran Church of Germany (VELKD) published a statement entitled *Ecumenism According to an Evangelical Lutheran Understanding*.[1] So what are the relevant passages for our question of church communion from a Lutheran perspective?

First of all, the VELKD stresses the importance of the proper relation between church unity and church communion. We read:

> The communion of the believers of all times and in every place, which is hidden from us, is the invisible unity in which we believe which is based on the *one* Lord, the *one* faith and the *one* baptism (Eph. 4, 5). On the other hand, the visible, institutionally established churches do not exist as a unity but as different local, regional or confessional congregations and churches.[2]

---

[1] The VELKD follows an earlier statement of the Evangelical Church in Germany (EKD) called *A Protestant Understanding of Ecclesial Communion*, which explains the EKD's model of ordered relations between churches of different confessions and in fact describes a very similar concept to the one of the VELKD paper. See *Kirchengemeinschaft nach evangelischem Verständnis* (Hannover, 2001 = EKD Texte 69); This version is published as: *A Protestant Understanding of Ecclesial Communion*, www.ekd.de/english/22_30_ecclesial_communion_2001.html. For a critical discussion of the text see O. Schuegraf, "Notwendige äussere Ordnung in unterschiedlichen Vorstellungen?" *Ökumenische Rundschau* 51 (2002): 463-68.

[2] *Ökumene nach evangelisch-lutherischem Verständnis: Positionspapier*

Since the church is understood as communion, a gathering of all believers – hidden, with boundaries not known to us, and the object of faith – "it is sufficient for the 'true unity' of the Church, as well as necessary, to agree on the right understanding of the Gospel, i.e. on proclamation in harmony with the Scriptures and on the administration of the sacraments."[3]

It is more than evident that these considerations are based on the famous definition in Article VII of the *Augsburg Confession*: "Et ad veram unitatem ecclesiae satis est consentire de doctrina evangelii et de administratione sacramentorum."[4] Therefore, for the VELKD the preconditions for church communion are these two criteria, which also constitute the church in general: true unity is given where the Gospel is rightly taught and the sacraments are rightly administered.

Consequently the VELKD paper continues: "Any additional condition would be a fundamental renunciation of the Lutheran understanding of the constitution of faith and the church."[5] The German Lutherans then go on to draw conclusions from this insight. The establishment of true unity is always God's work.

> The goal of ecumenism is rather *the declaration and practice of church communion on the basis and condition of the "true unity" of the church brought about by God and found in a common understanding of the gospel in harmony with the Scriptures.*[6]

True unity can never be achieved by the churches; rather, it can be declared a fact. So, if churches recognise the existence of a common understanding of the Gospel in their churches, then

---

der Kirchenleitung der VELKD (Hannover, 2004 = Texte aus der VELKD 123), § 3.1.a.

[3] *Ökumene* § 3.1.d.

[4] *Die Bekenntnisschriften der evangelisch-lutherischen Kirche*, herausgegeben im Gedenkjahr der Augsburgischen Konfession 1930, 10th edition (Göttingen, 1986), p. 61. The VELKD also uses the same biblical reference as the *Augsburg Confession*: Article VII closes with the same quotation with which the paper of the VELKD started its paragraph on church unity: Eph. 4:5.

[5] *Ökumene* § 3.1.d.

[6] *Ökumene* § 3.2.a.

they "must do justice to it by declaring and practising *church communion in word and sacrament* among themselves."[7]

Churches in communion with one another have the possibility of searching for closer cooperation, common structures and carrying out the church's task together. The term "visible unity," however, is not used at all in the document.

Churches that are not able to recognise a common understanding of the Gospel should also work together on all possible levels and participate in ecumenical conversations to search for that necessary common understanding of the Gospel. And above all, according to the VELKD they can still invite "members of such churches to share in the word and the sacraments in [their] own church."[8]

This short overview of *Ecumenism According to an Evangelical Lutheran Understanding* shows that the Lutheran Churches in Germany favour the model of "Church Communion" or "Ecclesial Communion" as it has been developed by the Leuenberg Church Fellowship and found expression in the *Leuenberg Agreement*.[9] Due to a common understanding of the Gospel and the realisation that the doctrinal condemnations of the confessional documents do not correspond to the present state of the doctrines of the assenting churches, over 100 churches of the Reformation in Europe have granted one another "table and pulpit fellowship," including "the mutual recognition of ordination and the freedom to provide for intercelebration."[10]

---

[7] *Ökumene* § 3.2.b.

[8] *Ökumene* § 3.2.f.

[9] Note that the German word *Kirchengemeinschaft* used to be translated as "church fellowship." However, there is the danger that church fellowship might be misinterpreted in the sense of a loose and non-binding relationship. It seems, therefore, that the word "church communion" or "ecclesial communion" is preferred for indicating that the sharing of Word and Sacrament is the highest form of unity. Thus, in line with this, in November 2003 the Leuenberg Church Fellowship was renamed the Community of Protestant Churches in Europe (CPCE).

[10] *Agreement between Reformation Churches in Europe* (Leuenberg Agreement). Trilingual Edition with an Introduction (Frankfurt a.M.,

Lutherans in Dialogue

Enough is enough. Is this all that can be said about a Lutheran understanding of church communion and should I stop my reflections right here? Actually, I take *Leuenberg* as my cue to broaden the perspectives. An overview of some dialogues helps us to grasp with what concepts for unity and models of union various Lutheran churches have engaged with other denominations.[11]

Conversations with the Methodists

The *Leuenberg Agreement* not only proved to be a very successful model in bringing together the Lutheran, Reformed, United and pre-Reformation Churches in Europe. It also became the sponsor for the ordered relations of these churches with the Methodists in Europe:

In Vienna 1994 the General Assembly of the Churches Participating in the Leuenberg Agreement decided that on the basis of an additional joint declaration the Methodists could become part of the Leuenberg Church Fellowship as soon as two-thirds of the existing member churches gave formal consent to this enlargement of the fellowship. In 1997 this new church communion between Methodists and the Leuenberg churches was publicly expressed in a Eucharistic service in Tallinn, Estonia.

This had been preceded by various national agreements. Back in 1987 the Evangelical Church in Germany and the Evangelical Methodist Church had already declared "pulpit and altar fellowship" (*Kanzel- und Abendmahlsgemeinschaft*), thus es-

---

1993), § 33. For a helpful account of the basis and principles of this concept see the statement *The Church of Jesus Christ*, issued by the 4th General Assembly of the Leuenberg Fellowship in Vienna in 1994.

[11] For an overview of the various bilateral dialogues with Lutheran involvement see O. Schuegraf, *Der einen Kirche Gestalt geben: Ekklesiologie in den Dokumenten der bilateralen Konsensökumene* (Münster, 2001 = Jerusalemer Theologisches Forum 3): with Anglicans, pp. 76-92; with Old Catholics, pp. 137-43; with Baptists, pp. 161-69; with Methodists, pp. 204-15; with Mennonites, pp. 216-22; with the Orthodox Churches, pp. 223-39; with the Reformed, pp. 240-54; with the Roman Catholic Church, pp. 255-87.

tablishing church communion.¹² Similarly, in 1994 the Church of Sweden and the Methodists signed an agreement on "full fellowship in preaching and sacraments" (*full förkunnelse- och sakramentsgemenskap*).¹³ And in 1997 Lutherans and Methodists in Norway followed suit. Their agreement has established "broadened church fellowship" (*utvidet kirkefellesskap*).¹⁴ All these official documents participate in the methods set out by Leuenberg but also take up the specific contexts in which the churches live.

Conversations with Baptists and Mennonites

The model of church communion granting fellowship in Word and Eucharist is also the leading model for the conversations of the VELKD with Mennonites and Baptists. The official dialogue group between German Lutherans and Mennonites asked their authorities in 1992 to declare table and pulpit fellowship. However, the VELKD did not follow this vote, since it still saw a need for clarification regarding the differences in the baptismal teaching. Therefore the two denominations offered each other Eucharistic hospitality instead, which in 1996 was made visible in two official Eucharistic services (one according to the Lutheran order, one according to the Mennonite tradition). On both

---

¹² For the history of the conversations and the agreement see Lutherisches Kirchenamt / Kirchenkanzlei der Evangelisch-Methodistischen Kirche (eds), *Vom Dialog zur Kanzel- und Abendmahlsgemeinschaft: Eine Dokumentation der Lehrgespräche und Beschlüsse der kirchenleitenden Gremien* (Hannover, 1987).

¹³ The agreement is based on the recommendations of *Svenska kyrkan / Metodist kyrkan i Sverige, Rapport från den andra samtalsdelegationen* (1991, ms.), p. 21.

¹⁴ Broadened church fellowship "means a fellowship which is expressed in a clearer and more binding manner than is the case in relationship between our churches today" *Fellowship of Grace: Report from the Conversations between Church of Norway and the United Methodist Church in Norway. Final Report and Proposal for an Agreement* (Oslo, 1994), § 38). However, all the characteristics of church communion according to *Leuenberg* can be found.

occasions both sides pledged to continue to strive for full communion.[15]

In a similar way the VELKD stated that as long as there is no common understanding of the sacrament of baptism with the Baptists the necessary preconditions for church communion are not yet met. However, the Lutherans officially recognised Baptists as part of the Church of Jesus Christ.[16]

---

[15] *Eucharistische Gastfreundschaft* (Hannover: VELKD, 1996 = Texte aus der VELKD 67).

[16] See *Stellungnahme der VELKD und des DNK zum Dokument 'Baptisten und Lutheraner im Gespräch'*, 3rd edition (Hannover, 1992 = Texte aus der VELKD 49), p. 9. The International Conversations between Lutherans and Baptists had already recommended in 1990 that both sides should recognise each other as parts of the one church of Jesus Christ (see *Baptists and Lutherans in Conversation: A Message to our Churches* [Geneva, 1990], § 90). This leads, however, to an interesting question. It can be assumed the German Lutherans wanted to express the fact that they in no way consider the Baptists a sect but rather a part of the Christian family, even though church communion cannot yet be established. But unfortunately the VELKD statement does not explain how it recognises another denomination as part of the one Church of Christ as long as there is no common understanding of baptism – the sacrament that is usually considered to be the rite of admission into the Church. Lutherans acknowledge the Baptist practice of adult baptism. But are they truly able to accept *all* Baptist baptisms? How can Lutherans acknowledge the baptism of an adult convert who has been already baptised as a child? This would mean to accept re-baptism. Therefore, Lutherans have to consider the same ritual act, which not only has the same form in each case but also for the Baptists the same theological foundation, to be valid in one instance (if the adult is a non-convert) and in the other case as invalid re-baptism (if the adult is a convert). This is a problem on which Lutheran theology has not reflected thoroughly enough. The dialogue between the CPCE and the Baptist European Federation briefly addresses the problem in its statement *The Beginning of the Christian Life and the Nature of the Church* but does not, however, resolve it. It only asks the Baptist congregations in Europe: "Would it be possible for them to avoid any appearance of re-baptism when believers come from a CPCE church which practises infant baptism? One way forward might be the following. While most Baptists would certainly consider infant baptism as inappropriate, they might not explicitly question its validity, and in

Both conversations with Baptists and Mennonites are good examples that the model of church communion accepts steps on the way to the final goal. If not all the necessary preconditions (in our case a common understanding of baptism) are met, then both sides are obliged to order their relations in a way that is appropriate to the consensus already reached (e.g. recognising each other as church and offering Eucharistic hospitality).

Conversations with Anglicans

We continue with some of the dialogues in which Lutherans are engaged with churches of the Anglican Communion. Here, too, some of the dialogues led to official and authorised agreements between the churches involved.

In 1988 the formal dialogue between the Evangelical Churches in both German republics and the Church of England published the *Meissen Common Statement*.

Bearing in mind, that "full visible unity" is a term and concept of unity usually not used in German Protestantism, it is quite remarkable that *Meissen* committed itself to exactly this idea. Paragraphs 6-8 are entitled "Growth towards full, visible unity" and in paragraph 7 we read that "[p]erfect unity must await the final coming of God's Kingdom …. But in a fallen world we are committed to strive for the 'full, visible unity' of the body of Christ on earth."[17]

However, this goal was not achieved with the official and solemn signing of the *Meissen Declaration* in 1991. Due to still remaining differences the churches were only able to take a step towards it, even though it was a very significant one.

---

these cases might make a confession of faith alone the requirement for recaption into a Baptist congregation, thus completing the path of Christian initiation" (*The Beginning of the Christian Life and the Nature of the Church*, www.leuenberg.net, 2004, § IV.11). This is, as a rule, precisely the practice of the German Mennonites, when a convert is received into a Mennonite congregation (see *Bericht vom Dialog VELKD / Mennoniten* [Hannover, 1993 = Texte aus der VELKD 53], p. 11).

[17] *The Meissen Agreement: Texts* (London, 1992 = CCU Occasional Papers 2), § 7.

Two different sets of preconditions for unity were a key problem in the conversations. The German churches brought their model of church communion, discussed above, into the dialogue. For the Church of England, however, the historic episcopate has to be considered as a further key element for unity.[18] Thus we read in the *Meissen Common Statement*:

> Lutheran, Reformed and United Churches, though being increasingly prepared to appreciate episcopal succession "as a sign of the apostolicity of the life of the whole church", hold that this particular form of episcope should not become a necessary condition for "full, visible unity". The Anglican understanding of full, visible unity includes the historic episcopate and full interchangeability of ministers. Because of this remaining difference our mutual recognition of one another's ministries does not yet result in the full interchangeability of ministers.[19]

It is interesting to note that in paragraph 8 both sides agree that full visible unity must include not only "a common confession of the apostolic faith in word and life" and "the sharing of one baptism, the celebration of one eucharist" but also "the service of a reconciled, common ministry" and a "bond of communion

---

[18] The so-called *Lambeth-Quadrilateral* shows that the historic episcopate is one of the cornerstones of the ecumenical endeavour of the Church of England. Its four points read in the version of 1888: "(a) The Holy Scriptures of the Old and New Testament, as 'containing all things necessary to salvation' [quotation from the 39 Articles], and as being the rule and ultimate standard of faith. (b) The Apostles' Creed, as the Baptismal Symbol; and the Nicene Creed, as the sufficient statement of the Christian faith. (c) The two Sacraments ordained by Christ Himself – Baptism and the Supper of the Lord – ministered with unfailing use of Christ's word of Institution, and of the elements ordained by Him. (d) The Historic Episcopate, locally adapted in the methods of its administration to the varying need of the nations and people called to God into the Unity of His Church" (*The Lambeth Conferences [1867-1948]: The Reports of the 1920, 1930 and 1948 Conferences, with Selected Resolutions from the Conferences of 1867, 1878, 1888, 1897 and 1908* [London, 1948], pp. 296f.).

[19] *The Meissen Agreement*, § 16.

which enable the Church at every level to guard and interpret the apostolic faith."[20] It seems that the German side recognises that a common understanding of the ministry is of at least derived necessity. Here in 1988 the Germans were able to stress the value of common structures more than *Ecumenism According to an Evangelical-Lutheran Understanding* seems to imply in 2004.

We now turn to the Nordic and Baltic Lutheran Churches. In September 1996 these churches officially ordered their relationships with the Anglican Churches of the British Isles with the signing of the *Porvoo Declaration*.

Compared to *Meissen*, the churches of the *Porvoo Declaration* had an easier starting point since most of the Nordic and Baltic Lutheran Churches had remained in or reintroduced the historic episcopacy. Thus they were able to reach a common understanding of apostolic succession and the laying on of hands with the Anglican churches. The *Porvoo Common Statement* states that the sign of the laying on of hands is "rather a means of making more visible the unity and continuity of the Church at all times and in all places."[21]

Porvoo remains slightly ambiguous about the question of whether "full, visible unity" has been reached with the signing of the declareation. Paragraph 60 speaks about the "form of visible unity" made possible by the agreement. Yet, at the same

---

[20] *The Meissen Agreement*, § 8.

[21] *Conversations between The British and Irish Anglican Churches and the Nordic and Baltic Lutheran Churches: Together in Mission and Ministry. The Porvoo Common Statement with Essays on the Church and Ministry in Northern Europe* (London, 1993), § 53 It is interesting to note that the Church of Norway Council on Ecumenical Relations in its evaluation of *Porvoo* picks up some critical responses in Norway to *Porvoo* on the "necessity" of the episcopal ministry. The Council admits that this matter was given more attention than is usual in the Church of Norway. But it comes to the clear conclusion that this does not impose a church-dividing difference (see *Statement on the Porvoo Common Statement by the Church of Norway Council on Ecumenical Relations* [Oslo, 31st of January 1994]; ms, p. 7). Evidently, this special focus on a particular form of ministry was still within the framework of Lutheran teaching, at least for Norwegian Lutherans.

time, both churches consider this only to be "a step towards visible unity" and they talk about their move to closer (!) communion. In my opinion, this has to be interpreted as stating that full communion has been achieved with the *Porvoo Declaration*, yet further steps should be to make this unity more visible.

In 1982 the American Lutherans and Episcopalians signed *The Lutheran-Episcopal Agreement*, which officially called for Interim Sharing of the Eucharist between the two denominations.[22] This step was taken, although this Eucharistic sharing "does not intend to signify that final recognition of each other's Eucharist or ministries has yet been achieved."[23] Once again we see that full doctrinal agreement does not have to be reached in order to step forward to some kind of unity. A sufficient agreement in Eucharistic teaching is reflected by an Interim Sharing of the Eucharist. The full recognition of each other's ministries was not a precondition for the step taken.

It took both churches almost twenty years before full church communion was indeed reached. In January 2001 the decisive agreement *Called to Common Mission* was signed by the Evangelical Lutheran Church in America (ELCA) and the Episcopal Church (ECUSA). This agreement is of special significance, since its adoption meant that a Lutheran Church – at present not in apostolic succession – agreed to move slowly into

---

[22] Signatory churches from the Lutheran side were the three churches that later formed the Evangelical Lutheran Church in America (the American Lutheran Church, the Lutheran Church in America and the Association of Evangelical Lutheran Churches). The Lutheran Missouri Synod was not part of the agreement.

[23] "The Lutheran-Episcopal Agreement: September, 1982," in: J.A. Burgess and J. Gros (eds), *Growing Consensus: Church Dialogues in the United States, 1962-1991* (New York / Mahwah, 1995 = Ecumenical Documents 5), p. 200. The presiding bishops of the churches involved define this Interim Sharing not as a reciprocal intercommunion "but rather a new and unique interim relationship, which looks toward future steps in that direction" and express their joy that the churches "are now willing for their ordained clergy to stand together at the altar, although not yet in place of each other" ("Statement: Joint Lutheran and Episcopal News Conference, September 28, 1982," *Ecumenical Bulletin* 56 [1982]: 22).

the historic episcopate for the sake of unity. The ELCA agreed that from now on the pastor who presides at ordinations will be an ELCA synodical bishop. Furthermore, at least three of the persons present for installations of future bishops will be bishops previously installed into the historic episcopate.[24] Thus the ELCA will eventually grow freely into the historic episcopate without thereby affirming that it is necessary for the unity of the church.[25] In order to enter into full communion at once the ECUSA, on the other hand, agreed to acknowledge the full authenticity of all Lutheran pastors immediately (!) without re-ordination, even though this meant the temporary suspension of Anglican ordination rites until all future Lutheran ministers are integrated in the historic succession.[26]

Even though the ELCA and the ECUSA are both churches in the USA, *Called to Common Mission* does not call for a shared ministry or an organic union. Rather, both sides agreed that the two churches once in full communion "become interdependent while remaining autonomous."[27] Full communion, however, includes the establishment of recognised organs of regular consultation and communication.

Before we leave the Lutheran-Anglican conversations it is worth having a look at the African continent. *The Interim Committee of the African Anglican Lutheran Consultation* stated in 1999:

> The vision, which guides our deliberation, is that of a united African Church with an African identity, in which Anglicans and Lutherans are in full communion and visible unity with one another. We look forward to a unique liturgical unity so that we may worship God as one church.[28]

---

[24] *Called to Common Mission*: www.elca.org/ea/Relationships/episcopalian/ccmresources/text.html, § 19f.

[25] *Called to Common Mission*, § 18.

[26] *Called to Common Mission*, § 14.16.

[27] *Called to Common Mission*, § 2.

[28] "Report of the Interim Committee of the African Anglican Lutheran Consultation, Harare 1999," quoted in: *Growth in Communion*:

Here the creation of a common African identity is apparently more important than the maintenance of denominational identities. A church union with a common liturgy is envisioned as goal. This is certainly a model of union that cannot be found in the context of the European or American Lutheran churches.

Conversations with the Orthodox Churches

So far, Article VII of the *Augsburg Confession* with its two criteria for the church (common understanding of the Gospel and sacraments), has been the ecumenical principle for the Lutheran side, even though the conversations with the Anglicans have focussed on different issues than the ones that followed closely the *Leuenberg Agreement*. The Lutheran-Orthodox conversations on the international level, as well as the conversations in Finland and those of the EKD with various Orthodox churches, hardly refer to this principle at all. Rather than quoting the Lutheran confessional statements, Lutherans refer to the Holy Scripture and the early Fathers. They make the effort to show their continuity with the undivided early church. None of these Lutheran-Orthodox dialogues has discussed precise concepts for church unity at length yet, but it can be assumed that this continuity with principles of the early church will also be the focus rather than the *satis est* of the *Augsburg Confession*, Article VII.

Conversations with the Roman Catholic Church

The Lutheran-Roman Catholic conversations have produced a remarkable amount of statements both at the national as well as at the international level. Some observations about them will round off this overview.

Church and Justification, the most recent statement of what is now called the Lutheran-Roman Catholic Commission on Unity did not produce significant results about the nature of unity and how unity might be realised. We have to turn to the document "Facing Unity" from 1984. It examines the different models of union offered on the ecumenical market. Weighing the strong and weak points of the various models, the commission

---

Report of the Anglican-Lutheran International Working Group, 2000-2002 (Geneva, 2003), § 16.

develops categories that it considers important for the shape of unity: joint witness to the apostolic faith, unity of faith in the diversity of its forms of expressions, removal of doctrinal condemnations, a common sacramental life, a structural community of service and a common ordained ministry.[29] The document puts its focus on the last aspect: A true *koinonia* demands a communion in ministry, which is more than the mere recognition of each other's ministry. Rather, it requires a joint practice of ministry, which "ultimately, means acceptance of the fellowship in episcopal ministry which stand in apostolic succession" and which "Lutherans are fundamentally free and open to accept."[30] The paper even draws a precise schedule of how this goal can be reached in four steps.[31]

It is evident that the statement assumes three preconditions for unity. Actually, this is put into words right at the beginning of the paper: "The unity of the church given in Christ and rooted in the Triune God is realised in our unity in the proclaimed word, the sacraments and the ministry instituted by God and conferred through ordination."[32]

With this sentence the Lutheran members of the Commission accept a model of union and preconditions for unity that go beyond any of the other documents discussed. It is not surprising that this raised substantial criticism. The VELKD, for example, denied in its response to "Facing Unity" that the ministry in a certain episcopal shape is on an equal level with word and sacrament and has the rank of a *plene esse* (instead of a *bene esse*) of the church.[33] And indeed one has to question if the very narrow structural framework regarding the ministry still meets

---

[29] "Facing Unity: Models, Forms and Phases of Catholic - Lutheran Church Fellowship," *The Secretariat for Promoting Christian Unity, Information Service* 59 (1985), §§ 46f.; in greater detail: §§ 55-145.

[30] "Facing Unity," § 98.

[31] "Facing Unity," §§ 120-41.

[32] "Facing Unity," § 3.

[33] *Stellungnahme der VELKD und des DNK/LWB zum Dokument der Gemeinsamen römisch-katholischen/evangelisch-lutherischen Kommission 'Einheit vor uns'* (Hannover, 1989 = Texte aus der VELKD 37), p. 11.

the space for legitimate diversity, which "Facing Unity" itself calls for on various occasions. The balance between visible unity in common structures and necessary diversity is lost. The strong criticism might also explain why the international dialogue has been rather careful on statements about unity ever since.

Preconditions for Church Communion

Where does this overview leave us? What are the essential paradigms for church communion from a Lutheran perspective?

Confessio Augustana VII

It has become evident that there is a great consensus that Article VII of the *Augsburg Confession* has to be the central starting point for any Lutheran concept of church unity.[34] This is the framework within which the Lutheran churches order their relations with other churches. Enough is enough, and for Lutherans the right understanding of the Gospel and the right administration of the sacraments therefore grant unity and are the two preconditions for unity. In many cases this has led to altar and pulpit fellowship.

However, pulpit fellowship is more than just agreement on the day-to-day preaching. The "consentire de doctrina evangelii" (*Confessio Augustana* [= CA] VII) calls for a basic doctrinal consensus. From a Lutheran standpoint, an adequate model of union therefore has to include a communion in confession. Communion in confession does not mean that both sides have

---

[34] We have already seen that the arguments of the VELKD paper centre around this article. Other Lutheran churches take a similar stance. In 1970 the Fifth Assembly of the Lutheran World Federation had already affirmed: "For the extension of church fellowship beyond the Lutheran family the only prerequisite should be a basic agreement on the gospel and the sacraments according to the Scriptures (*satis est*, CA VIII)" (*Sent into the World: The Proceedings of the Fifth Assembly of the Lutheran World Federation, Evian, France, July 14-24, 1970* [Minneapolis: Augsburg, 1971], p. 77). See also *Guidelines for the Ecumenical Work of the Church of Sweden:* Adopted in 1992 by the Central Board of the Bishop's Conference: www.svenskakyrkan.se/SVK/eng/ecuguide.htm, § 6.1 or *Ecumenism: The Vision of the ELCA* (Minneapolis, 1994).

to agree on the same confessional texts. Different confessional traditions can be in communion as long as there is a consensus that the differences in confessional traditions are a legitimate diversity of the same Gospel.

And if this need for a communion in confession is taken seriously, then doctrinal questions will automatically influence the model. Each bilateral dialogue has to wrestle for a form of union that takes into consideration the diversity in teaching of the churches involved as well as their specific history and geographical peculiarities. Therefore, Lutherans rightly envision unity as oneness in reconciled diversity. It is the logical consequence, then, that reconciled diversity is not only the goal but is also taken seriously on the way towards that goal, allowing different models to achieve unity.

A Ministry Serving Word and Sacrament

If we accept diversity in models, then we also have to accept that for many of our ecumenical partners Article VII of the *Confessio Augustana* is not enough. Often the value of ministry becomes the test case.

For Lutherans, ministry is not on the same level as Word and Sacrament but rather exists to serve them. In that sense it has a central role: "institutum est ministerium docendi evangelii et porrigendi sacramenta" (CA V).[35] Since it is the task of the whole church – meaning ministry in the most general sense of the word – to ensure that the good news is passed on and since the *communio sanctorum* has no authority to decide whether the Gospel should be proclaimed at all in Word and Sacrament, the institutionalised and public ministry is appointed, in order to ensure the execution of these two means of salvation that constitute the church. In that sense and only in that sense the church needs the ordained ministry or to use the words of the Lutheran World Federation: "The ordained ministry belongs to God's gift to the church, essential and necessary for the church to fulfil its mission."[36] Therefore, it is essential and consistent

---

[35] Cf. *Bekenntnisschriften*, p. 58.

[36] *The Episcopal Ministry within the Apostolicity of the Church: A Lutheran Statement, 2002* (Geneva, 2003), § 14.

that the *Leuenberg* model of granting church communion includes the mutual recognition of ministries.

However, we can even go a step further. Lutheran ecclesiology has never seen a particular form of ministry as the only possible way to fulfil its essential role. Lutherans should, therefore, show a great openness in taking into account the doctrinal particularities of their ecumenical partners and this might also include talking about particular forms of ministry, in other words, about episcopal structures.

According to the Apology of CA XIV, Lutherans had to do without bishops, since the later effaced God's word, left the right doctrine, and persecuted those teaching what is right. At the same time this paragraph stresses, that it is "our deep desire to maintain the church polity and various ranks of the ecclesiastical hierarchy, although they were created by human authority."[37] Today, however, it is safe to assume that the bishops in apostolic succession as we find them – let us say, for example, in the Anglican Church – do not persecute Lutherans, but indeed safeguard and spread God's Word.[38]

So I would like to argue that it is possible for Lutherans to reintroduce the historic episcopacy if this helps to comply with the promise given by the signers of the *Augsburg Confession* to

---

[37] Theordore Tappert (ed.), *The Book of Concord: The Confessions of the Evangelical Lutheran Church* (Philadelphia, 1959), p. 214 (= *Bekenntnisschriften*, pp. 296f.). See also: "It is not our intention that the bishops give up their power to govern, but we ask for this one thing, that they allow the Gospel to be taught purely and that they relax some few observances which cannot be kept without sin" (CA XXVIII, 77 lat. = Tappert, *Concord*, p. 94; *Bekenntnisschriften*, p. 132).

[38] *Confessio Augustana* describes the office of bishops as follows: "According to divine right ... it is the office of the bishop to preach the Gospel, forgive sins, judge doctrine and condemn doctrine that is contrary to the Gospel, and exclude from the Christian community the ungodly whose wicked conduct is manifest. All this is to be done not by human power but by God's Word alone. On this account parish ministers and churches are bound to be obedient to the bishops according to the saying of Christ in Luke 10:16, 'He who hears you hears me'" (CA XXVIII, 21f. [Tappert, *Concord*, p. 84; *Bekenntnisschriften*, p. 123f.).

the Emperor stating that they "shall not omit doing anything, in so far as God and conscience allow, that may serve the cause of Christian unity" (CA Preface 13).[39] This view is found not only in Melanchthon's rather irenic *Augsburg Confession*, but can be also backed by Luther's *Smalcald Articles*. Luther observes that if bishops "were concerned about the church and the Gospel," Lutherans could accept their authority to ordain and confirm "for the sake of love and unity, but not of necessity."[40]

So where does all this leave us? I suppose some Lutherans fear that taking up the historic episcopate implies that the ecclesiological reality of their particular church is being retrospectively questioned. And indeed, Lutherans are not able to accept any structural and doctrinal changes that might imply that they had not been part of the continuity and apostolicity of the one church and that their orders have been null and void.[41] In addition, safeguards must be found to ensure that the historic episcopate is not of equal rank as the two criteria for the church set out by Article VII of the *Augsburg Confession* and is thus not a necessary precondition for unity.

On the other hand, Lutherans are free to value the historic episcopate as *one* possible means of making more visible the

---

[39] Tappert, *Concord*, 26; *Bekenntnisschriften* 46f. In that sense the episcopal order can be understood as one of the adiaphora, "which are neither commanded nor forbidden in the Word of God, but have been introduced into the church in the interest of good order and the general welfare" and which only have to be resisted if required of it under persecution or duress (Epitome X [Tappert, *Concord*, pp. 492-94; *Bekenntnisschriften*, pp. 813-16]; see also *Solida Declaratio* X [Tappert, *Concord*, pp. 610-16; *Bekenntnisschriften*, pp. 1053-63]).

[40] *Smalcald* III.10 (Tappert, *Concord*, p. 314; *Bekenntnisschriften*, 457)

[41] This conviction explains the reactions to the declaration *Dominus Iesus* issued by the Congregation for the Doctrine of Faith in 2000. The statement that "ecclesial communities which have not preserved the valid Episcopate ... are not Churches in the proper sense" (*Declaration Dominus Iesus: On the Unicity and Salvific Universality of Jesus Christ and the Church* [Rome, 2000], § 17) implies that it is impossible for churches without the apostolic succession to have maintained the full apostolicity of the church, a claim to which Lutheran churches have to object.

unity and continuity of the church. If other churches are able to accept this Lutheran position as a possible one, then Lutherans are able to take up or to maintain apostolic succession for the sake of love and unity. *Porvoo* and *Called to Common Mission* are two good examples where, in a certain context, this was the way forward.

Steps and Stages on the Way to Church Communion

This leads us to another important point. A Lutheran concept of unity includes a model of union in stages. The already reached consensus has to be matched with a respective step on the way to unity.

However, the churches have to be aware that this interaction in various and diverse steps and stages can lead to unexpected "eternal triangles." For whenever one church declares church communion or any other form of official relationship with more than one church at the same time, then this will also have consequences for the now indirectly linked denominations, which one may call "churches-in-law." It can happen that members of "churches-in-law" practise degrees of fellowship under the roof of a third church on which their own churches have never agreed directly.[42] The latest Anglican-Lutheran document raises these issues and – borrowing a term from logic and mathematics – calls the phenomenon "intransitivity."[43] This anomaly of an imperfect web of communion has to be accepted if we take the insight seriously that all bilateral relations are contextual and if the churches want to avoid ecumenical paralysis.

However, "eternal triangles" or intransitivity always have to remain "the thorn in the side of any bilateral relation, keeping us 'from being too elated' (II Cor. 12:7)" – to cite once time the Anglican-Lutheran document just mentioned.[44] They only ought to be accepted, if the process of steps and stages is

---

[42] O. Schuegraf, "Ist der Freund meines Freundes auch mein Freund? Strukturelle Probleme ökumenischer 'Dreiecksverhältnisse'," *Ökumenische Rundschau* 48 (1999): 347-60.

[43] *Growth in Communion*, §§ 156-65.

[44] *Growth in Communion*, § 165.

backed by the deep conviction that at the end the churches will discover their God-given unity and be able to grant church communion.[45] It would be helpful, if ecumenical dialogues address this essential connection between intermediate steps and full unity more thoroughly and directly and considerations regarding already existing agreements are an integral part of any new agreement.

Striving for Full, Visible Unity

Finally, I would like to return to the term 'full, visible unity' which is a key phrase in most bilateral dialogues or official statements issued by churches to describe their ecumenical commitment.[46] Strikingly enough, this term is missing in the VELKD document *Ecumenism According to an Evangelical Lutheran Understanding*. This document stresses, rather, the invisibility of unity, as we have seen.

The document is right in the sense that the *una sancta* is an object of faith and the God-given unity of all believers will only be revealed at the end of times. This is the difference between the church and God's kingdom. Unity is solely God's work and cannot be made by humankind.

However, in my opinion, a Lutheran understanding of unity can never accept churches just living side by side. This is not enough. The institutionally established churches cannot contradict their core beliefs as expressed in their creeds. The confession of the *una sancta* is relevant for the visible church on earth. When Paul asks the Ephesians to "make every effort to maintain the unity of the Spirit in the bond of peace" (Eph. 4:3), this cannot be seen as a reference to the invisibility of the church's unity as the document of the VELKD seems to imply. Rather, it shows that Paul envisions unity in visible and concrete terms.

---

[45] One should simply recall the already mentioned *Lutheran-Episcopal Agreement on Interim Eucharist Sharing* in the USA. It states that the final recognition of each other's Eucharist or ministries has not *yet* been achieved, implying that both sides are convinced it will be one day. And indeed *Called to Common Mission* was able to establish both.

[46] For an overview regarding the goal of visible unity in the various Lutheran-Anglican conversations see *Growth in Communion* §§ 111-21.

The declaration and practice of table and pulpit fellowship is such an act of giving evidence of visible unity. But the churches are unceasingly called by God to make this church communion even more visible to the world. *Called to Communion and Common Witness*, the latest document of the Lutheran World Federation and World Alliance of Reformed Churches reminds us of this insight:

> Often, the view is held that declaring communion does not call for any further steps. We believe that mutual recognition implies a commitment to work together towards greater visibility. Lutherans and the Reformed need therefore to engage in a common reflection on the appropriate forms of the visible unity of the church.[47]

This striving for "full, visible unity" might in some cases be best served when the institutionally established churches keep existing as different local, national or confessional churches. In other cases, however, it might make sense to work towards a common ministry and joint structures of oversight to serve this goal best or to start a process of uniting churches. Within the framework of Article VII of the *Augsburg Confession* the Lutheran churches have an exciting scope to give witness and shape to the unity that is already given through God's reconciling work in Christ and that arises from the sharing in the trinitarian unity and communion. They are obliged to use their given freedom and flexibility to show this unity with each of their ecumenical partners as fully and visibly as possible in obedience to God's will "ut unum sint" (John 17:21).

---

[47] *Called to Communion and Common Witness: Report of the Joint Working Group Between the Lutheran World Federation and the World Alliance of Reformed Churches, 1999-2001* (Geneva, 2002).

Part II

Notions of Catholicity and Communion

This section offers four essays which directly or indirectly reflect on the notion of catholicity and its meaning for any discourse on the matter of unity.

Martien Brinkman, from the Vrije Universiteit in Amsterdam (the Netherlands), approaches the theme from the viewpoint of contemporary debates on inculturation. He looks first at questions of identity and nationalism, and their relationship to evangelisation. Attention is drawn to the constant ambiguity present in discussions of inculturation, and the need for challenges to be mutual – from culture to Gospel but also from Gospel to culture. Hence there can be no naïve attempt to separate context and catholicity. Thus, he moves on to address the concept of catholicity and the various implications this has in terms of the relationship between local and universal church, the role of ministry in determining the catholicity of the local church and the fact that "catholic" cannot simply be understood as "universal."

Anton Houtepen, from the University of Utrecht (the Netherlands), takes as his theme the new catholicity. He argues that this concept allows for local churches in interior communion, forming a church that is catholic, universal, precisely because it is local. What unites these churches is their "shared matrix of faith and life," an idea, however, that should not be allowed to take on an exclusivist colouration. Valid diversity has always included accepting the ministry and sacraments of those churches gathered in council. This is simultaneously a wider and narrower field than is sometimes proposed.

The third essay in this section addresses a different problem or, at least, approaches the matter of catholicity from a very different angle. Eddy Van der Borght, from the Vrije Universiteit in Amsterdam, looks at the relationship between faith and ethnicity in Europe. Thus, the question is perhaps more one of what happens when "context" prevails over "catholicity," when the local – especially in its socio-political but thus also religious forms – has priority over the universal. The essay deals with three documents, the Oxford Life and Work Conference of 1937, the Leuenberg document of 2001 and the *Charta Oecumenica*. For each of these documents he offers, first, a summary of their history and conclusions and then a critical analysis of their content. At the end of his essay Van der Borght summarises his conclusions, drawing particular attention to the reactive nature of the documents and their lack of sound theological, and especially ecclesiological, grounding.

Finally, Johannes Oeldemann of the Möhler Institut in Paderborn, Germany, examines the question as to how the model of gradual church communion might be employed to construct a way forward in the field of ecumenical endeavour. He offers seven theses on which he expands briefly, looking first at the problems and possibilities inherent in the various confessions and traditions and secondly at the potential of this model as a means for reinforcing the ecumenical movement. Underlying Oeldemann's attempts is, perhaps, a certain disquiet at the apparent paradox of a situation where church leaders can endorse a document such as the *Charta Oecumenica* while at the same time issuing pronouncements which seem rather to make a problem of the whole idea of ecumenical cooperation and progress.

Thus, Oeldemann takes church leaders to task for turning their backs on the model of gradual church communion, demonstrating that it is actually supported by their own traditions, and arguing for the reviving of this model as an apt agent for furthering dialogue and promoting the growth of unity. Oeldemann deals directly with problems at the level of church leadership. But, in doing so, he draws attention to related problems that need to be addressed seriously if the ecumenical endeavours of the churches are not to cease altogether or at best relegated to the safe backwater of specialist interest groups whose deliberations and findings do not impinge on each church confession as a whole.

The Modern Inculturation Debate and the Catholicity of the Church

Martien E. Brinkman

The Modern Inculturation Debate

The modern inculturation debate confronts us with the transcultural effects of the Christian message:[1] God's Word always comes to people in a specific culture as the "milieu" of human living.[2] The Gospel cannot be identified with any particular culture and no culture can claim to have grasped the fullness of God. In the confrontation with new cultures new aspects of the Gospel can illuminate but can be kept hidden as well. Hence, in the modern ecumenical inculturation debate the importance and ambivalence of the theological meaning of the context are often simultaneously emphasised. In new approaches of the relation between Gospel and culture, the challenging character of the interaction in this two-way relationship is especially stressed. Culture challenges the Gospel and the Gospel challenges cultures.[3] This twofold approach can clearly be recognised in the so-called *Colombo Statement*, arising from a consultation of the World Alliance of Reformed Churches (WARC) with the participation of the World Council of Churches (WCC) and the Lutheran World Fed-

---

[1] For a survey see J. van Butselaar, "The Gospel and Culture Study: A Survey," *Exchange* 27 (1998): 236-47.

[2] There is a great deal of literature dealing with the meaning of the concept of culture. One of the most well-known definitions is that of C. Geertz in *The Interpretation of Cultures: Selected Essays* (New York, 1973), p. 89, who describes culture as "a historically transmitted pattern of meanings embodied in symbols, a system of inherited conceptions expressed in symbolic forms by means of which men communicate, perpetuate, and develop their knowledge about and attitudes toward life."

[3] For the discussion within the WARC see *Gospel and Cultures: Reformed Perspectives* (Studies from the WARC No.35) (Geneva, 1996), esp. pp. 133-48, "Report of the Consultation."

eration (LWF) on "Ethnicity and Nationalism," held in Colombo (Sri Lanka) in 1994. It states that, as the Gospel has been preached to many nations, the church has taken root in many cultures, transforming them as well as being profoundly shaped by them. Yet the church does not have its own specific culture; rather, to be church is a way of living the life of the new creation within a given culture. Therefore, the church must have its feet firmly planted in any culture in which it lives but have its arms stretched out towards God and God's future, the new creation.

Referring to Pentecost, the *Colombo Statement* confirms that this event is not a reversal of the experience of cultural diversity to which the story of the Tower of Babel refers. It states:

> We wish to affirm not only the unity of humanity but also the cultural diversity that ethnic groups bring to our societies. One of the tasks of the church in a given culture is to contribute to the flowering of that culture, as well as to make sure that the salutary sense of ethnic belonging does not turn into ethnic aggressions towards the "stranger who is within the gates" or towards neighbouring ethnic groups. It is therefore the responsibility of the church to work towards genuine community, in which each ethnic group remains faithful to its dynamic and changing identity and yet is enriched by and enriches others.[4]

The statement speaks about ethnic identity not as a entity of static, unchangeable characteristics but as a dynamic reality. In an appendix containing an explanation of the terms used, it is recognised that many factors shape human identity, including religion, culture, gender and class. In relation to all these factors it can be said that identity "is about a sense of belonging." Every person from birth requires socialisation in a culture for his or her development. Identity is therefore derived in part from membership in a socio-cultural system.

This acknowledgement confronts us, however, immediately with the question of what primarily determines our Christian identity. In all parts of the world for the last two decades we have been witnessing a search for cultural roots, a stress on cul-

---

[4] "Ethnicity and Nationalism: A Challenge to the Churches," *The Ecumenical Review* 47 (1995): 225-31, esp. pp. 227-28.

tural uniqueness and an insistence on a group's right to its own particular development. As a vehement protest against the overriding power of the "message" of globalisation communicated by the Western mass media and multinationals, the plea for ethnic identity can be understood as an expression of the concern to protect the integrity of peoples, nations, etc. Hence, the report of the conference on World Mission and Evangelism in Salvador, Bahia (Brazil) in 1996 states, that "the positive values of ethnicity and sovereignty of peoples and nations in the face of the forces of globalization are to be affirmed."[5] In this regard the African theologian John Pobee is undoubtedly the spokesperson for many in the South when he says that "there is in the North an almost pathological fear of nationalism" and that

> we should eschew any pathological fear of the ideology of nationalism, however much pain and destruction have in history gone with the upsurge of nationalism. For different cultures require different symbols.[6]

In the current inculturation debate the references to the creation, the incarnation and the gifts of the Spirit play an important role.[7] It underscores that inculturation is not a luxury, a surplus, an added extra, but the very way in which the Gospel enters into the lives of people. The recognition, however, that the life of a local congregation should be rooted authentically in its particular context confronts us – as the *Riano Statement* of the WCC and the Vatican of 1985 states – with the same ambivalent evaluation as articulated in the analysis of the nationalism debate in the 1930s.[8]

---

[5] Cf. C. Duraisingh (ed.), *Called to One Hope: The Gospel in Diverse Cultures* (Geneva, 1998), pp. 45-49, "Gospel, Ethnicity and Identity Politics," esp. p. 48.

[6] J.S. Pobee, "Churches Between Nationalistic Endeavor and Ecumenical Demand," *Mission Studies* 8 (1991): 177-89, esp. pp. 180 and 185.

[7] Cf. C. Duraisingh, "Gospel and Cultures: Some Key Issues," in: P. Réamonn (ed.), *Break the Chains of Injustice*, Studies of the WARC 33 (Geneva, 1996), pp. 30-55.

[8] Cf. for a brief survey of that debate, especially at the second meeting of the International Missionary Council at Tambaram (India) in 1938, M.E. Brinkman, "From Nationalism to Inculturation Debate," in:

On the one hand there is the affirmative aspect of the Gospel:

> The gospel transforms people and cultures to bring to fruition the possibilities inherent in them; the best in them is realized when they have authentic self-identity and self-expression. Thus, the denial of opportunity for self-identity and authentic self-expression impedes the gospel.[9]

On the other hand, however, every culture is called by the Gospel to conversion. Christian identity is, therefore, always a new identity. The self-affirmation wrought by the Gospel must be understood as the result of a lifelong process of the dying of our "old Adam" and the rising of our reborn "self" as a new creation in Christ, the "second Adam." Hence, the real identity of Christians all over the world can be found only in the reference to the implications of their baptism, including a "new ethical orientation," as the WCC *Lima Text on Baptism, Eucharist and Ministry* has it. Even in the case of the indiscriminate baptism of infants in the so-called established churches the meaning of baptism is always derived from the life-changing "model" of adult baptism and, to quote the *Lima Text* once again, implies that

> by baptism, Christians are immersed in the liberating death of Christ where their sins are buried, where the "old Adam" is crucified with Christ, and where the power of sin is broken .... Thus, those baptized are pardoned, cleansed and sanctified by Christ, and are given as part of their baptismal experience a new ethical orientation under the guidance of the Holy Spirit.[10]

E.A.J.G. Van der Borght, D. van Keulen, M.E. Brinkman (eds), *Faith and Ethnicity*, Vol. 2, Studies in Reformed Theology 7 (Zoetermeer, 2002), pp. 256-67, esp. pp. 256-60.

[9] "Gospel and Culture: The Working Statement Developed at the Riano Consultation," *International Review of Mission* 74 (1985): 264-67, esp. p. 266. This consultation consisted of an international group of forty-six people meeting at Riano (Italy) in 1984, by invitation of the WCC Commission on World Mission and Evangelism and the Vatican Secretariat for the Promotion of Christian Unity to consider the theme "Gospel and Culture," which resulted in this short *Riano Statement*.

[10] Cf. *Baptism, Eucharist and Ministry*, Faith and Order Paper 111

This baptismal experience cannot be limited to a strictly individual experience. It can be applied to Christian groups as well. Hence, the French ecumenical dialogue commission Groupe des Dombes speaks, referring to this Christian experience of baptism, about the conversion not only of individual believers but also of churches and stresses the point that without this preparedness for conversion there can be no real Christian identity.[11] What conversion in different situations exactly implies can only be, however, formulated in relation to the biography of the persons involved within the framework of their social circumstances and can never be universally articulated and indiscriminately imposed.[12]

This conversion aspect of Christian baptism gives a peculiar flavour to the inculturation debate. It implies that no plea for the incorporation of contextual factors can be naive. In every context there is a potential ambiguity about the way in which the Gospel is proclaimed. Contextual differences have helped shape confessional divisions, but the diversity of contexts calls also for authentic engagement with the diverse riches of Scripture. Hence, we cannot play the one concept (contextuality) off against the other (catholicity).

(Geneva, 1982), p. 2.

[11] Cf. *Pour la Conversion des Églises: Identité et changement dans la dynamique de communion* (Paris, 1991), p. 21 (no.8): "Bien loin de s'exclure, identité et conversion s'appellent l'une l'autre: il n'y a pas d'identité chrétienne sans conversion; la conversion est constitutive de l'Église; nos confessions ne méritent le nom chrétiennes que si elles s'ouvrent à l'exigence de conversion." See also P. Lengsfeld, "Ökumenische Spiritualität als Voraussetzung von Rezeption," in: P. Lengsfeld and H.G. Stobbe (eds), *Theologischer Konsens und Kirchenspaltung* (Stuttgart *et al.*, 1981), pp. 126-34, esp. p. 132; and P. Lengsfeld, "Ökumenische Theologie als Theorie ökumenischer Prozesse," in: P. Lengsfeld and H.G. Stobbe (eds), *Ökumenische Theologie* (Stuttgart, 1980), pp. 36-68, esp. pp. 60-68.

[12] *Bangkok Assembly: Minutes and Report of the Assembly of the Commission on World Mission and Evangelism* (Geneva, 1973), pp. 70-86, "Culture and Identity," esp. p. 76.

The document of the Faith and Order Commission of the WCC on intercultural hermeneutics, *A Treasure in Earthen Vessels*, gives a good impression of this two-sided aspect of contextuality. It begins with a rather neutral definition of contextuality: "The dimension of contextuality refers to the interpretation and the proclamation of the gospel within the life and culture of a specific people and community."[13] It continues immediately, however, with a strong emphasis on the double, critical and affirmative, role of this concept. With regard to the critical function, it states that a contextual proclamation of the Gospel "can seek to judge the cultural context, it can seek to separate itself from the culture in which the church is set and it can seek to transform culture."[14]

It is precisely in this transforming capacity, however, that the Gospel plays its affirmative role as well. Referring to a WCC consultation on intercultural hermeneutics at Jerusalem in 1998, it quotes the sentence that real contextuality "appears whenever the gospel works like salt and leaven, not overwhelming a context, but permeating and enlivening it in distinctive ways."[15] This function of the Gospel might be described as a purifying function in which the critical and affirmative roles are integrated.[16] In this way the Gospel demonstrates its liberating power.

> When the church's faith is genuinely contextual, the shame and stigma imposed on oppressed people begins to be lifted. They find a new dignity as they see not only their own lives but also their culture in God's redeeming light. When faith is contextual,

---

[13] *A Treasure in Earthen Vessels: An Instrument for an Ecumenical Reflection on Hermeneutics*, Faith and Order Paper 182 (Geneva, 1998), p. 30 (No. 44).

[14] *A Treasure in Earthen Vessels*, p. 30 (No. 44).

[15] "On Intercultural Hermeneutics: Report of a WCC Consultation Jerusalem 5-12 December 1995," *International Review of Mission* 85 (1996): 241-51, esp. p. 245.

[16] The report of the 1996 International Missionary Conference held in Salvador, Bahia, Brazil, identifies the Gospel's role in "illuminating" and "transforming" cultures and considers the "purification" of certain elements of cultures as one of the aspects of this transformational role; cf. C. Duraisingh (ed.), *Called to One Hope*, pp. 34-35.

there is a recognition that the gospel speaks to Christians in their language, connects with their symbols, addresses their needs and awakens their creative energies.[17]

The main thesis of this present essay is that this concept of contextuality need not be interpreted or understood in contrast or opposition to the concept of catholicity but rather in conformity with it.

The Catholicity of the Church

The catholicity of the church implies an interrelatedness and interdependence among local churches. That means in the first place that once a local church turns in upon itself and seeks to function completely independently from other local churches, it distorts a primary aspect of its ecclesial character. In other words, catholicity belongs to the definition of the local character of the church. Only in this openness to communion does the local church fully live its own catholicity: "Catholicity enters into the very concept of church and refers not simply to geographic extension but also to manifold variety of local churches and their participation in the one *koinonia.*"[18]

The same interpretation was already to be found at the Fifth Assembly of the WCC in Nairobi in 1975, which emphasised in Section II of its report, "On What Unity Requires," that "each local church possesses, in communion with others, the fullness of catholicity."[19] As the Second Vatican Council's Constitution on the Church, *Lumen Gentium*, states, the variety of local churches demonstrates with even "greater clarity the catholicity of the undivided church" (23). This catholicity can be and is experienced wherever the Word of God is announced and received in faith, where baptism is administered, where the Eucharist is celebrat-

---

[17] C. Duraisingh (ed.), *Called to One Hope*, pp. 34-35.

[18] Cf. the document "The Church: Local and Universal," No. 19, in: Joint Working Group between the Roman Catholic Church and the World Council of Churches, *Sixth Report* (Geneva, 1990), pp. 23-37, esp. p. 29.

[19] Cf. G. Gassmann (ed.), *Documentary History of Faith and Order 1963-1993* (Geneva, 1993), p. 3.

ed, where the ministers serve the Lord's flock, where the Spirit bestows his gifts. There the one Church of Christ is present and visible. Hence, the document "The Church: Local and Universal" is able to conclude:

> All Christian World Communions can, in general, agree with the definition of the local church as a community of baptised believers in which the word of God is preached, the apostolic faith confessed, the sacraments are celebrated, the redemptive work of Christ for the world is witnessed to, and a ministry of *episcope* exercised by bishops or other ministers is serving the community (No. 15).[20]

In the second place, that implies that wherever ordained ministers preach the Gospel and administer the sacraments, we can recognise the church. As such, these local communities express the presence of the church of all places and all times, i.e., the catholic church.

In the third place, it must be underscored that this catholicity of the church cannot simply be equated with universality. The catholic church as a communion of saints (*communion sanctorum*) has at least two dimensions: a less visible diachronic, historical dimension and a more visible synchronic, universal dimension. Protestants especially face the problem of concretely manifesting the second dimension of visible, synchronic universality among their churches. They often have only weak structures beyond the confines of their own congregation, although the foundation of the WCC has certainly heightened their awareness of belonging to a world communion of churches.

If indeed – as stated above – real catholicity implies the participation of the local in the global and of the global in the local, catholicity is not the destruction or overwhelming of the local but the local in communion. It can be ascribed to each local community, inasmuch as each community expresses in its faith, life and witness this fullness that is nowhere yet fully realised. Catholicity grows from the commitment of local churches to communion, both with other churches in the present (synchronically) and

---

[20] *Sixth Report*, p. 27.

with the church throughout the ages (diachronically). Hence, the report of the Jerusalem consultation concludes:

> If the church's life is to be healthy, it must be characterized by a dynamic interaction between catholicity and contextuality. Otherwise the identity of the gospel as transforming story is compromised. If catholicity is emphasized at the expense of contextuality, the gospel may not fully connect with the life of the people and cease to be good news. If contextuality is emphasized at the expense of catholicity, division and instability may undermine the gospel's expression of God's reconciling purpose for the world as a whole.[21]

Just as a contextual interpretation of the Gospel does not in itself imply a legitimation of the local situation, so it is also not, by definition, bound to a specific context. When, for example, an interpretation of the Gospel in a particular context points to injustice or to liberation, this interpretation is not simply a contextual claim. It may provide an insight to be tested and amended or applied in other contexts. The reflections of people such as Bonhoeffer, King, Gandhi and Mandela on their particular contexts are instructive examples of the universalising potentialities of many human situations. No contextual interpretation, however, can claim to be absolute. It is especially catholicity that binds Christian communities together and that makes possible the awareness of possible limitations of one's own experiences as well as the possible enrichments through the experiences of others.[22]

Conclusions

Just as catholicity also belongs to the definition of the local church, so contextuality belongs to the definition of the catholic church. The local, contextual church is indeed not an independent, self-sufficient reality. It is church in a diachronic and synchronic relation with other churches of its own tradition and those of others and in this *koinonia* every local church is a consti-

---

[21] "On Intercultural Hermeneutics," p. 246.

[22] *A Treasure in Earthen Vessels*, pp. 31-32 (No. 48).

tutive part of the universal church throughout the ages i.e. the catholic church. This implies that there is no universal church without local churches. This interconnectedness is a direct corollary of the character of the Gospel itself. Any authentic understanding of the Gospel is both contextual and catholic. The Gospel is contextual in that it is inevitably embodied in a particular culture; it is catholic in that it expresses the apostolic faith handed down from generation to generation within the communion of churches of all places and all ages.

Therefore, the main question is not the supposed contrast between catholicity and contextuality, but what the outcome of this cross-fertilisation of local and catholic aspects of the Christian message might be. Which cultural aspects will survive in the (baptismal) process of dying and rising with Christ? What kind of consequences will that have for the structure, liturgy, theology, etc. of the catholic church?

This implies that no church can claim that its own ministry, liturgy, doctrine, church order, etc. is the unique biblical one. Within an ecumenically composed "hierarchy of truths" the church order and ministry, etc. of every church might be interpreted as an – in principle – authentic, contextual interpretation of the Gospel and, as such, it might claim catholic meaning. But only as such: as a contextual and therefore, by implication, limited interpretation.

Hence, first of all, every church tradition has to show the biblical character of its church order, ministry, etc. Secondly, every church tradition has to engage in ecumenical dialogue with other traditions in order to put its own interpretation of the Gospel in balance with those of other churches.

Then, in an atmosphere of comprehensiveness, rather than one of exclusiveness, churches can enrich one another and legitimately interpret their own church life as one of the many rich contributions to the catholicity of the church. For future decades it is realistic to expect that especially the churches of the southern hemisphere will – in the abovementioned sense – enrich the concept of the catholicity of the church with their own, local, contextual interpretations of the Gospel and its ecclesiological implications.

The Catholicity of the Church

A Matrix of Faith and Life in View of God's Final Kingdom

Anton Houtepen

A New Catholicity

At the beginning of the third millennium we are witnessing a new worldwide "ecclesiogenesis": in ecumenical dialogue among the various Christian traditions, in the encounter with other living faiths, in the challenging re-reception of the heritage of Israel, in daring new responses to socio-economic, cultural and political contexts in Asia, Latin America and Africa, in the "reconstructive hermeneutics" of the idea of church within feminist theology and in the search for a "foundational theology" of the church in secularised Europe and North America. Ecclesiological reflection on the church, local and universal, today implies a real intercultural approach. Within the Christian family the missionary and ecumenical movements have brought together people of all tribes and nations in a continuous exchange of customs, ideas and forms of community life. At the same time all of them are related to the common heritage of the faith of Abraham and the Gospel of Jesus Christ, sent out by the Father of all on a mission of salvation reaching out to all.

Every form of the church, therefore, should be *catholic* – not, however, in the sense of any centralised, universalist or global geographical concept of a so-called worldwide church but in the sense of a *new catholicity*, as Robert Schreiter[1] has called it. Nor should it be local in the sense of territorial limitations (e.g, by claiming a *canonical territory* for a certain church or by appealing to the anachronistic feudal principle of regalism (according to the

---

[1] R. Schreiter, *The New Catholicity: Theology between the Global and the Local* (Maryknoll, 1997).

principle *cuius regio, eius et religio*), or in the sense of ethnic chauvinism or racist segregation. The *ekklèsia tou theou*, according to Acts 2 and Matt. 28:19-20, is gathered from among all peoples of the earth or, according to the *Didachè* (X.; cf IX. 4), from the four winds and the ends of the earth. Christians are at home anywhere in the world and are aliens and strangers – *paroikoi* – passing through in every country.[2] They have *une patrie portable* (H. Heine), a portable fatherland.

No Global Church; Local Churches in Interior Communion

But this does not imply that they are the same everywhere nor that there should be something like a "global church," let alone some Platonic idea of an original universal church, disseminated over the world in a myriad of particles of the universal church and called particular churches. Just as economic, cultural and political globalisation should not imply the imposition of one economic or political system or one dominating culture on all parts of the world, so Christian catholicity is not well served by a fully centralised church order, theology and discipline. Western Latin Christianity, and Roman Catholicism especially, through its long legal tradition and cultural dominance over the centuries, is in danger of imposing its universalist claims on all particular, local churches. Such centralism harms the creativity and blocks the right of initiative of the local churches within the Roman Catholic communion of churches. If applied to all particular churches of Eastern and Western Christianity and to the newly emerging churches in the southern hemisphere, it would destroy the conciliar community of the churches participating in the one Ecumenical Movement. In its heavily criticised *Letter to the Bishops of the Roman Catholic Church on Some Aspects of the Church Understood as Communion*, the Congregation for the Doctrine of the Faith stated:

> The Church of Christ, which we profess in the Creed to be one, holy, catholic and apostolic, is the universal Church, that is, the worldwide community of the disciples of the Lord, which is present and active amid the particular characteristics and the

---

[2] *Ad Diognetum* IV, 6-VI, 3. *Sources Chrétiennes* 33 bis (Paris 1965), pp. 61ff.

diversity of persons, groups, times and places. Among these manifold particular expressions of the saving presence of the one Church of Christ, there are to be found, from the times of the Apostles on, those entities which are in themselves Churches, because, although they are particular, the universal Church becomes present in them with all its essential elements. They are therefore constituted "after the model of the universal Church," and each of them is "a portion of the People of God entrusted to a bishop to be guided by him with the assistance of the clergy.[3]

The quotation "after the model of the universal Church" refers to *Lumen Gentium* 23 ("… Ecclesiis particularibus, ad imaginem Ecclesiae universalis formatis …") and *Ad Gentes* 20. In both cases however, the emphasis is on the role of the local bishops for the unity and mission of the particular churches: "…in quibus et ex quibus una et unica Ecclesia catholica exsistit."[4] The universal church exists *in* and consists *of* local, particular churches. The unity and mission of the church of Christ, the one Body of Christ, consists of many members cooperating with the Head of the Body, Jesus Christ, in *his* mission, which is the *Missio Dei*. Vatican II did not speak of any "ontological priority" of the "universal Church" or of a "mother-daughter" relationship between the universal and the particular churches, as does § 9 of the *Letter on Communion*:

> In order to grasp the true meaning of the analogical application of the term *communion* to the particular Churches taken as a whole, one must bear in mind above all that the particular Churches, insofar as they are *"part of the one Church of Christ,"* have a special relationship of *"mutual interiority"* with the whole, that is, with the universal Church, because in every particular Church *"the one, holy, catholic and apostolic Church of Christ is truly present and active."* For this reason, *"the universal Church cannot be conceived as the sum of the particular Churches, or*

---

[3] Congregation for the Doctrine of the Faith, *Letter to the Bishops of the Catholic Church on some Aspects of the Church understood as Communion*, (28 May 1992), *Acta Apostolicae Sedis* 85 (1993): 838-50.

[4] *Lumen Gentium* 23

as a federation of particular Churches." It is not the result of the communion of the Churches, but, in its essential mystery, it is a reality *ontologically and temporally* prior to every *individual* particular Church. Indeed, according to the Fathers, *ontologically*, the Church-mystery, the Church that is one and unique, precedes creation, and gives birth to the particular Churches as her daughters. She expresses herself in them; she is the mother and not the product of the particular Churches. Furthermore, the Church is manifested, *temporally*, on the day of Pentecost in the community of the one hundred and twenty gathered around Mary and the twelve Apostles, the representatives of the one unique Church and the founders-to-be of the local Churches, who have a mission directed to the world: from the first the Church *speaks all languages*.

Footnote 42 to this passage refers to the authority of "the Fathers," mentioning Shepherd of Hermas (*Vis.* 2, 4: PG 2, 897-900) and Clement of Rome (*Epist. II ad Cor.*, 14, 2: Funck, 1, 200). Both texts, however, deal with the idea of a pre-existent *spiritual* (Clement) or *heavenly* (Hermas) church, together with Christ embodied in the flesh, i.e. in the Mystical Body of Christ. This analogy transcends the ecclesiological relation of the local and the universal and has nothing to do with a temporal or ontological priority of the universal church.

The Church Catholic: Local and Universal

What Hermas and Clement of Rome had in mind was much better understood by the Joint Working Group of the Roman Catholic Church and the World Council of Churches in its Sixth Report, "The Church: Local and Universal":

> The Church is the icon of the Trinity, and the Trinity is the interior principle of ecclesial communion. From the resurrection to the *parousia*, communion is willed by the Father, realized in the Son, and caused by the Spirit in and through a community. Every authentic Christian community shares in this communion and is part of the mystery of God unfolded in Christ and the Spirit. Thus, the eschatological reality is already present, and ecclesial communion expresses the "fellowship of the Holy Spirit." At the same time the church has an inner dynamism towards that unity

that rests in the Holy Spirit. In the words of Cyprian, "the church is a people made one with the unity of the Father, the Son, and the Holy Spirit."[5]

The document of the Joint Working Group stresses the fact that there is only one church in God's plan of salvation, but this one church "is present and manifested in the local churches throughout the world."[6]

> The local church is not an administrative or juridical sub-section or part of the universal church ... the local church is the place where the church of God becomes concretely realised. It is a gathering of believers that is seized by the Spirit of the risen Christ and becomes *koinonia* by participating in the life of God.[7]

It is clear that the church is catholic in the sense that this *koinonia* of salvation has a universal, eschatological validity and is offered as a Gospel to the whole inhabited earth (Matt. 24:12). But it must be realised, as was already the case in Jerusalem in the event of Pentecost, in local communities:

> In the concrete historical situation of the foundation of the church, the local had priority and will keep it until the second coming of Christ, because the gospel is preached each time in a determined place; the faithful receive baptism and celebrate eucharist in this determined place, even though it is always and necessarily in communion with all the other local churches in the world. There is no local church that is not centred on the gospel and not in communion with all other churches.[8]

The true meaning of catholicity is not being of a global or universal geographical nature.[9] It is not to be explained in terms of

---

[5] "The Church: Local and Universal," in: Joint Working Group between the Roman Catholic Church and the World Council of Churches, *Sixth Report* (Geneva, 1990), pp. 23-37 , §§ 1, 24.

[6] "The Church: Local and Universal," § 2.

[7] "The Church: Local and Universal," § 14.

[8] "The Church: Local and Universal," § 23.

[9] "The Church: Local and Universal," § 19: "The universal church is the communion of all the local churches united in in faith and worship

time and space as such but refers, like the concept of *koinonia* itself, to a shared *matrix of faith and life*, passed on to us through the ages, inherited, first, from the faith and life of Israel and then from the apostolic community of disciples around Jesus: a common confession of the one God, Father, Son and Holy Spirit, a common sacramental life through baptism and the Eucharist, a shared pattern of ministerial oversight (*episkopè*) and of a communal congregational life and, finally, a way of life in society which corresponds with the commands of the covenant of Israel and with the new commandment of love given by Jesus Christ.[10] Such catholicity is realized first of all at the local level. In the words of the Joint Working Group:

> All Christian World Communions can, in general, agree with the definition of the local church as a community of baptised believers in which the word of God is preached, the apostolic faith confessed, the sacraments are celebrated, the redemptive work of Christ for the world is witnessed to, and a ministry of *episcope* exercised by bishops or other ministers is serving the community.[11]

This *shared matrix of faith and life* has been and is still to be incarnated, inculturated in the languages, customs, rites of local communities that we call cultures. This inculturation process is not a one-way street, as if it were only a matter of translating a fixed *depositum fidei* and an unchangeable *moral code* into ever new cultures. It is rather a permanent *interaction* of tradition and culture, which results in changes and varieties of both of them. That is why we have to deal with so many traditions within the one Tradition, as the IVth World Conference of Faith and Order at Montreal in 1963 had already stated.

---

around the world. However, the universal church is not the sum, federation or juxtaposition of the local churches, but all together are the same church of God present and acting in this world .... Catholicity enters into the very concept of church and refers not simply to geographic extension but also to the manifold variety of local churches and their participation in the one *koinonia*.

[10] "The Church: Local and Universal," §§ 25 and 31.

[11] "The Church: Local and Universal," § 15.

Catholicity implies, thus, the recognition of *legitimate diversity* within Christianity, which is a precondition for ecumenism and the unity of the Christian churches. No form of the church of Christ in whatever cultural setting may be excluded from the Christian *koinonia,* as long as its variety is *legitimate,* i.e. in accordance with the *matrix of faith and life* that regulates its catholicity. This legitimacy must be presumed when a local church community intends to be faithful to this *matrix* as it was kept through the ages and adopted in the statements on unity of the successive Assemblies of the World Council of Churches in New Delhi, Uppsala, Nairobi and Canberra as well as by the Second Vatican Council of the Roman Catholic Church.

There is one clear exception with regard to the legitimacy of diversity, already formulated in the New Testament and continuously applied in the conciliar decisions of the Christian churches. Excluded from the *koinonia* of legitimate diversity are those who refuse to recognise members and ministers, the proclamation of the Word and the faithful administration of the sacraments of the *sanior pars ecclesiae. Sanior* here does not mean the most saintly, most pure and certainly not the most powerful or simply the majority of the churches, but it means the churches gathered in council, deciding in unanimity. Those who refuse the decisions of the ecumenical councils, do not accept the members and ministers of the churches present there or are not willing to participate in the conciliar deliberations to which they are invited are to be considered *anathema.* They do not belong to the body of the church catholic. Their churches, like those of Novatus or Donatus, no longer "subsist" because they have broken off the *koinonia,* precisely by refusing to accept the others into *their* community of Word and Sacrament, although the declaration of *anathema* is meant for their penitence and hopefully their conversion to the fullness of the Body of Christ.

This criterion for *reception of and submittal to the conciliar structures of decision making* in the church – the *conciliar principle* – is valid and accepted in the ecumenical movement in multiple ways and highly relevant for the intercultural religious pluralism of today.

First of all, only those churches can call themselves "catholic," according to the qualifications set by the Nicene Constantinopolitan Creed, that accept this Creed as an ecumenical creed for the churches. All Eastern Orthodox Churches, the Roman Catholic Communion of Churches, the Churches of the Anglican Communion, the Churches of the Reformation and the Old Catholic Churches of the Union of Utrecht are rightly labelled catholic churches. But Nestorians and Monophysites who accept Nicea are, thus, catholic churches as well, sharing the catholic matrix of faith and life. Their churches are sister churches of all other catholic churches.

Not all Christian churches, however, even if they are members of the World Council of Churches, would meet this criterion. Ecumenism suffers from a trend to stress the proper identity of local communities and cultures and to treat separatism as a method of evangelisation. Classic Unitarian traditions and many newer forms of Christian churches, like part of the African independent churches, the Afro-Brazilian churches, the Neo-Pentecostal churches and various evangelical movements do not want to be measured by this conciliar standard of catholicity. Some would even claim that to be faithful to the Gospel one must meet quite other criteria of faith and life than this traditional *matrix* of the historical churches thus far. They would claim to adhere to "a fuller Gospel" and a more radical conversion, the fruits of which can be distinguished in the gifts of the Holy Spirit. Of course, they have a point insofar as the *matrix of catholicity* is interpreted in a rather formal and rationalistic way: as consonance with dogmatic formulations, ritual rules, moral codes or even adherence and obedience to the teaching ministry of the church, while the fruits of the Spirit would be neglected or considered irrelevant. But when the criterion of fruitfulness or inner experience of the Spirit *replaces* the set conciliar *matrix of faith and life*, instead of being *added to* it as a correcting principle, such churches and movements can no longer be called catholic.

Similar things could be said of churches with a closed and exclusive membership, such as white or black racially bound churches, exclusive gay or women's churches, churches only accessible to rich people or even only for their own shareholders.

Finally, I suggest, we should remove the title of catholic church from any congregation or communion of churches that refuses to accept baptised and confessing members of other catholic churches who have adopted the matrix of catholic faith and life as their honoured guests at the Table of the Lord. They would come under the verdict of the presbyter John in his third letter to the Johannine communities on the bishop Diotrephes (3 John 10). Those who subscribe to the conciliar matrix of catholicity should be welcomed, whenever they want to share in a catholic community elsewhere, with the words of the presbyter, as follows:

> My dear friend, I hope everything is going happily with you and that you are well both physically as you are spiritually. It is a great joy for us, that our brothers have told us of your faithfulness to the truth and of your life in the truth .... My friend, you have done faithful work in looking after your brothers and sisters, even if they were complete strangers to you. They are a proof to the whole church of your charity and it would be a very good thing if you could help them on their journey in a way that God would approve. *It was entirely for the sake of the name that they set out, without depending on the pagans for anything; it is our duty to welcome people like them and contribute our share to their work for the truth.* (3 John 1-8)

There can be no competition or strife among those who are witnesses to the covenantal gospel of Christ and the carriers of it to strange lands. There must be utmost hospitality and solidarity among those who work for the sake of the name, so that the world may believe (John 17:21). Those who refuse such hospitality and solidarity, however, are to be blamed:

> I have written a note for the members of the church, but Diotrephes, who seems to enjoy being in charge of it, refuses to accept us. So if I come I shall tell everyone how he has behaved, and about the wicked accusations he has been circulating against us. As if that were not enough, he not only refuses to welcome our brothers, but prevents the other people who would have liked to from welcoming them, and expels them from the church. My dear friend, never follow such a bad example, but keep following the good one; anyone who does what is right is a child of God, but the person who does what is wrong has never seen God. (3 John 9-11)

How could a Christian be called catholic, when he refuses to admit other Christians to the Table of the Lord, who intend to work for the sake of the Name of Jahweh/Adonai and want to share in the same covenant of the Lord Jesus Christ and enjoy the fruits of life of the Holy *Pneuma* of God according to the Scriptures of the prophets and apostles of old, as laid down in the conciliar *matrix of faith and life* we have received and adopted through the ages?

In a similar mood the historic churches should be ready to engage in dialogue and offer communion to those emerging churches which spring up under difficult societal circumstances in house communities as in China, in human base communities as in India, in charismatic communities all over the world or in tribal communities as with many African Instituted Churches. True catholicity, indeed, does not reject diversity of forms, should have patience and offer assistance for the building up of these communities. It should presume the good will and the right intention of faith in these emerging churches (*intentio fidei, intentio faciendi quod facit ecclesia*). But even in such situations, the readiness of such communities to be in touch with the other and older churches as their sister churches, to receive members and leaders of other churches in their midst and to come together in council for deliberation on *"the faith of the church through the ages,"* would be a sound criterion for mutual reception within the one *koinonia* of faith and an antidote against the disease of separatism.

Intercultural ecclesiology implies the exchange of contextual theologies in interconfessional and interreligious dialogue as well, without, however, forgetting that theology, in whatever form of conceptualisation, has to adhere to its proper focus and final referential object: the God of Abraham, Isaac and Jacob, the Father of Jesus and the Source of the life-giving *Ruach* of JHWH, whose fruits of justice and peace we may enjoy in the hope of God's kingdom and the final integrity of creation.

As such, catholicity remains an *eschatological ecumenical quality of the Church*, nowhere yet completely realised, but given to us provisionally in Word and Sacrament, sharing there in the full *koinonia* of the life of the Triune God.

Uniting Europe as a Challenge to the Future of National Churches

Eddy Van der Borght

Introduction

In its original form this paper presented me with the challenge of discussing the issue of "church and nation" in a concrete place, namely Sibiu, Transylvania. This is an area that has a long tradition of different peoples who live together and claim to belong to the region but adhere to different confessional traditions. People of German origin are expected to be Lutherans, those of Hungarian origin claim Reformed identity and those of Romanian origin refer to the Orthodox tradition. In Transylvania ethnic differences intertwine with confessional strains. As a consequence, the quest for the visible unity of the church in that region must deal with theological divisions in addition to allegiances to specific ethnic groups. The theme of the *Societas Oecumenica* conference at which this paper was first given, "On the Way to Koinonia," provides a second reason for discussing the topic. Is the ethnic or national element in the identity of local, regional churches a stumbling block for the unity of the churches – especially in Europe? The location and theme of this conference, along with the growing awareness among social scientists that national identity is linked with ethnicity and with religion,[1] may stimulate Christian theologians to reconsider the link between ethnic and/or national allegiances to Christian faith and Christian churches.

---

[1] See especially the ethno-symbolists among the theorists on nation and nationalism: A.D. Smith, *Nationalism and Modernism: A Critical Survey of Recent Theories of Nations and Nationalism* (London and New York, 1998) pp. 170-98. Recently, Smith developed the concept of a nation as a chosen people in religious terms in *Chosen Peoples* (Oxford and New York, 2003).

I plan to report here on research I did on how the ecumenical movement has treated the issue of faith and ethnicity until now. I will examine the results of the Oxford conference of Life and Work in 1937, the Leuenberg document on the issue of 2001 and the *Charta Oecumenica* of 2002 in particular. This will be followed by general conclusions about how the ecumenical movement has dealt with the issue.

Oxford Revisited[2]

In 1925 nationalism was already an issue at the first World Conference of Life and Work in Stockholm. In April 1934 Life and Work organised a consultation on "The Church and the State Today" in Paris as a response to the rise of authoritarian states – especially in the Soviet Union and Germany.[3] Because of the fast deterioration of the situation in Germany, Life and Work decided (a few months later) to organize its second World Conference on the theme of "Church, Community and State." The word "community" was the inadequate translation of the German word *Volk*. After Life and Work had nominated J.H. Oldham to the position of Chairman of its Research Committee, an impressive worldwide study programme began that included the contributions of many eminent theologians and non-theologians.[4]

In December 1934 Oldham wrote an introductory booklet for the conference, *Church, Community and State: A World Issue*.[5] This booklet functioned as a type of personal "manifesto for the Oxford conference and, moreover, for the programme of study

---

[2] E.A.J.G. Van der Borght, "Oxford Revisited: A Re-reading of the Report on Church and Volk at the Life and Work Conference in Oxford 1937," *Exchange* 33 (2004): 4.

[3] A. Houtepen, "A God without Frontiers: Ecumenism and Criticism of Nationalism," *Exchange* 22 (1993): 235-49.

[4] Theologians such as E. Brunner, R. Niebuhr, C.H. Dodd, H.G. Wood, H.D. Wendland, M. Dibelius, H.H. Farmer, M. Boegner, M. Huber, C.E. Raven, W. Temple, P. Tillich, E. Bevan and S. Zankov and non-theologians such as J.F. Dulles and T.S. Elliot.

[5] J.H. Oldham, *Church, Community and State: A World Issue* (New York and London, 1935).

leading up to and (he hoped) beyond it."⁶ He was not only aware that he was living at a turning point of history, linked with the growth of the modern state, but he was also aware of a growing global crisis that was connected to the rise of the totalitarian state and modern paganism. Digging deeper into the causes of the actual crisis, Oldham referred to nationalism. The actual crisis demanded Christian reflection not only on the state and its nature, authority and functions but also on the community. The questions concerning state and community obliged the church to think about its own identity. As to the relation to the community, he sums it up in the following questions:

> What is the relation of the Church as a body of believers and practising Christians to the rest of the nation? How far ought the Christian Church to be a *Volkskirche*? How is the membership in the one body or the universal Church of Christ related to the fact that Christians become members of it through membership of national Churches united by a multitude of ultimate ties to the distinctive historical life of the communities to which they belong?⁷

Oldham stresses that these questions are fundamentally theological questions that supersede the traditional confessional differences.

It is remarkable that Oldham gave prominence to the theme of the church in a study programme of Life and Work. He did so because he was convinced that the social stance of Christianity in Life and Work was related to the understanding of the church, which was the traditional theme of Faith and Order.⁸

---

⁶ K. Clements, *Faith on the Frontier: A Life of J.H. Oldham* (Edinburgh and Geneva, 1999), p. 311

⁷ Oldham, *Church, Community and State*, p. 29.

⁸ The manner in which Oldham included the church as a theme in the programme of Life and Work contributed to the growing together of Life and Work and Faith and Order in the World Council of Churches in the following years. See also "6. The Future," in J.H. Oldham, "Introduction" in J.H. Oldham (ed.), *The Churches Survey Their Task: The Report of the Conference at Oxford, July 1937, on Church, Community and State*, Church, Community and State Vol. 8 (London, 1937), pp. 48-

Of course, the focus of attention of the Oxford Conference was not on the identity of the church but on the church and its function in society.

Originally, he planned nine areas of research: the three topics implied in the title (the church and its function in society, church and community, church and state), three related areas (concerning education, economic order and the universal church in relation to the world of nations) and three fundamental, theological topics (the Christian understanding of man, the kingdom of God and history, and Christian faith and common life). Eventually seven volumes would be published that covered seven of the nine research areas. Only church and state and the issue of the economic order were excluded as separate subjects.[9] At the conference the discussions took place in five sections: church and community; church and state; church, community, and state in relation to the economic order; church, community, and state in relation to education; the universal church and the world of the nations. Instead of the three years allotted, he considered the programme to be a process that demanded twenty or thirty years of hard work by the churches because the ambitions were so high, the issues so fundamental

---

50 and Appendix B "Report of the Committee of Thirty-five" concerning a future World Council of Churches in Oldham, *The Churches Survey Their Task*, pp. 276-82.

[9] Eight volumes in the series Church, Community and State would appear in the years 1937 and 1938: vol. 1, *The Church and its Function in Society*; vol. 2, *The Christian Understanding of Man*; vol. 3, *The Kingdom of God and History*; vol. 4, *The Christian Faith and the Common Life*; vol. 5, *Church and Community*; vol. 6, *Church, Community, and State in Relation to Education*; vol. 7, *The Universal Church and the World of Nations*; vol. 8, *The Churches Survey their Task: The Report of the Conference at Oxford, July 1937, on Church, Community and State* (London, 1937). The issue of the relationship church-state had already been the topic of the conference in Paris in 1934 and in 1937. N. Ehrenström, one of the directors of the Research Department of *Life and Work*, expanded that material and it was published in an English translation, *Christian Faith and the Modern State* (London, 1937).

and the implications so far-reaching. In spite of this, he made sure that the deadlines were respected.[10]

Looking back on the documents and their history, I am impressed by the correct analysis made by Oldham and his fellow workers. By 1934 they saw that much more was at stake than the well-known discussions on the responsibilities of church and state in the post-*corpus Christianum* era. Consequently, the conference did not only discuss the roles of church and state in society extensively but also looked into the theological evaluation of *Volk* and nation and the responsibility of the church.

Within the Ecumenical Movement the Oxford Conference of 1937 is still remembered for its clear "no" to an extreme nationalistic or racist approach to humanity.[11] In our conclusions we want to dig deeper, based on the detailed analysis of the text of the two reports on church and nation. We will try to answer the question of whether an adequate answer to the challenge of nation and nationalism was found at the Oxford conference in seven points.

We are fortunate that not only the shorter report of the conference but also the longer report of the first section on church and nation were published. At the heart of the shorter report stands the condemnation of a nationalism that transgresses borderlines: when the nation is given divine status, when other nations are disrespected, and when the church is subordinated to the national life. The report calls upon individual Christians, churches and civil authorities to refrain from promoting loyalty to the nation as the highest duty in life.

The longer text is more argumentative and reveals that the unity of the common confession of the participants at the conference was limited. The degree of disunity is striking. The members disagree not only on fundamental issues such as the

---

[10] Clements, *Faith on the Frontier*, p. 315.

[11] Houtepen, "A God without Frontiers," pp. 246-47; M.E. Brinkman "The Theological Basis for the Local-Universal Debate," in: L.J. Koffeman and H. Witte (eds), *Of All Times and of All Places: Protestants and Catholics on the Church Local and Universal* (Zoetermeer, 2001), pp. 178-79; M.M. Thomas and P. Dekar, "Nation," *Dictionary of the Ecumenical Movement*, 2nd ed. (Geneva, 2002), p. 806.

involvement of Christians in society and the possibility of compromises but also on the interpretation of the nation: a mere human organization or a God-given *Ordnung* with almost absolute claim on individuals. I came to the following conclusions as a result of my analysis.

The Mixed Assessment of Nationalism

The longer report reveals that even in 1937 the judgement of the nationalism that had developed in Central Europe was suspended and certainly was not completely negative. Nationalists had returned pride, confidence and a new vitality to the people. The contempt for the erosion of the Christian heritage in the countries of the West that had not been taken over by the nationalists seemed stronger than the unease about some of the more extreme aspects under nationalist regimes. It looked as if a movement that provided a sense of community, remembering the common roots of the past, could perhaps counter the crisis caused by modernity. Without doubt, many Christians in the West felt attracted to a nationalism that seemed to confer the old Christian identity of society.

The Central Theological Concept: *Ordnungen*

The reports on church and *Volk* use one theological argument for the nation: the creation theological notion of *Ordnungen*. Already in his introductory manifesto of 1934 Oldham had referred to E. Brunner's work *Das Gebot und die Ordnungen*. In spite of the vague definition and the uncertainty about the theological weight of the nation as an *Ordnung,* all agreed that the nation is partly God-inspired and partly sin-infected. Because of this God-inspired element, all are called on to loyalty and service to the nation. Some participants at the conference promoted the equation of duty of *Volk* with duty to God. Based on the interpretation of the nation as a God-given order, they attributed an almost absolute claim of the nation on the individual.

The Different Treatment of Nation and Race.

The Oxford report does not distinguish between *Volk* and nation but does make a distinction between nation and race. In spite of the fact that both are analysed as *Ordnung,* they are treated differently. The very positive attitude towards *das Volk* contrasts with the neutral and even negative focus on race. Focus on race can easily lead to prejudice and racism. The value of the nation is supported by a creation argument, while emphasis on race is dismissed through creation, Christological and ecclesiological arguments. In addition, the history of the Ecumenical Movement reveals a different treatment of nation and race. Not only was a programme to combat racism launched, but the South African Reformed segregated churches were banned as well. The Ecumenical Movement never felt the challenge to start a programme to combat nationalism and no church was banned because of strong links with a nation or a nation state.

The Absence of the Universal Church.

The report on education begins with a description of the church as a supranational fellowship in contrast to state and nation. In addition, the report on the universal church and the international order presents the church as a good partner to contribute to the international order because of its universal and ecumenical scope. Nevertheless, the report on church and nation does not develop the universal aspect of the church. This is even more remarkable because, by stressing its universal character, it could have proven that its own identity goes contrary to nationalism.

The Silence about the National Church.

Why is the nation treated so fundamentally positively? Why is the universal church absent? In our judgement, this has to be explained in relation to the national church. As can be seen from the list of the churches present at the conference, they are identified according to nation.[12] In fact, most churches of the Protestant and Orthodox tradition are linked to nations. As national churches, they felt committed to their respective nation and/or nation-state. Consequently, we should not be surprised that the nation is approached positively. We assume that the drafters considered it to be inopportune to raise the issue of national churches in a report that condemns extreme nationalism.

---

[12] Oldham, *The Churches Survey their Task*, pp. 290-94.

In addition, they may have considered it unwise to discuss the universal church if they could not develop the theme of the national church.

The Identity of the Church.

The Oxford document remains silent on the identity of the church. We have tried to explain this from strategic motivations. The looming war was not the right context to discuss the status of the national church. Nevertheless, after World War II the issue was left undeveloped and only reconsidered – with an unsatisfactory outcome – after new nationalistic eruptions of violence.

The Study Document Church-People-Nation-State
of the Leuenberg Church Fellowship (2001)[13]

We will now turn our attention to another document that is strikingly different in two ways: it is a recent ecumenical contribution to the theme and it offers a specifically Protestant approach. The fifth General Assembly of the LCF (Leuenberg Church Fellowship) in Belfast (June 2001) adopted the study document, *Church-People-State-Nation*.[14] It is not surprising that they have been conducting their own investigation on this topic, because Reformation Churches are traditionally divided along national lines.[15] The previous General Assembly commissioned this study in 1994 at the height of the renewed outbreak

---

[13] Cf. E.A.J.G. Van der Borght, "The Leuenberg Document 'Church – People – State – Nation': A Critical Assessment," *Exchange* 31 (2002): 278-98.

[14] *Kirche, Volk, Staat, Nation: Ein Beitrag zu einem schwierigen Verhältnis. Beratungsergebnis der Regionalgruppe der Leuenberger Kirchengemeinschaft Süd- und Südosteuropa*. Lembeck, 2002.

[15] In the first half of 2002 LCF counted 103 member churches. Often, their names reveal not only that they belong to a specific confession but also their relation to a nation-state (e.g. the Reformed Christian Church in Croatia, the Evangelical Lutheran Church of Denmark, Estonian Evangelical Lutheran Church, etc.), a region (Church of Scotland,) and languages (German-speaking Evangelical Church in Greece). In 2003 the LCF changed its name to the *Community of Protestant Churches in Europe*.

of nationalist conflicts in Central and Southeastern Europe and in the aftermath of the political turning point of 1989. In 1995 the Executive Committee of the LCF entrusted the Southern and Southeastern Europe Regional Group to undertake this study. This group, which was founded more than twenty-five years ago against the background of the continuing East/West conflict, drafted a document that consisted of six chapters. After an introduction (1) and a clarification of terminology (2), a historical review (3) and some specific examples (4) are presented. For our purposes, the section on biblical evidence and fundamental theological insights (5) is most important. The last chapter (6) faces the current challenges.[16]

In the fifth part of the document a biblical orientation (5.1) is followed by a consideration of fundamental theological elements for understanding the church (5.2), the people(s) (5.3) and the nation (5.4) and concludes with a short paragraph on potential tensions (5.5). I will recall some elements of my analysis of this document. The short biblical orientation gives a good introduction to the theme of the relationship between God, Israel and the other peoples. But the result of these three paragraphs on the church is very disappointing. (1) A biblical evaluation of the church is lacking. Only the first paragraph contains two explicit references to the Scriptures. References to the letters to the Galatians, Romans and Ephesians concerning the surmounting of the opposition between Jews and Gentiles in Christ and in the church, which are very relevant in this context, are completely absent. (2) Through the absence of a biblical (especially New Testament) analysis, the incentive for a critical evaluation of the current situation of the (Protestant) churches divided along confessional, territorial and national lines is lost. The partition is admitted but not evaluated negatively. The eschatological perspective leads to a church with a provisional nature that can only exist in a broken form in this era. (3) Because the pain of the sin of individual Christians is softened in this eschatological perspective, a call for repentance is also lacking. The sin is stated in general terms and not bound

---

[16] Van der Borght, "The Leuenberg Document."

to the disunity in and among the churches. (4) The reference to the creeds is too general – not connected to the place of peoples within the church – and too specific – the unity and the apostolicity of the church are not mentioned.

The paragraphs on the theology of a people are challenging. But I also made the following observations and critical remarks on this theme. (1) Aspects of creation theology and Christology prevail in this section on the theology of the people(s). This makes it even more remarkable that in the previous section on the church the Christological approach was completely absent. (2) The dominant approach is that of the theology of creation. The Christological accent and its consequences determine only the fourth paragraph. Here its revolutionary impact surfaces: "Jews" and "Greeks" have, through faith and baptism, become one people in Christ Jesus. But in the fifth and sixth paragraph the power of God's saving action in Christ is expressed in general concepts and is strongly determined by the limitations of creation. From the seventh paragraph onwards the approach of creation theology and its ethical consequences have completely taken over. This leads to an open, sociological definition in the last paragraph. What the consequences of our belonging to Christ are for our identity and attitude towards the peoples in which we are rooted has disappeared. (3) The ethical criterion for judging the developments of a people – the ability to serve life – is general and leaves so much room for interpretation that its practical value is considerably reduced. (4) The references to the Scriptures are few (only two) and weak. The document has some valuable paragraphs on the nation, but they lack theological depth.

The last chapter of the document provides numerous considerations on the attitude the churches should take when confronted with extreme nationalism (6.1), on criteria for different aspects of their relationship towards people, nation, state and society (6.2), and on their position towards European integration (6.3). I made the following observations and critical remarks.

a. The warning against the tide of nationalism in Europe (6.1) is unambiguous.
b. The tools offered to the churches for dealing with nationalism in 6.2 are less convincing, because one very important

element in the existence of many Protestant churches is skipped: the way in which a specific people, a specific nation-state, a specific language or the relation to the state co-determine the structure and identity of most Protestant churches. The notion of *koinonia* is indeed an inspiring biblical concept that challenges the churches to live an exemplary way of life (6.2.5), but it also challenges the churches to reconsider their links with people, nations, states and languages that might be an obstacle to *koinonia* for those who do not belong to the people, the nation, the state or a specific language. This problem challenges the Protestant churches to reconsider how they give shape to their local as well as their global identity (6.2.6). Is their participation in international, ecclesiastical organisations more than symbolic? Or is their participation free of obligation? Is it not remarkable that the way in which a church is related to the nation is not named as an element that can enhance the credibility of the church towards nationalism (6.2.7)? And is not a church less sensitive to manipulations if she is minimally dependent on a people, nation, state, or language in her structures and identity (6.2.8)?

c. The LCF considers European integration to be an alternative to nationalism and one-sided economic globalisation. It advocates the role that the Protestant church can play in a uniting Europe: the Reformed tradition is connected to European history (6.3.1) and the awareness of the presence of God in different traditions (6.3.2), the sensitivity for the rights of the individual and the protection of minorities (6.3.3) and the Protestant ethics of individual responsibility (6.3.4) – all Protestant accents that can contribute to the development of a uniting Europe that preserves diversity. It is remarkable how some elements of Protestant theology and ethics are brought together to suggest a natural inclination to European integration. But the historical reality was more ambiguous, even often anti-European. Indeed, the Reformation is deeply embedded in European history – not as a uniting force (for the most part) but as a force that was used to support the ongoing partition of Europe. Protestantism let itself be used by governments to determine the identity of a nation-state over against other nation-states and over against residents who adhered to other religions or convictions. The Protestants' zeal was directed, in many cases, not towards tolerance of other opinions but to the protection and preservation of rights and interests of their own congregations and structures. In general, Protestant churches have not been in the forefront of European integration. If one reads between the lines, this is admitted in the text.[17] Would it have been more credible if the LCF, as an expression of Protestantism with its strong European roots, had confessed its co-responsibility for the evolution towards a dangerous nationalism in Europe in the past centuries and if it had called for repentance and a rethinking of the identity and the structure of the church within the Reformation traditions?

d. The choice for a uniting Europe seems to be ethically and politically motivated in order to avoid a dangerous nationalism and to avoid one-sided economic globalisation. We share this choice. However, we feel the argumentation misses the most important element connected directly to the heart of the Christian message, viz. that in Christ there is no Jew, nor Greek (Gal. 2:28).

This document is the result of a valuable initiative. In the context of the nationalistic upsurge in Europe after the shift in the geopolitical power balances at the end of the 1980s, the European Protestant churches felt challenged to re-define their position towards that actual evolution through theological contributions on the relationship between the church and the people/nation/state. It is clear that the history of the last century has made the Protestant churches more aware of the negative potential of nationalism. They consciously turned away from describing peoples in terms of divinely instituted elements of the created order, in contrast to the approach at Oxford. This

---

[17] In 6.3.1: *"Die protestantischen Kirchen beginnen erst allmächlich, sich mit dem Europagedanken und der Geschichte des zusammenwachsenden Europas auseinanderzusetzen"* and in 6.3.5: *"Das derzeitige Europa ist, wie beschrieben, für den europäischen Protestantismus ein relativ neues Thema ...."*

opened the way for a positive evaluation of the European integration process. The (church) political choice of the Leuenberg Church Fellowship is a clear "no" to renewed extreme nationalism and "yes" to ongoing European integration. The real importance of this document lies within the option for European integration, especially because this option is not self-evident for the often nationally organised Protestant churches.

But as a theological contribution, it only presents a description of the generally accepted positions and of the status quo. It offers no new perspectives on the theme of the church in its relationship to people, state and nation. It is a missed opportunity in the context of the worldwide need for a better theological evaluation of the relationship between faith and ethnicity and the need for a renewed self-understanding of the church from a Reformation perspective. The structure of the theological chapter of the document reveals where its fundamental weakness lies: in the theology of the church (5.2). Where the text is not able to describe the novelty of the ecclesiological community in Jesus Christ with baptismal and Eucharistic notions, our identity as members of other communities is not put into perspective and is not transcended. That is why the identity of the church remains too closely connected with the people and nation through phrases such as *"eingebunden in, Einwurzelung in"* and "being an integral part of" (5.5). The document is not able to re-define "the potential tensions" between our identity as members of the church and members of people, nation and state. It is remarkable that the text always shifts from Christological discourse to that of creation theology on the most important point. The core of the identity of the church is thus left undisclosed. The issue of the relationship between the church and people/nation/state leads us to the question of the identity of the church.

The Protestant tradition is in need of a re-evaluation of its ecclesiology. If it is more assured about its own identity, then it will be less problematic to formulate its local expression and structure in a more relaxed way. This exercise will require a thorough biblical investigation of the meaning of the church – a striking lack in this document – and a willingness to repent and to change. A tradition that carries the adage *ecclesia semper reformata* cannot strive for less.

Being a Protestant theologian, I feel very comfortable in making this critical analysis of the Protestant churches' relationship towards ethnicity and faith. I imagine a critical assessment of the way that Orthodox churches relate towards people, nation and state waits to be written and published by some Orthodox theologians. This is not only a problem with which Protestant and Orthodox churches have to deal. Coming from Flanders in Belgium, I have experienced the identification of being Flemish with being Roman Catholic. Although the Roman Catholic Church has a strongly developed universal aspect of its concept of church, the way it understands the link between the local church and the nation also needs special attention. I am convinced that this is a problematic issue that the mainstream Christian confessions have to face head-on.

The Charta Oecumenica *on Divisions*

Most of these churches belong to the Conference of European Churches (CEC), which includes almost all Orthodox, Protestant, Anglican, Old Catholic and independent churches in Europe, or to the Council of European Bishops' Conferences (CCII), which represents all Roman Catholic Bishops' Conferences in Europe. In 2001 they published the *Charta Oecumenica: Guidelines for the Growing Cooperation among the Churches in Europe*.[18] In its introduction the *Charta* defines Europe as extending "from the Atlantic to the Urals, from the North Cape to the Mediterranean." With this description the *Charta* indicates that it opts for a broad understanding of Europe. Not the European Union with its twenty-five members but the Council of Europe with its forty-two members – or even, the Organisation for Security and Cooperation in Europe with fifty-three members – offer a better scope for the delimitation of Europe. The churches offer their cooperation in order to reconcile peoples and cult-

---

[18] V. Ionita and S. Numico (eds), *Charta Oecumenica: A Text, a Process and a Dream of the Churches in Europe* (Geneva, 2003).

ures in the process of the unification of Europe as understood in this broad way.

But these good intentions ask for a critical evaluation of the role that the churches can play in this process, because the divided churches are part of the divisions in Europe. Europe has been divided into a Byzantine East (with the Orthodox churches) and a West under the influence of the Roman Catholic Church and the churches of the Reformation, creating two distinct cultures with differing systems of philosophy and law and influencing the churches and their theologies. But the divisions go even deeper. I quote Reinhard Frieling,

> Overall, everywhere in Europe, churches have been closely connected with national cultures. The churches became "cultural factors" through their influence, for example, on "Catholic Poland", "Orthodox Russia" or "Lutheran Scandinavia". Even the widespread secularisation and disappearance of the church's effect on public life in most European countries has not removed the cultural influences. At the same time the churches became themselves "products of culture", since for example French Catholicism, Greek Orthodoxy and German Protestantism are today each still characterised by a certain mentality and spirituality.[19]

So the religious divisions are not only linked to the Eastern and Western parts of Europe but also to the system of nation-states that has divided Europe until now. It challenges the churches in Europe to rethink their relations to homelands, nations, people and state. But has the *Charta Oecumenica* actually addressed this issue? Does it deal with the links of churches with nations and ethnic groupings with? Has it become part of their guidelines in growing European ecclesiastical cooperation? Or did the drafters felt the need to keep silent on the issue? I will continue with a short analysis of the references to this issue in the *Charta*.

In the introduction to this document, the CEC and the CCEE express the wish to continue growing in ecumenical cooperation and fellowship and the will to overcome the divisions

---

[19] R. Frieling, "Our Common Responsibility in Europe," in: Ionita and Numico, *Charta Oecumenica*, p. 63.

that still exist among them. The nature of these divisions is not elaborated. What the drafters of the document have in mind becomes clear when we continue with the first part on the common calling to unity in faith. The triune God calls the churches to be one, holy, catholic and apostolic church. But because of the existing fundamental differences in faith, the visible unity of the church is still problematic. The text explains: "There are different views of the church and its oneness, of the sacraments and ministries." So, in the added commitment the accent is on the mutual recognition of baptism and Eucharistic fellowship. We note the silence in relation to ministries. In general, we can say that the first part on the unity of the church is less developed than the two following parts and that dividing issues among the churches are identified as being of a theological nature: the understanding of the church, its unity, its sacraments and its ministries.

The second part on the visible fellowship of churches provides new clues for understanding the divisive history of European churches. Paragraph 3 blames the schisms, hostilities and even armed conflicts of the past not only on human guilt and lack of love in general but more specifically on the frequent abuse of faith for political interests. Here a first indication is offered that the divisions cannot be attributed only to theological elements. Paragraph 4 on churches acting together commits the churches to defend the rights of minorities and to help reduce misunderstandings and prejudices between majority and minority churches. Here an opportunity for further development of the theme is lost. The text links minorities to majority and minority churches without further explanation. Paragraph six deals again with the historical divisions, stating:

> Rather than seeing our diversity as a gift which enriches us, however, we have allowed differences of opinion on doctrine, ethics and church law to lead to separations between churches, with special historical circumstances and different cultural backgrounds often playing a crucial role.

But this explicit link of theological with historical and cultural aspects is not developed further in the next sentence that calls for continuing dialogue in order to reach a consensus in faith.

The accent is on dialogue and the implied content seems to be merely theological.

The third part on the common responsibility of the churches starts with a paragraph (7) of support for the integration of the European continent. The last of the three commitments of this paragraph reads: "We commit ourselves to resist any attempt to misuse religion and the church for ethnic or nationalist purposes." This frank statement is surprising because it was not indicated in the main text of the paragraph that possible links of religions (in general) or churches (specifically) to ethnic or nationalistic communities might be a problem on the way to an integrated Europe. The main text is vague. A shared responsibility is confessed for the guilt in not preventing suffering and destruction by Europeans, both within Europe and beyond, but a deeper analysis of the cause of this suffering and destruction is lacking. Secondly, blame is imputed to Christians as individuals rather than churches. Thirdly, the confession of sin is weakened because the active participation of Christians or Christian churches is not admitted. They are accused only of not doing enough to prevent the violent behaviour of others. The next paragraph (8), "Reconciling peoples and cultures," indicates that churches are called to promote reconciliation among peoples and cultures in Europe in the spirit of the Gospel. So, the first commitment is "to counteract any form of nationalism which leads to the oppression of other peoples and national minorities and to engage ourselves to non-violent resolutions." Can churches do this? Yes, says the main text, but only if there is peace among them. Possible causes for this lack of peace among the churches are not investigated.

By way of conclusion, we can observe that the *Charta Oecumenica* is outspoken in its commitment to the opposition of extreme nationalism. This is in line with ecumenical documents on this issue in the past. What is new is the engagement to the reconciliation of peoples and cultures in Europe as part of their participation in the building of Europe. But in its analyses of the cause of the past divisions in Europe, the main text lacks clarity as to the responsibility of the Christian churches. It seems to be viewed as an external problem, a problem caused by others, individuals or groups. It might be labelled a political, social or cultural issue but not an ecclesiological one. The fundamental conflicts and divisions in Europe are of a political, social and cultural nature, and the nature of the conflicts in the church is labelled "theological." The first chapter identifies the stumbling blocks for the visible unity of the churches as related to the ecclesiological issues and refers to the mutual recognition of baptism and to Eucharistic fellowship. It is remarkably silent on the topic of ministry. The idea is that if European churches commit themselves to resolving these outstanding theological and ecclesiological differences, they will be able to contribute to the reconciliation of peoples and cultures in Europe.

This analysis cannot stand the test for two reasons. First of all, the history of Europe and its divisions cannot be separated from the history of the European churches and their divisions as though they are two fundamentally different issues. Both divisions are linked much more than is admitted in the text. The division of churches in Europe lies not only along confessional lines but also along ethnic and national lines. Secondly, questions of the relationship between local churches and peoples and nations, their territories, their histories and their languages make this a fundamental ecclesiological problem and thus a theological problem. The issue of nationalism and ethnicities is not just an issue for society but for the church as well.

I will end this analysis of the *Charta Oecumenica* with an issue in the document that illustrates why the text does not meet expectations on the topic of the issue of faith and ethnicity. In the paragraph on reconciling peoples and cultures (8), a reference is made to the issue of asylum seekers: "Together we will do our part towards giving migrants, refugees and asylum seekers a humane reception in Europe." No doubt we are all able to tell beautiful stories of Christian congregations working together to give asylum seekers and migrants a hospitable reception. But there is a downside to this. Many brothers and sisters coming from Central and Eastern Europe or from Africa, Latin America or Asia as asylum seekers in Western Europe do not feel at home in our churches, even if they have mastered our languages or even if they are from the same confessional background. They establish their own Ghanaian Methodist congregations in Amsterdam, Russian Orthodox parishes in London or Korean Presbyterian congregations in Brussels that are directly dependent on the churches in the mother country. They do not feel at home in our Western European churches, which are too closely linked to specific cultures. The most problematic feature, they say, is that the traditional European church members are not interested in them. Hospitality to asylum seekers is not only a social issue for society but also an ecclesiological issue for the church. It is linked to the question of how much a local church can be adapted to local cultures without losing its ability to receive Christians from other cultures?

Conclusion

I will summarize the approach of the Ecumenical Movement in the past to ethnicity and nationalism in terms of three aspects.

The Limitation to a Pastoral Approach.

In the past the Ecumenical Movement reacted only when a major nationalistic or ethnic upsurge occurred. In these cases major international crises asked for a careful, diplomatic and – in the case of the churches – a pastoral response. Although the pre-World War II conferences of the Ecumenical Movement condemned an extreme nationalist or racist attitude, they were always very careful not to state positions that could unnecessarily hurt the churches and individual Christians who where suffering under nationalist violence (especially in fascist Germany.) When the crisis was over, the Ecumenical Movement returned to its own agenda on which nationalism was not considered to be a key issue. So the discussion on the value of nation and country for global society and the church was not carried out in depth. The Ecumenical Movement of the twentieth century has left us with a heritage of mainly pastoral reactions to nationalism in situation of crises.

The Absence of Faith and Order.

The Conferences of Life and Work (Stockholm 1925 and Oxford 1937) and of the International Missionary Council (Edinburgh 1910 and Tambaram 1938) responded to the threat posed by nationalism. Accordingly, the response was practical and strategic with respect to missions. Life and Work and the International Missionary Council should not be blamed for this. On the contrary, they did what was expected of them and performed their task well. The problem is that the third pillar of the twentieth-century Ecumenical Movement, Faith and Order, was absent from the debates. The theological department allowed the opportunity to pass. We can only note that the second World Conference of Faith and Order held in Edinburgh (August 1937) one month after the Oxford Conference of Life and Work, did not discuss the theme of the identity of the church in relation to the nation. The national church is mentioned only under the heading of obstacles to church unity which are partly theological or ecclesiological and equally sociological or political: "Such obstacles are met in the case of a national Church which hallows the common life of a given people, but is at the same time exposed to the perils of an exclusive provincialism or of domination by a secular state." After giving examples of obstacles due to historical factors, we read about churches of different cultural origins agreeing on doctrinal matters.

> These Churches are not conscious of any obstacles to such union because of mutually exclusive doctrines. They are, however, kept apart by barriers of nationality, race, class, general culture, and, more particularly, by slothful self-content and self-sufficiency.[20]

It is remarkable that in these two quotes descriptive language is mixed with normative language. Because it is grouped under non-theological obstacles to church unity, it suggests that this is to be understood as a cultural, non-theological element that does not influence the identity of the church. Fortunately, Faith and Order decided to start a research project on the issue in the 1990s. As the title, *Ethnic Identity, National Identity and the Search for the Unity of the Church*, indicates, the project is intended to deal with the ethnic issue as an ecclesiological issue. We are awaiting the results.

The Weaknesses of the Theological Argumentation.

The line of reasoning always travels from a universality that is

---

[20] L. Hodgson (ed.), *The Second World Conference on Faith and Order held at Edinburgh, August 3-18, 1937* (London, 1938), pp. 258-59.

based on creation theology and soteriological elements towards a supranational world order with a need for international solidarity. What is, striking, however, is the lack of ecclesiological argumentation. Therefore, the line of argumentation always begins from the theology of the world and its structure. Not the church but the world has to learn its theological lesson.

Through re-reading the harvest of theological argumentations a second weakness becomes obvious. The conferences of Paris (1934) and Oxford (1937) focussed more on the threat posed by the state than by that of the nation. Both state and nation are elements of the new type of nationalism that emerged – together with the appearance of the new phenomenon of the nation-states – during the nineteenth century.[21] The Paris Conference has the relationship between church and state as its theme. The Oxford Conference chose the title "Church, Community and State." However, the main challenge was to give an answer to the claims of totalitarian states, such as the fascist state in Germany and the communist state in the Soviet Union. Oldham was well aware of the particular challenge posed by the nation as an identification marker for people, but aggressive types of states constituted the main framework of his perception. It is not by chance that the Ecumenical Movement reacted more strongly to the state than to the nationalist challenge. In the first half of the twentieth century the Ecumenical Movement was almost solely a Protestant cause. And Protestants were better equipped to deal with the issue of state than that of nation. Since their origin the Protestant churches had discussed their authority vis-à-vis the state after the decline of the religious monopoly position of the Roman Catholic Church in Western and Central Europe from the end of the Middle Ages. But how to relate to a country, a nation, a people was a far less certain issue for most Protestant churches. It is obvious from the preceding analysis that Uniting Europe challenges the national churches politically and theologically. Nothing less than the identity of the church(es) is at stake.

---

[21] Cf. Smith, *Nationalism and Modernism*.

Gradual Church Communion as an Ecumenical Model?

Some Remarks from a Roman Catholic Perspective

Johannes Oeldemann

"On the Way to *Koinonia*: Church Communion in Transition". This was the theme of the 13th Academic Consultation of the *Societas Oecumenica*, held in August 2004 in the Romanian city of Sibiu. It was there that the following theses on the understanding of church communion as a gradual ecclesial reality and its significance as an acceptable model for different Christian traditions were first presented. "On the Way to *Koinonia*" could, moreover, serve as a motto for all ecumenical endeavours. *Koinonia* in its broad biblical sense[1] is undoubtedly the goal of all our efforts towards unity. The aim of ecumenism is an *ekklesia ton ekklesion*, a community of churches in the sense of mutually linked local churches, as the groundbreaking first Munich document of the International Orthodox-Catholic dialogue commission put it.[2]

"Church communion" is then – and this is my initial thesis – an apt description of the aim of our ecumenical efforts, not only from a Protestant but also from an Orthodox and Roman Catholic perspective.[3] The subtitle of the *Societas Oecumenica*

---

[1] Cf. T. Söding, "Ekklesia und Koinonia. Grundbegriffe paulinischer Ekklesiologie," *Catholica* 57 (2003): 107-23.

[2] Cf. the document "The Mystery of the Church and of the Eucharist in the Light of the Mystery of the Holy Trinity," in: J. Gros *et al.*, (eds), *Growth in Agreement II*, Faith and Order Paper 187 (Geneva, 2000).

[3] Cf. W. Thönissen, "Kirchengemeinschaft als ökumenisches Einheitsmodell? Eine katholische Perspektive," in: P. Walter *et al.* (eds),

consultation was, significantly, "Church Communion in Transition." This points to the fact that a change in the understanding of church communion is starting to emerge. In what does this change consist? I will consider this question in the form of seven theses, which may offer a stimulus for a deeper discussion.

1. The goal of all ecumenical striving is the visible unity of the church, which is to be realised in the form of mutually recognised church communion being carried out in practice.

This thesis, which at first sounds so self-evident, must surely be placed at the beginning. For recently an increasing number of voices have been raised, claiming to find a contradiction between the striving for visible unity of the church and the concept of church communion.[4] These voices find a clear echo in the well-publicised 2001 vote of the Council of the Protestant Churches in Germany (EKD) on "Church Communion in Protestant Understanding." There it is stated that the "Roman Catholic idea of the full, visible unity of the churches is not compatible with the understanding of Church communion developed here."[5] From a Roman Catholic perspective this declaration must be firmly rejected, for the incompatibility that is postulated here does justice neither to the allegedly "Protestant" concept of church communion nor to the allegedly "Catholic" understanding of visible unity. Thus with my first thesis I want to underline that I am convinced that a striving for visible unity is compatible with the model of church communion.

The paper from the EKD quoted above affirms the opposite, when it sets the model of church communion as the "Protestant model of unity" over against the "Catholic model of unity," namely that of visible unity. Were both concepts indeed so op-

---

Kirche in ökumenischer Perspektive, Festschrift für Kardinal Walter Kasper (Freiburg i.Br., 2003), pp. 163-77.

[4] Cf. K. Koch, "Kirchengemeinschaft oder Einheit der Kirche? Zum Ringen um eine angemessene Zielvorstellung der Ökumene," in: P. Walter *et al.* (eds), *Kirche in ökumenischer Perspektive*, pp. 135-62.

[5] Kirchenamt der EKD (eds), *Kirchengemeinschaft nach evangelischem Verständnis. Ein Votum zum geordneten Miteinander bekenntnisverschiedener Kirchen* (= EKD-Texte 69) (Hannover, 2001), 13.128

posed, the EKD would logically have to leave the World Council of Churches (WCC). For in the latter's constitution, Paragraph III, in setting out the aims of the WCC, states that the main goal of the Council is "to call one another to *visible unity* in one faith and in one eucharistic fellowship expressed in worship and common life in Christ, through witness and service to the world."[6] I do not believe that a member of the Protestant churches in Germany would seriously question this description of the goal of unity.[7] The incompatibility stated between the allegedly "Catholic" model of visible unity and the allegedly "Protestant" model of Church communion is due, in my opinion, to the authors of the EKD paper failing to make the necessary distinction between the understanding of unity and the models of unification – something which Harding Meyer, in his study on "Ideas on the aims of Ecumenism," has clearly demonstrated.[8] The aim of visible unity is not necessarily linked with the model of an organic union but is open to other unification models, including that of church communion.

2. In order to draw nearer to this goal of the ecumenical movement we need to discover interim stages on the path towards full church communion. The model of gradual church communion offers a theological basis for such interim stages.

The ecumenical dialogue of the past decades has shown that the way to the visible unity of the churches is more laborious and longer than some would have hoped after the ecumenical en-

---

[6] *Constitution of the WCC*, III.2.

[7] There were also, and not without reason, numerous critical responses from the Protestant Churches in Germany to the EKD paper. See, for example, G. Wenz, "Kirchengemeinschaft nach evangelischem Verständnis. Eine Stellungnahme zum Votum der Kammer für Theologie der Evangelischen Kirche in Deutschland zum geordneten Miteinander bekenntnisverschiedener Kirchen," *Ökumenische Rundschau* 51 (2002): 353-66.

[8] H. Meyer, *Ökumenische Zielvorstellungen* (=Bensheimer Hefte 78) (Göttingen, 1996).

thusiasm of the 1960s and 1970s. Because of the length of the journey, it makes sense to look for intermediate staging posts. The more distant the goal, the more urgently we need signposts which give us directions on the way to that which still lies beyond our horizon. In the history of the ecumenical movement a few such signposts have been evident. I will name only two examples: the so-called "lifting," on December 7, 1965, of the mutual anathemas from 1054, which was aimed at a "healing of memories" with regard to the symbolic date of the division between the Eastern and Western churches, and the signing of the *Joint Declaration on the Doctrine of Justification,* on October 31, 1999, in which it was possible to formulate a basic consensus on one of the central conflict areas of the Reformation period. Such interim stages on the way to visible unity represent necessary reference points which, to borrow an image from mountaineering, secure the point of the ascent that has already been reached, the shared level, and thus prevent us from falling back down into the valley of confessional polemic. Carefully considered interim stages on the journey to full church communion are something like transitional goals on the way to the visible unity of the church.

Interim stages on the way to full church communion are thinkable and desirable not only from a Protestant but also from a Catholic perspective. This was recently underscored by Bishop Brian Farrell, for some two years now Secretary of the Pontifical Council for Promoting Christian Unity, in a lecture given at the Möhler Institute in Paderborn, in which he referred to the fact that "on the way to that goal there are many intermediate destinations to be reached".[9] It goes without saying that such interim stages cannot, from the perspective of the churches, be based only on tactical moves and diplomatic skill. If they are really to mark a substantial change in the relationship of the churches to one another, then they must be constructed on a theological base. The model of gradual church communion offers such a theological basis, which allows us to make the corresponding interim steps on the way to full unity.

---

[9] B. Farrell, "Der Päpstliche Rat zur Förderung der Einheit der Christen im Jahre 2002," *Catholica* 57 (2003): 83-106, here p. 84.

3. Protestant as well as Catholic and Orthodox Church traditions contain points of contact for the concept of gradual church communion.

At first glance, it would seem more accurate to consider the concept of gradual church communion as a model for the Protestant sphere. Indeed, it is among the churches of the Reformation that the most varied forms of church communion are to be found. These range from the very narrow forms of church communion based on a common confession (as, for example, in the Lutheran World Federation) or on common structures (as in the German United Protestant Churches for example), through looser forms (as, for example, within the Leuenberg community) to the extremely broad forms of church communion (as, for example, between the Church of England and the German Protestant Churches). There is, undoubtedly, a qualitative difference between these different forms of church communion. The Protestant sphere thus offers ample illustrative material for a deeper reflection on the possible concretisations of the concept of gradual church communion. Unfortunately, to the best of my knowledge, the Reformed community still lacks an appropriately differentiated theological concept that would be generally recognised (i.e. beyond specific regional or confessional boundaries) as a basis for the understanding of church communion.

For the Catholic Church, a glance at the documents of the Second Vatican Council suffices to establish that the concept of a gradual church communion is in no way alien to Catholic thinking. I would like to point here in the first instance to the relation between the Roman Catholic dioceses of the Latin Rite and the Eastern Catholic churches. The relationship between "Roman" (Latin) and "Greek" (Eastern) Catholics is – at least today – an example of an extremely close form of church communion between local churches with very different ritual, cultural and disciplinary characteristics. From this it follows directly that, from a Catholic perspective, the Orthodox churches are churches in the full sense of the word, even though they do not stand in communion with the Roman See. On these grounds Paul VI had already described the Orthodox churches as sister churches, whereby a certain degree of church communion is established.[10]

With regard to the Protestant churches, it is well known that the Decree on Ecumenism differentiates between churches and ecclesial communities, whose ecclesial status is, however, not more precisely defined in the Council documents. Nevertheless, the fundamental ecclesial character of these non-Catholic communities is clear from the ecclesiological expressions of the Council's Decree on Ecumenism and the Constitution on the Church. Both documents point first to the sacrament of baptism through which the faithful are incorporated into the body of Christ.[11] The Council considers baptism as "a sacramental bond of unity,"[12] thus emphasising the baptismal basis of church communion. All the baptised are "in communion with the Catholic Church, even though this communion is imperfect."[13] This expression of the Decree on Ecumenism forms the theological basis for a concept of gradual church communion from the Catholic side.

There are also points of contact for the concept of gradual church communion in the Orthodox Church. This is true within the community of Orthodox churches but also for relations with non-Orthodox churches. In intra-Orthodox terms there are – not, it is true, in theory but *de facto* – different degrees of relationship between the eparchies of one and the same Patriarchate and the eparchies of different Patriarchates. There are still clearer differentiated degrees of church communion between the canonically recognised Patriarchates in full communion with one another and the non-canonical Orthodox groupings, such as those in the Ukraine and Macedonia.

---

[10] Cf. E.C. Suttner, "Die Anerkennung der Orthodoxen Kirche als Schwesterkirche durch das Zweite Vatikanische Konzil," *Der Christliche Osten* 56 (2001): 164-76; Zygfryd Glaeser has made a thorough investigation of the implications of a theology of sister churches in his habilitation work: *Ku eklezjologii "Kosciolów siostrzanych."* Studium ekumniczne, Ekumenizm i Integracja 3. (Opole, 2000).

[11] *Lumen Gentium* 14; *Unitatis Redintegratio* 3.

[12] *Unitatis Redintegratio* 22.

[13] *Unitatis Redintegratio* 3.

With regard to the relations to non-Orthodox churches, reference can be made to the document of the August 2000 Moscow Synod of Bishops on "Basic Principles of the Relationship of the Russian Orthodox Church to Non-Orthodox." This points to the existence of different liturgical rites of reception for non-Orthodox Christians as evidence "that the Orthodox Church has different forms of relationship to different non-Orthodox churches."[14] The document has been much criticised on the basis of some exclusivist statements. However, it says that the non-Orthodox churches are regarded as "never having completely lost the grace of God," so that "a certain incomplete communion has remained."[15] The parallelism of these formulations of the Moscow Bishops' Synod with the statements of Vatican II's *Decree on Ecumenism* is remarkable.[16] At least, then, with regard to Russian Orthodox theology it is possible to speak of a concept of gradual church communion, even if this concept would not meet with complete agreement on a pan-Orthodox level.

4. Within the Protestant world there are tendencies that question the concept of gradual church communion at a theoretical level.

The concept of church communion was, of course, first taken up in Protestant theology in the twentieth century in order to provide a basis for developing a model for the unification of previ-

---

[14] The text of this declaration was published in Russian in: *Zhurnal Moskovskoj Patriarchii* (2000): 22-30; an English translation is available in *Eastern Churches Journal* 7 (2000): 137-52; a (partial) German translation can be found in *Orthodoxie aktuell* 4 (2000): 6-15 and in *Ökumenische Rundschau* 50 (2001): 210-15. For the quotation cf. Section I.17.

[15] Cf. "Basic Principles of the Relationship of the Russian Orthodox Church to Non-Orthodox," I.15.

[16] Cf. J. Oeldemann, "An der Schwelle zu einem vertieften Dialog. Eine Stellungnahme zur 'Ökumene-Erklärung' der Bischofssynode der Russischen Orthodoxen Kirche vom August 2000," *Ökumenische Rundschau* 50 (2001): 178-90.

ously divided churches.[17] The Protestant concept of church communion finds its basic support in the understanding of the church as expressed in Article 7 of the *Confessio Augustana*. This would seem to offer a clear starting point for ecumenical conversation. Unfortunately in recent years a shift within the Protestant understanding of church communion has begun to emerge which makes its acceptance from a Catholic perspective increasingly problematic. Alongside the declaration of the EKD cited at the start, reference can also be made here to the position paper of the church leadership of the United Evangelical Lutheran Church of Germany (VELKD) on the theme "Ecumenism in Evangelical Lutheran Understanding," published in February 2004. Here we read:

> The aim of ecumenism according to a Lutheran understanding is neither the establishment of the true unity of the church, which can only be the work of God, nor the establishment of organisational unity between churches, which is a question of the possible and desired intensity of ecclesial cooperation. The aim of ecumenism according to a Lutheran understanding is much more the affirmation and practising of church communion.[18]

Even if this paper received considerable criticism from within the Lutheran community,[19] both it and the vote of the EKD must be taken seriously as official pronouncements of the respective churches by their ecumenical dialogue partners. It is hard, because the contradiction expressed in them between the concept of unity and that of church communion clearly does

---

[17] Cf. H. Meyer, "Zur Entstehung und Bedeutung des Konzepts 'Kirchengemeinschaft'. Eine historische Skizze aus evangelischer Sicht," in: J. Schreiner and K. Wittstatt (eds), *Communio Sanctorum. Einheit der Christen – Einheit der Kirche*. Festschrift Bischof Paul-Werner Scheele (Würzburg, 1988), pp. 204-30.

[18] *Ökumene nach evangelisch-lutherischem Verständnis* (= Texte aus der VELKD 123/2004) (Hannover, 2004), p. 9.

[19] Cf., for example, G. Wenz, "Ökumenische Kehrtwende? Zu einem Positionspapier der Kirchenleitung der VELKD," *Una Sancta* 59: (2004) 171-80; M. Hailer, "Zur Hermeneutik von Schrift und Bekenntnis. Eine Stellungnahme zu 'Ökumene nach evangelisch-lutherischem Verständnis,' *Ökumenische Rundschau* 53 (2004): 530-37.

not coincide with the spirit of Article 7 of the *Confessio Augustana*. For this article begins and ends with a confession of the unity of the church. If Article 7 is taken seriously as a base text for the ecclesiology of Reformation churches, then the affirmation of church communion alone cannot be the final goal of Protestant ecumenical efforts. Even from a Protestant perspective oriented to the confessional documents, the real goal of all ecumenical endeavours would have to be the unity of the Church.

The *Leuenberg Concordia* has in my view the correct understanding of Article 7 of this creed when it distinguishes between the affirmation and the realisation of church communion. The prerequisite for the affirmation of hurch communion is, according to the *Leuenberg Concordia*, the common understanding of the Gospel as well as the conviction that the doctrinal judgements of the Reformation no longer apply to the current doctrinal positions of the participant churches. The *affirmation* of church communion achieved by the signing of the *Concordia* must, however, be followed by the *realisation* of church communion by, as no. 35 of the *Concordia* puts it, the "strengthening and deepening of the communion that has been won." The *Concordia* itself names four areas in which such a deepening of church communion is required. This shows that the authors of the *Leuenberg Concordia* understood this not as the final goal of the internal Protestant ecumenical effort but rather as an interim stage that should become a starting point for further steps on the way to the unity of the church. I would like here to quote briefly Günther Gassmann, who refers to the fact that the *Leuenberg Concordia*, and the church communion established through it, are an "important stage" in the efforts to bring about the unity of Christians "but still only a stage and not the goal."[20] The impression this statement from one of the fathers of the *Leuenberg Concordia* gives makes me think that it contradicts their intention when "Leuenberg" is presented in the most re-

---

[20] G. Gassmann, "Die Leuenberger Lehrgespräche und der umfassendere ökumenische Dialog. Zur Frage der Kompatibilität von Lehrgesprächen," in A. Birmele (ed.), *Konkordie und Ökumene* (Frankfurt a. M., 1988), pp. 118f.

cent pronouncements of the EKD and VELKD as *the* Protestant model of unity. I would rather characterise the *Leuenberg Concordia* as one model of unification, with the help of which a certain, albeit relatively far-reaching, form of church communion has been achieved. This, however, should not be identified with the full realisation of church communion. Such an identification would, in the end, lead to a theoretical abandonment of the concept of gradual church communion in the Protestant sphere, although it is widespread in practice.

5. In the Catholic and Orthodox communities there are developments in practice which undermine the concept of gradual church communion.

In the Catholic and Orthodox churches there is, to some extent, an opposite development to the tendencies presented above in Protestantism. Although there is a sound basis for the concept of a gradual church communion in theory, that is, in Catholic and Orthodox ecclesiologies, in practice tendencies can be observed which go against this concept. I will give a few examples of this as well.

The Second Vatican Council called emphatically for the liturgical and canonical independence of the Eastern Catholic churches and argued that "each individual Church or Rite should retain its traditions whole and entire."[21] Accordingly, the Council urges the Eastern churches "to return to their ancestral traditions."[22] However, in practice there is still a strong inclination for the Roman Curia to intervene in the life of the Eastern Catholic churches, seen most clearly in Rome's pushing through the promulgation of a Canon Law for the Eastern Catholic churches. Despite all good intentions, the *Codex Canonum Ecclesiarum Orientalium* is not able to do justice, as a single lawbook for all twenty-one Eastern Catholic churches, to the liturgical and canonical plurality of the Eastern traditions.[23]

---

[21] *Orientalium Ecclesiarum* 2.

[22] *Orientalium Ecclesiarum* 6.

[23] Cf. D. Schon, *Der Codex Canonum Ecclesiarum Orientalium und das authentische Recht im christlichen Orient* (= Das östliche Christentum, N.F. Vol. 47) (Würzburg, 1999).

A second example is the growing number of Roman directives over the past few years by means of which the independence of the local churches of the Latin rite has also been restricted even more.[24] This goes against the Council's affirmation of the "plurality of the local churches" which "enjoy their own discipline, their own liturgical usage, and their own theological and spiritual heritage," as the Constitution on the Church says with reference to the Patriarchate structure of the early church.[25] The Council's indication that Bishops' Conferences could fulfil a similar role nowadays has never been put into practice. Behind this development there lies the ultimately unfinished debate within Catholicism over the correct relationship between the local churches and the universal church, which recently re-emerged in the dispute between Cardinals Kasper and Ratzinger on the interpretation of *Lumen Gentium*.[26]

I would like to avoid giving concrete examples from Orthodoxy here, so as not to stick fingers in another's pie. It should suffice to point to the intra-Orthodox disagreements over the way of recognising the autonomy or autocephaly of a local church as well as those concerning the church structures in the diaspora for it to be clear that here too the concepts which are theoretically to hand for gradual church communion are not always followed through consistently in practice.

---

[24] See, for example, in the area of liturgy, the instruction published in March 2001 by the Congregation for Divine Worship and the Discipline of the Sacraments, *"Liturgiam Authenticam"*. Latin-German edition (= Verlautbarungen des Apostolischen Stuhls 154) (Bonn, 2001); English translation available at, for example, http://www.vatican.va/roman_curia/congregations/ccdds/documents/rc_con_ccdds_doc_20010507_liturgiam-authenticam_en.html.

[25] *Lumen Gentium* 23.

[26] Cf. K. McDonnell, "The Ratzinger/Kasper Debate: The Universal Church and Local Churches," *Theological Studies* 63 (2002): 227-50; M. Kehl "Zum jüngsten Disput um das Verhältnis von Universalkirche und Ortskirchen," in: P. Walter *et al.* (eds), *Kirche in ökumenischer Perspektive*, pp. 81-101.

6. To put strong emphasis on baptism as the basis for the unity of all Christians or to press for closer Eucharistic fellowship can both lead to a situation in which careful thought about interim stages on the path towards full church communion is neglected.

In the contemporary ecumenical discussion there is still too little reflection on the chances which the model of gradual church communion offers. With regard to ecumenical coexistence, the debates centre mostly on the possibilities and limits of Eucharistic fellowship.[27] Church leaders are thus faced with an unproductive alternative of "either/or": *either* having to consider the conditions for mutual admission to the Eucharist as met *or* rejecting it. Given that Catholics and Orthodox regard Eucharistic fellowship as an expression of full church communion, they will agree to the mutual admission to the Eucharist only after the completion of all the requisite interim stages on the way to full church communion. For their part, the churches of the Reformation tradition, drawing on Article 7 of the *Confessio Augustana* and the *Leuenberg Concordia*, repeatedly demand admission to the Eucharist on the basis of a common understanding of the Gospel. In doing so, they marginalise the still unresolved questions of the understanding of church and ministry, which, on the one hand, fails to do justice to Catholic and Orthodox self-understandings and, on the other, runs counter to the actual declarations on the incompatibility of the particular understandings of church and unity (see the vote of the EKD cited above).

Those who do not consider the time ripe for any form of Eucharistic fellowship have, in recent times, increasingly had recourse to baptism as the "sacramental bond of unity."[28] Both the request to Catholic Bishops' Conferences from the Pontifical Council for the Promoting of Christian Unity to devote efforts to appropriate official declarations on mutual recognition of

---

[27] From the vast list of publications on this theme reference can be made, for example, to the paper published by three member institutes of the *Societas Oecumenica*: "Abendmahlsgemeinschaft ist möglich". *Thesen zur eucharistischen Gastfreundschaft* (Frankfurt a.M., 2003) and to J. Brosseder and H.-G. Link (eds), *Eucharistische Gastfreundschaft. Ein Plädoyer evangelischer und katholischer Theologen* (Neukirchen-Vluyn, 2003).

[28] *Unitatis Redintegratio* 22.

baptism in their areas, as well as the apt closing speech of Konrad Raiser at the Ecumenical Church Assembly in Berlin[29] witness to this tendency to stress the baptismal basis of the unity of all Christians. The emphasis on the linking of all Christians through baptism does, however, neglect – in addition to the difficulties that those Free Churches that reject infant baptism have with the mutual recognition of baptism – the practical relevance of ecumenism, which strives for visible forms of expression of growing communion. The stress on baptism is not able to clarify which elements in addition to baptism already bring Christians together and what has been achieved in relation to this understanding in the previous decades.

7. The degree of communion in the one Christian faith, which we have been rediscovering in ecumenical dialogue, now needs to be expressed both in liturgical and in other living forms, which will help us to identify the interim stages on the path to full unity.

Those interim steps which are possible on the basis of the concept of gradual church communion and which, with respect to the deepening of ecumenical relations, are necessary on the path to full unity should not be limited to an official church reception of the results of ecumenical doctrinal dialogue, as happened with the *Joint Declaration on the Doctrine of Justification* nor to formal declarations of church communion, such as took place with, among others, the documents of Leuenberg, Meissen, Porvoo and Waterloo. The community in faith rediscovered and "fostered by the grace of the Holy Spirit"[30] needs, in addition to theoretical recognition, other forms of expression, too, through which it will be experienced in the lives of Christians and local communities. Opening up the possibility of ecumenical religious services or that of the participation of the priest of anoth-

---

[29] Cf. K. Raiser, "Der Weg der Ökumene: Dank und Verpflichtung," in: T. Bolzenius *et al.*, (eds). *Ihr sollt ein Segen sein. Ökumenischer Kirchentag, 28. Mai – 1. Juni 2003 in Berlin. Dokumentation* (Gütersloh-Kevelaer, 2004), pp. 416-28, esp. pp. 426ff.

[30] *Unitatis Redintegratio* 1.

er church in the marriage of a couple from different traditions were first steps in this direction after the Council. Since then agreement in faith has grown still more, without having been transformed into corresponding liturgical or other forms of expression. It is something to be desired of practical theology and liturgical studies that they take up this challenge and develop appropriate models.

A glance over the border of one's own country or own confession can perhaps be of further help in this respect. So, for example, one might ask whether the preacher exchanges, which have been undertaken with success in some countries, could not become a more widespread practice. So far the Catholic Church has rejected this, pointing to the fact that the president of the Eucharistic celebration must also give the homily, in order to safeguard the unity of the Liturgy of the Word and the Celebration of the Eucharist. However, if even at a Eucharist celebration presided over by the Pope a representative of another confession is permitted to preach – as was the case not long ago in Rome on the Solemnity of St Peter and Paul with the Ecumenical Patriarch Bartholomew – then the question arises as to why this cannot be possible on a local level. If Catholics and Protestants agree on the heart of the Gospel, as the *Joint Declaration on the Doctrine of Justification* affirmed, then it should basically also be possible for a Lutheran pastor to preach in a Catholic Mass.

With respect to liturgical forms, which can express different grades of communion, a glance at the Orthodox tradition will be helpful. In the Byzantine rite of the *antidoron* the Orthodox Church also has the rite of *artoklasia*, the blessing of the bread, which is open for the participation of believers of different confessions. The celebration of blessed bread that is offered to all believers at the end of the Holy Liturgy represents an important sign of communion, whose significance should not be underestimated. Moreover, Morning Prayer is a remarkable rite, in which holy oil is traced on the foreheads of the faithful with a brush in the form of a cross. This rite contains a liturgical gesture that goes beyond a mere memorial of baptism but still does not enter into the realm of Eucharistic service.

Finally, in this connection attention should be drawn to the "Guidelines for Admission to the Eucharist between the Chaldean Church and the Assyrian Church of the East," issued by the Vatican in 2001.[31] This document is remarkable from an ecumenical perspective for two reasons. The first lies in the way it takes the particular nature of another tradition so seriously that it even considers a Eucharistic celebration valid that does recite the words of institution (something which goes contrary to the regulations of the Latin tradition as these were formulated, for example, at the Council of Florence).[32] Moreover, it contains an interesting innovation with regard to Eucharistic fellowship between churches that do not yet stand in full church communion. In this connection, on the one hand, the document takes up the well-known formulation of the documents of Vatican II with respect to a limited *communicatio in sacris* between the faithful of the Catholic Church and those of the Eastern Churches,[33] while on the other hand it brings forth a new emphasis, inasmuch as it limits this possibility – within the Eastern Syrian rite – to the faithful of the Chaldean and Assyrian churches. It is in this limitation that the particularly explosive ecumenical element lies. For if these Vatican guidelines make admission to the Eucharist in a non-Catholic church possible only for a determined group within the Catholic church while other Catholics are excluded from these regulations, then this raises the question of whether a corresponding "partial" admission to the Eucharist may not be conceivable in other particular church contexts. Then, a gradual Eucharistic fellowship could correspond to the model of gradual church communion.

These few examples may suffice to show that there is a whole range of possibilities to express and celebrate the rediscovered and deepened communion in faith through different liturgical forms. Such practical interim steps on the way to full unity are necessary, so that the will to move towards one an-

---

[31] Cf. *Information Service* (ed. by the Pontifical Council for Promoting Christian Unity), no. 108 (2001/IV): 148-52; also published in *Eastern Churches Journal* 8 (2001): 130-34.

[32] Cf. *Dignitatis Humanae* 1321, 1352.

[33] Cf. *Orientalium Ecclesiarum* 27.

other does not wane. An ecumenism of deeds must ultimately follow the ecumenism of words, or, as Cardinal Kasper put it at the German Catholic Assembly in Ulm in June 2004, an "ecumenism of life", which is oriented on the three basic functions of the church: the witness to faith, the celebration of the liturgy, and charity towards all humankind. If we "act together at all levels of church life wherever conditions permit and there are no reasons of faith ... mitigating against this," as the *Charta Oecumenica*[34] formulates it following the so-called "Lund Principle," then we could, under the leadership of the Holy Spirit, make further steps "on the way to *Koinonia*," as the theme of the 13th Academic Consultation of *Societas Oecumenica* put it.

---

[34] See *Charta Oecumenica* II.4 in the appendix to this volume.

Part III

The Sacramental Road to Unity

This section contains two essays, the first by Maria Clara Bingemer from the Pontifical Catholic University in Rio de Janeiro, and the second by Ivana Noble from the Charles University in Prague. Both authors examine questions of sacramentality and how a renewed understanding of the nature of sacrament could help bring about a growing unity.

Bingemer seeks to locate her reflection on sacramentality within several contexts. The first is that of the crisis of modernity, or postmodernity. Among the challenges this raises is the need to encounter and dialogue with other religions, the second part of her contribution. Thirdly, this leads to an emphasis on experience as a key hermeneutic key for talking about religious belief. She then proceeds to reflect on the sacraments, or the sacramental, as the symbolic representation or manifestation of Christian experience, necessarily linked to the concrete living out of Christian life.

In her paper Noble examines two sacramental theologians, a Russian Orthodox, the late Alexander Schmemann, and a French Catholic, Louis-Marie Chauvet. With each theologian she begins with epistemological questions, concerning their understanding of relational and symbolic knowledge of God, before discussing their concepts of sacramentality and the way in which the world and church are combined in their theologies. From each writer she draws positive points, whilst also pointing to some of their shortcomings. In her conclusion she suggests ways in which they can complement each other and seek help from other sources to help promote a greater unity among churches which, at the same time, is not destructive of the individual.

The Roman Catholic Understanding of Sacramentality and Its Potential for Church Unity

Maria Clara Lucchetti Bingemer

The Western world lives today in a time that can only be understood within the framework of a process that is not, properly speaking, recent but has been going on for a long time and that appears today in the form of a crisis of models, paradigms, and values. The impact is very strong on those who live it and especially on the generations who have already experienced another world and who find their certainties and all their most fundamental supports – family, religion, etc. – threatened.

In this article I will analyse more specifically *one* of the aspects of this crisis of modernity, namely, its impact on the manner of living out religion. I shall reflect on the contours of the profile of religious identity, on the ways followed by what is termed religious experience, which lies at the heart of the present historical moment. To help achieve this aim, I will start by briefly outlining what constitutes the so-called crisis of modernity, conscious, however, of the fact that this, like any attempt to describe the subject, will necessarily be limited and partial. This is not only due to the diversity of points of view and possible angles for analysis, but even more to the diversification of the tendencies of those authors who have dedicated themselves to the subject over the last few years.[1]

Conscious of this limitation, I will begin with a first stage which intends to locate the reflection within a framework of

---

[1] For the basis of what I say about modernity as a globalising and enveloping phenomenon, see, e.g., J. Baudrillard, "Modernité," in: *Encyclopaedia Universalis*, vol. 11 (Paris, 1980) 139-41; J. Maradones, *Postmodernidad y Cristianismo* (Santander, 1988); M. Gauchet, *Le désenchantement du monde: Une histoire politique de la religion* (Paris, 1989).

more or less understandable contours. Following this, I propose to characterise the question, initially seeking to understand and reflect on the phenomenon named (rightly or wrongly) "the return of the sacred" or "the return of the religious" in secularised society. Using the data thus acquired, I will continue, restricting my attention to historical Christianity as opposed to focussing on religion in general. At the turn of the millennium Christianity is engaged in the process of finding its deepest identity again and discovering an adequate way of expressing it to a world that is at the same time secularised and multireligious.

The experience of God appears to be the main way ahead for the dialogue that Christianity so greatly desires, not only with the modern world but also with other religious traditions.[2] Likewise, it seems to be the privileged way for Christianity to advance always further in search of its own identity and the adequate means to make it known and proclaim it in language understandable to contemporary ears. The final objective of my presentation will thus be to look further into the characteristics of this experience at the heart of Christianity and especially in sacramentality and to make it the subject of my reflection, which will allow us to come to some conclusions that I hope can contribute to the contemporary ecumenical debate.

The Modern Crisis and Postmodernity: Attempting a Description

At a time when paradigms and models are collapsing and changing noticeable in today's society is a rediscovery of the self-understanding of human beings as relational beings, open to a heteronymous autonomy, that is to say, to an autonomy gov-

---

[2] The question of God is proving today to be the path of possibility for dialogue between religions. Cf. the reflections in some recent works on a *theocentrism*, which succeeds *christocentrism* in the attempts of Christianity to dialogue with other religions: J. Dupuis, *Jesus Christ à la rencontre des religions* (Paris, 1989); (English translation: *Jesus Christ at the Encounter of World Religions*, transl. Robert R. Barr (Maryknoll, 1991); J. Dupuis, "Les religions comme voies de salut?" *Spiritus* 33 (1992): 5-14; M. Fitzgerald, "Panorama du dialogue interreligieux et questions théologiques," *Spiritus* 33 (1992): 92-103. See also J. Dupuis, *Vers une théologie du dialogue interreligieux* (Paris, 1997).

erned by otherness. This can be understood in terms of the seduction of the sacred, in as far as the otherness in question is nothing else than the Transcendent, the divine otherness, the completely Other or a plurality of countless divinities. We Christians call it God.[3]

The re-sacralisation of that same world in which modern reason hastened to proclaim disenchantment and secularity complicates the question. The reappearance, the re-emergence – more than the return – of the religious, of the sacred, the thirst for mystery and for the mystical in different forms, appearing as they do after the "fading out" attempted by secularisation, denotes a return (or the permanency) of the contemplative necessity, an apparently new emergence of values such as gratuity, desire and feeling, and the rediscovery, in a new dimension, of nature and of people's relationship with the planet.

Even after the whole process of secularisation and of modernity and of the categorical declarations of the masters of suspicion concerning religion, we still meet people who spend hours and hours of their time in rituals, celebrations and ceremonies of praise; people who invest all their affective potential and the entirety of their time, energy, creativity and resources in religious rituals, who sing hymns of praise, participating in long assemblies for many hours, who look for therapy and bodily and spiritual cures, searching for communion with the universe and nature, reciting mantras or looking for different forms of therapy, for ways of breathing and posture which help them to find what they are looking for in terms of the integration of the self.

There is a process of new religiosity happening under our eyes, one that is becoming more and more popular. It is a product of the complexity of our times. It is less a new historical time of religion to be lived than a new way of living religion. At this same peak of secularisation there is also occurring in diverse places the widespread return of the sacred. It is what is customarily described as the postmodern phenomenon.[4]

---

[3] Cf. K. Rahner, in *Escritos de teología VII* (Madrid, 1972), pp. 90-96.

[4] Cf. M. Carvalho Azevedo, "América Latina: perfil complexo de

Consciously or unconsciously, people are affected by the conjugation of these two elements and they are beginning to adopt a new paradigm of perception and analysis and a new world vision. One can observe the presence in different urban contexts – squares, shopping centres, highways, stores in middle-class neighborhoods – of activities and practices which were supposed to be carried out privately, in enclosed spaces. Things which concern the most intimate restlessness and deepest secrets of the human being (future, final destiny, health, and happiness) have gained a place in the public square and are no longer restricted to private places, discreet, favourable to mystery. Rather, they are on offer at stalls peddling mysticism in shopping centres. Meanwhile, the techniques and structures that surround these services are true managerial enterprises.[5]

Beneath this complex and plural phenomenon of religious explosion are hidden several matters of extreme importance, not only for theological reflection but equally for all the social and human sciences that intend to work seriously with this problem – more than purely human – of religious experience or experience of the Sacred. On the one side, there is a veiled criticism of the traditional historical churches that they have lost a good part of their initiatory or mystical character and are characterised almost solely by their institutional aspect as articulators of community or ethical transformers of reality. In this sense, this fact can be seen right in the heart of institutionalised Christianity, where the use of techniques belonging to Oriental traditions, self-help therapies, or the search for resources largely identified with the New Age appear and become visible in

---

um universo religioso," in "Novas Experiências Religiosas," *Cadernos Atualidade em debate* no. 26 (1996): 13: "Let us take the term 'postmodern' here in one of its technical meanings: as a cultural paradigm, in relative contrast, although co-existent, with non-modern and modern paradigms. Owing to a question of space and time, we will not specify the content and expressions of those other two paradigms. But we are using the term post-modern as an expression of the exotic or psychedelic, as has been done by some publications or by the media."

[5] J.G. Cantor Magnani, "O neo-esoterismo na cidade," *Revista da USP* 31 (1996: 8.

the living of spirituality. On the one hand, if those facts are cause for concern, they can be viewed, on the other, as symptomatic of a new way or effort of recovering initiatory and mystagogical Christianity.

The question that remains, however, is whether our contemporaries' almost frantic search for mystic experiences corresponds to a real search for a deep encounter, to an openness to being affected by the alterity of the other. To search for more or less religious or spiritual sensations does not necessarily imply a desire to be open to an experience of alterity and may not leave space or place so that otherness and the difference of the other can reveal freedom in everything, disclosing the relationship of each sign and each step.[6]

It seems, then, to me that Christian experience today finds itself dealing with the question of its identity, sometimes lost or broken into fragments among an ocean of different religious experiences which do not necessarily imply the Otherness that, in absolute liberty, reveals itself as Holiness, that is to say, as the Otherness of the absolute other. If we too easily call mystical experience every and any search for spiritual sensations, achieved sometimes with artificial resources, other than and not in relation with what is established and deepened only in gratuity, in hearing and in desire, we will betray the mystical conception that to this day has marked the Western tradition and is at the heart of what is and has always been understood by "mystical." If we very easily legitimise any experience of seduction by the Sacred, we run the risk of baptising many divinities with this name and not, perhaps, the True One, who does not surrender His/Her Sacred name so lightly.[7]

---

[6] Cf. the lives of saints, mystics and especially martyrs and the huge amount of literature that investigates this phenomenon in Christian tradition. See *Dictionnaire de Spiritualité* vol. X, cols 727-28, under the entry "Martyre," the word which refers to the experience of martyrdom as experience of deep union and identification with Christ. Cf. A.J. Festrugière, *La sainteté* (Paris, 1949) in which the author does a comparative research and reflection between the Greek hero and the Christian saint.

[7] Cf. J. Ladrière, "Approcio filosofico alla mistica," in: J.M. Van

Christianity and Dialogue among Religions

The other line of questioning addressed to Christianity today concerns ecumenism and the ecclesial dialogue. It is not only about the intra-ecclesial dialogue among the various trends found inside of one church but even more about a dialogue among religions in which Christianity and other religions seek together points of reference for a convergence that can lead to common ground.[8] This includes the lines of questioning addressed to the traditional Christian churches from the great non-Christian religions as well as from new religious movements. Although they have been criticized many times because their morals do not strictly conform to the doctrinal and ethical principles of Judaism and Christianity, the fact is that several of the new religious movements have a rather strict moral code, sometimes even more so than the one found in the Judeao-Christian frame of reference.

The figure of Jesus, central to Christianity, also appears in these movements but from a point of view other than the one in Christian tradition: his death and resurrection are questioned, and, consequently, so is his divinity.[9] Other figures of Christian-

---

Cangh (ed.), *La mistica* (Bologna, 1992), p. 83.

[8] Cf. the ever more numerous works over the last years on this subject. As examples I cite the following: H. Küng, *El Cristianismo y las grandes religiones* (Madrid, 1987); A. Gesché, "Le Christianisme et les autres religions," *Revue théologique de Louvain* 19 (1988): 315-41; Dupuis, *Jesus Christ à la rencontre des religions* Cf. also F. Couto Teixeira, *Teologia das religiões. Uma visão panorâmica* (Sao Paulo, 1995), with an extensive bibliography. On the dialogue from a pneumatological perspective see also my: "A pneumatologia como possibilidade de diálogo e missão universais," in: F.Couto Teixeira (ed.), *Diálogo de pássaros* (Sao Paulo, 1993), pp. 111-21; (in English: "The Holy Spirit as Possibility of Universal Dialogue and Mission," in: L. Swidler and P. Mojzes (eds.), *Christian Mission and Interreligious Dialogue*, Religions in Dialogue 4 (Lewiston/Lampeter, 1990), pp. 34-41.

[9] On the way in which the figure of Jesus is present in the new religiosity see J. Vernette, *Jesus dans la nouvelle religiosité. Esotérismes, gnoses et sectes d'aujourd'hui* (Paris, 1987) as well his most recent article by the same name in: *Research Project on New Religious Movements – Dos-*

ity, such as Mary and the saints, are invoked by several of these movements, without, however, filling the same roles there as they do in Catholicism.

In these movements the communitarian dimension is very strong; it is surprising to note that certain new Christian groups who search for some form of community (the Charismatic Revival and other groups formed by Catholics and non-Catholics) are similar both in terms of motivation (marked by a strong affectivity) and with respect to the expression of strongly connected relationships. It should, however, be recognised that these groups, criticised for "alienation" by others more aware of and engaged in the historical churches, show several features similar to those of the so-called new religious movements, while remaining inside the institution of the church, and having, like them, a great capacity for attraction and recruitment.

In an analysis of this situation, the sects constitute a phenomenon apart.[10] Of a rather fundamentalist stamp, they always maintain, if in a veiled way, an attitude of protest towards traditional Christianity, especially the Catholic Church, which is reproached for soiling the purity of the Gospel. At the present time, by accentuating the eschatological principle in its millenarian guise, as well as the pneumatic spiritual principle, in opposition to what they see as the preponderant role of dogma in the traditional churches, the sects enjoy a very marked seductive power and are gaining ever-increasing contingents of peo-

---

sier (Rome, 1990), pp. 245-72.

[10] We employ the term "sects" here according to Max Weber's definition, which opposed the concept of "sect" to that of the "church," but ascribe to it the characteristic that seems to fit better with the mode of organization of religious groups in Brazil and other parts of the world, that are called "sects": people who believe in Jesus, gather around the Bible, with rituals that are marked by the affective and emotional, claiming direct inspiration from the Holy Spirit who speaks through the mouth of the faithful, whoever that might be, without hierarchical rigorism. On the discussion of the concept see P.F.C. De Andrade, "Sinais dos tempos. Igrejas e seitas no Brasil," *Perspectiva Teologica* 23 (1991): 223-40, especially pp.224-25.

ple who participate in their rituals in a more and more intense way.

Even given all their ambiguous aspects, one can legitimately wonder if the growing seduction exerted by the sects, even over former members of the historical Christian churches, might not be equated to a serious questioning of these same churches, linked to the methods they use to evangelize. Also one may wonder if the success of these religions in the diffusion of their message is not due to the content and means employed, and would not have something to say to the historical Christian churches about the coldness of their liturgies, about the bureaucratisation of their institutions, about the necessity of reconsidering the affective dimension of the communication of what they have to offer.[11]

Basically, the great challenge, the great scandal for Christianity in the multireligious world nowadays continues to be faith in Jesus Christ, Son of God and Universal Saviour. Recognising and proclaiming the singularity of the event of the incarnation of the God whom no one has ever seen and yet who is revealed in the historical particularity of Jesus of Nazareth is an inescapable requirement of Christianity. On the other hand, this is what is increasingly contested by other religions that support the thesis that there are mediations other than that of Jesus for

---

[11] See on this subject R. Bergeron, "Les sectes et l'Eglise catholique," in *Research Project on New Religious Movements- Dossier* (Rome, 1990), pp. 599-616. See also my text "A sedução do Sagrado," in: C. Caliman (ed.), *A sedução do sagrado* 2nd ed. (Vozes, 1998), pp. 79-115, esp. pp. 82-93. See, moreover, what J. Hortal says in his address to the 30th General Assembly of the Episcopal Conference of Brazil (CNBB). Although referring more closely to Brazil, his comments have, in my view, wider relevance. The accusations that he enumerates of the sects against the Catholic Church, are, among others, the following: the weight of the institution, the quasi-federative structure of the Catholic Church, etc, Also, on pages 4-5, he gives some of the principle motivations of those who have abandoned the Catholic Church for the sects: deeper personal relationships, the emotion of the supernatural and the search for the wonderful, immediate solution to alarming problems, and the privatization of religion.

the revelation of God. And the same thing can be found in those currents inside Christianity that propose reconsidering the uniqueness of Jesus.[12]

However, interreligious dialogue does offer hope and prospects for Christianity at the present time. Without making concessions about the central point of the incarnation, Christianity, today as always, is called to find in the secularised, postmodern and multireligious world a new but faithful way of experiencing the God who is at the centre of its identity and of tracing the contours of his profile in a way that can be understood by our contemporaries.

From Seduction to Experience

Karl Rahner, rightly considered one of the greatest of twentieth-century theologians, affirmed that the Christian of the future (I would add, of the present) will be a *mystic*, that is to say, somebody who has experienced something, or will be nothing at all, even less a Christian.[13] Since time immemorial, and today more than ever, speaking of God, from the perspective of the Christian faith, means speaking about an experience, or better, starting from an experience: an experience that, in fact, because it is divine, is profoundly human from the moment when, in the fullness of time, as the Christian faith proclaims, God himself was made flesh, was made human, the Word Incarnate, in Jesus Christ.

If it appears – rightly or not – that Christianity may partially have lost the possibility of expressing itself through words, of proclaiming before the world of today, aloud and comprehensibly, the God who is at the heart of its experience, it would be to a great extent the result of the divorce which has

---

[12] Cf., for example, such works as P. Knitter, *No Other Name? A Critical Survey of Christian Atttitudes toward the World Religions* (Maryknoll, 1985). Cf. also the writings of M. Amaladoss, R. Pannikar and others. J. Dupuis also comments on this in his "Pour une théologie do dialogue," in Dupuis, *Jesus Christ à la rencontre des religions*, pp. 299-313.

[13] Cf. K. Rahner, *Escritos de teología VII* (Madrid, 1972), pp. 75-81.

slowly been established between the experiences and practices of faith on the one hand and, on the other, the important and significant human experiences that manage to move and to mobilize what is most profound in the human being. To the degree that these experiences, structural and full of meaning, lose their analogy with Christian experience, personal, communal and ecclesial, they cease to be experiences that make God real, cease to be salvific. In short they do not deserve, strictly speaking, to be called experiences of God. [14]

At the present time, religious pluralism and, consequently, the quest for a dialogue with religious traditions, which preoccupy – and perhaps worry – the traditional Christian churches, are finding fertile soil in the experience of God for possibilities of progress. Although one cannot, with regard to the experiences that occur within several religions, simply reduce one to another or identify one with the other, it is undeniable that religious and mystical experience can be used as a privileged ground for theological dialogue, insofar as it returns the human being to fundamental questions of meaning: Where do we come from and where will we go? What is the meaning of human existence, with its burden of suffering and death? What is the source of this movement that we share, that brings us into relationships, that carries us out of ourselves into solidarity and communion with the other and is *the* response to the call by an Absolute of which we are aware and in which we believe.

The answer – though mysterious and veiled – to these questions, and the simple fact that it concerns us, indicates that the *experience of God* is the indispensable criterion for Christianity, not only for advancing in the understanding of its identity but,

---

[14] Cf. on this subject the affirmation of M. De França Miranda, *A Igreja Católica diante do pluralismo religioso no Brasil. Avaliação teológica* (San Paulo, 1991), pp. 84-85. Moreover, and more explicitly related to Catholicism, I believe that it is possible to extend this to the level of Christian experience in more ecumenical terms. In my opinion, the core of this problem lies in the divorce between the expressions and practices of faith on the one hand and, on the other, the significant human experiences of our contemporaries. The present crisis in Catholicism is a result, in good part, of this rupture.

moreover, for going forward toward the other that challenges it and, paradoxically, renders it increasingly faithful to the core of its fundamental truth.

As a starting point for dialogue in a multireligious world, the experience of God also presents nothing less than the possibility, for the human being, of living out the fundamental anthropological dimension of gratuity. While walking on the road of the experience of God, human beings note that the One who their hearts desire does not at all surrender to the immediacies of their needs and even less to the consuming "frenzy" of certain psychological states and emotional conquests. The experience of God, while occurring on the level of desire, can only occur gratuitously, leaving the one who has felt it in the grip of an always unappeased desire and thus always capable of desiring and, consequently, of experiencing.[15]

The Judaeo-Christian tradition recognises and assumes the natural presence of this desire in the human being. Scripture does not fail to take into account this human desire deeply rooted in the force of the aspiration for life in its fullness, in which the fundamental element is the establishment of personal relations with God.[16] However, this experience does not consist, for Judaism and even less so for Christianity, either in a permanent satiety or in something incomplete.

---

[15] Cf. D. Bertrand, "La théologie négative de Michel de Certeau," in C. Geffré (ed.), *Michel de Certeau et la différence chrétienne* (Paris, 1991), pp. 120-21, in commenting on de Certeau with respect to the question of the experience of God. See also A. Vergote, "Verticalité et horizontalité dans le langage symbolique sur Dieu," in: A. Vergote, *Explorations de l'espace théologique* (Louvain, 1990), pp. 543-48.

[16] Cf. the number of biblical texts that express the corporeal repercussions of human desire: Ps. 42, Ps. 123:3, Ps. 63:2, Ps. 130:6, Ps. 73:25-28 and others. Jesus himself speaks to his disciples in terms of desire (cf. Luke 12:49-50; 22:15). The Bible itself ends with the cry of the impatient desire of the Bride who calls for her Beloved: "Maranatha! Come, Lord!" (Rev. 22:17.20). Cf. the beautiful commentary by M. Meslin, *L'expérience humaine du divin* (Paris, 1988), pp. 383-85, on these passages.

If, on the one hand, it is certain that "only desire is capable of qualifying the relationship of God with humanity,"[17] on the other hand, the relationship established by this desire places humankind before the very "difference" of God: a difference of the desire for the Other, the encounters of which can be made only in renouncing oneself, in conversion, in the examination of one's own desires. It is the only way, in the Christian experience, of opening a space for God to desire in us and consequently for allowing us to desire only God, by increasingly identifying our desire with the divine desire. It is thus the human being who, in experience, is *seized* by God, and not the other way around. And this experience, if it is true, entirely escapes his or her control.

So, if the experience of God occurs on the level of desire – not being able to occur otherwise – it is also necessary to say that it occurs as a *mystery*. It is, to be sure, a revealed mystery, the mystery of love that comes close in salvation, but yet a mystery. There is no natural logical transition between the daily experience of life and the experience of God, although the former is the place where the latter occurs. One may speak of an analogical knowledge, on the basis of the fundamental perception that nothing, no reality, is able to express transcendence. Also, with regard to any human experience of transcendence, the term "mystery" is the more appropriate one for defining the discovery of God as the Absolute who attracts and invites to experience.

And yet the incarnation of the Word in Jesus of Nazareth says to the Christian that, purely by the grace and mercy of God, time itself has received a new significance and this "afterwards" has been redeemed. Thus, his or her religious experience consists in the indissoluble union of two seemingly (humanly) irreconcilable poles: the theological fact that God allows himself to be experienced while at the same time being Absolute and Father. Defined as love from the very beginning of Christianity, this God reveals himself as a father in the personal

---

[17] On this subject see what Meslin says in *L'expérience humaine du divin*, p. 386. Cf. also my "A sedução do sagrado."

and intimate relationship that he maintains with humankind, a relationship whose primary point of reference is the loving union maintained with Jesus of Nazareth, in whom the Christian faith has recognised the Beloved Son of the God never seen by anyone.[18]

The mystery of the incarnation of God in Jesus Christ thus reveals not only that the divine Absolute is experienced by humankind as fatherhood but moreover that this experience makes it possible to glimpse a difference and a plurality even in the interior of God's existence, then experienced as Father, Son and Holy Spirit.[19]

The great difficulty of speaking intelligibly today to modern, postmodern and/or post-Christian ears about the God of Christian revelation results perhaps not only but mainly from the fact that, for some time, historical Christianity attached very little importance to experience and even to a *pedagogy* of the experience of God.[20] Fearing the intimacy and the subjectivism engendered by modern individualism, which could lead to alienation, to a disengagement from community and history – which, to a certain extent, has already occurred and is still occuring – Christians became excessively suspicious with regard to everything that comes from the domain of religious experience and has the appearance, however remote, of approximating so-called mystical experience. Apparently, this should be reserved for only a handful of privileged people, almost always dedicated to contemplation in a cloister, exposed to the most diverse

---

[18] Cf. the beautiful text by M. Perine, *Transcendência e mundo. Aproximação filosófica e cristã* (Belo Horizonte, mimeo., 1991), pp. 19-23.

[19] Cf. Meslin, *L'expérience humaine du divin*, pp. 404-05

[20] There are no lack of accusations on this matter, be they from within the Christian world (J. Sudbrack, *La nueva religiosidad* , esp. p. 99) or from outside (e.g, J. Needleman, *Lost Christianity* [San Francisco, 1985], pp. 102-03: "[W]hile Catholic monks and nuns are teaching all kinds of things, from botany to business, there are not so many who are teaching people how to pray." Needleman cites here William Johnston's *Christian Zen* (Dublin, 1979) and is in complete agreement with this statement. This subject is more extensively treated in my article "A sedução do sagrado."

psychological suspicions concerning their "normality" and "mental health."

The ethical attitude that the church calls love (*agape*) neither finds itself at odds with the experience of God nor denies the assertion that this God, revealed by grace, is an object only of desire and never of necessity. If on the one hand humanity, in the grace of contemplation and at the deepest level of the experience of God, can feel the proximity of the Ineffable Absolute never seen by anyone, on the other hand, humanity can perceive a depth – the home of the One who challenges by coming from the heart of reality – which is experienced as an authentic manifestation of the divine.

There is more. It is this dialectical movement – of the experience of the infinite in the finite, of the challenge that comes from the heart of the finite leading up to the ethical act, that by intervening in the finite and transforming it touches the edge of the infinite at the same time – that allows us to become aware of this Absolute which lovingly governs our life, the same One who reveals, in Jesus Christ, his name of Father. In going to the root of his human existence, poor and limited, marked by conflicts, injustices and restrictions of all kinds, we become aware of a divine origin which is always at one remove from the field of one's own experience, or better, from one's awareness, from the knowledge that one might have from this experience.[21]

Theology as Sacrament: The Vulnerability of Reason

At this moment of the crisis of modernity, of the diversification of the field of religion, which is becoming increasingly complex, theology is in turn questioned concerning its identity and the very meaning of its existence. If the identity of Christianity is at this time problematic, what about the language of theology, which claims with extreme boldness to organise discourse on God using poor, limited, and now somewhat diverted, human reason?

---

[21] Cf. Vergote, "Verticalité et horizontalité dans le langage symbolique sur Dieu," p. 545.

And yet it is perhaps more urgent than ever that theology rediscover its primordial vocation and its significance in order to be able to pronounce the word that is proper to it, witness to the covenant, conscious or not, of humanity. More concretely, theology must here and now concentrate its attention in a special way on that which is the central object of its content, the frame of its method: God himself. This is the only way that will lead theology to become what it truly is and what it is called to be, that is, theological.[22]

Thus, when it comes to true theology, reason has its citizenship, though this citizenship is or even wishes to be auxiliary, secondary, like that of a handmaiden. While daring to leap into and reflect on the mystery that graciously reveals itself to its proud reason, which modernity has set up as a definitive protagonist and which has arrived at the height of instrumentality and of claiming to explain everything, it will have no other path than that of *vulnerability*, which allows itself to be unceasingly demolished and reconstituted by the revelation of the mystery which always exceeds it.[23]

Thus, by assuming this constituent and foundational vulnerability, theology will fall in step with him who, throughout

---

[22] On the centrality of the theme of God in theology see G. Gutiérrez, *O Deus da Vida* (São Paulo, 1991).

[23] On the impossibility of reason accounting for the mystery of God cf. Meslin, *L'expérience humaine du divin*, p. 226, citing Pascal. See also Gutiérrez, *O Deus da Vida*; M. Mardones, *Postmodernidad y Cristianismo*, p. 144. See also my "Saber, sabor e sabedoria. A fé em meio ao conflito das racionalidades," in C. Caliman (ed). *Fé, política e cultura. Desafios atuais* (São Paulo, 1991), pp. 83-98. See also, more recently, my work on the God of revelation: with V. Feller, *Deus Trindade: a vida no coração do mundo* (Valladolid, 2002) and also *Alteridade e vulnerabilidade. Experiência de Deus e pluralismo religioso no moderno em crise* (São Paulo, 1993), "Abba: um pai maternal," in: G.B. Hackmann (ed.), *Deus Pai* (Porto Alegre, 1999), pp. 143-96, "A sedução do sagrado," "A alteridade e seus caminhos," in: M. Fabri dos Anjos, (ed.), *Teologia e perspectivas de futuro* (São Paulo, 1997), pp. 21-46, "A Post-Christian and Postmodern Christianism," in: *Liberation Theologies, Postmodernity, and the Americas* (London and New York, 1997), pp. 83-94.

his encounter with humanity, never preserved, never clung to his prerogatives, who laid himself bare and who could be encountered in all that is smaller, more humble, and less important according to the criteria of this world (cf. Phil 2:5-11).[24] Thus, if the experience of God is basically interrelational and one of vulnerability with regard to an Otherness which, from its absolute difference, in revealing itsel does not do so by overwhelming but by serving and saving, then the discourse on this experience will not have any other choice than the way of encounter with the same vulnerability, in letting itself be unceasingly influenced by the otherness inevitably present in the relationship that is grounded there.[25]

It is necessary, however, to pay attention to the symbolic, "sacramental" dimension that this *kenosis* of theological discourse entails today, which is perhaps different from yesterday. If, at the apogee of modernity and secularization, explicit language on God sought indirect ways of speaking, in the name of respect for plurality and religious freedom, trying the path of dialogue with modern atheism and agnosticism and opting often for mute testimony where only the gesture counted and

---

[24] Cf. what M. de Certeau says about the mystery of the revelation of God in Christianity, which operates "not without us" in "Autorités chrétiennes et structures sociales," in: M. de Certeau, *La faiblesse de croire* (Paris, 1987), p. 113.

[25] On this subject, see what is said by Vergote in "Verticalité et horizontalité dans le langage symbolique sur Dieu," p. 540 "L'etre soi-même et le devenir autre …. c 'est le paradoxe de la reaction a Dieu." On the humble and kenotic mode of God's presence in the world see also M. França Miranda, quoting F. Varillon (*L'humilité de Dieu* [Paris, 1978], p. 84, in "Salvação cristã na modernidade." *Perspectiva Teologica* 23 (1991): 19, n.9. "Il faut une longue expérience, il faut peut-etre toute une vie, pour comprendre un peu que, dans l'ordre de l'amour, comme la richesse est pauvreté, la puissance est faiblesse. L'homme s'incline toujours, quand il pense a son Dieu, a sortir de la sphere de l'amour. a imaginer des attributs qui ne seraient pas ceux de l'amour. Il a fallu des siècles pour que le Dieu des armées soit enfin adoré comme le Dieu desarmé."

where ethics was the sole common denominator driving towards dialogue, the situation appears different today.

It could be that the major and more demanding part of vulnerability at this moment consists in making proclamation explicit again, in using religious and mystical discourse when speaking about God – not out of opportunism or in order to make a place for oneself in the field of religion, which has been transformed into an immense supermarket of possibilities, where each can choose a recipe according to one's taste but rather to make, among the plurality of denominations which today invoke the thirst for transcendence and spirituality in which humanity is caught up, a Name resound that continues to love and call humankind to the permanent dialogue of love and communion.

It is this name that Jesus of Nazareth referred to as Father. And it is this name that, by taking root inside the most fundamental psychological necessities of the human being, expresses the most transcendent divine Being – the wholly Other. To name God as Father, to recognize his paternity and truly to express it, is to recognise that the foundation and origin of the human being is something outside of him and to allow all dimensions of life to organise themselves freely for relationships of true solidarity and fraternity. It is, in addition, to proclaim that divine paternity is not a projection of insecurity, frustration or a human construction, as has been endlessly repeated in so many critiques of religion, but the revelation of God as Father of the only Son, the Saviour of humankind.[26]

As long as we do not confuse this experience with the simple search for feelings or emotional compensation, which could characterise the appearance of many religious manifestations at the present time, it seems to me that theology finds itself – perhaps more than ever at this moment in history – put on the defensive by the fundamental question of God, the centre of its discourse, and by the way of talking about him to the contemp-

---

[26] On the experience of divine paternity cf. the important work by M. Meslin, "Désir du Père et paternité divine," in: Meslin, *L'expérience humaine du divin*, pp. 297-320.

orary world. It may, perhaps, be bold to claim to trace the profile of the unutterable and inexpressible God. But, if this same God lets himself be experienced in spirit and truth and even in human flesh assumed and redeemed by the incarnation of the Word, it will necessarily be possible to talk about this experience. This is what should be the primary occupation of theology now; it may be increasingly a mystical theology, not only because it is centred on the reflection on what is proper to it but also because it would increasingly take on the form not of abstracted speculation but of a witness of a sacramental visibility, of a narration of the interdependent, sympathising and loving relationships of humans with God.

The Catholic theology of the sacraments after Vatican II has returned to a closer affinity with the patristic and Eastern understanding. The fundamental sacrament is Jesus Christ, who is made present in the sacrament of the church, which in turn is realised as a sacrament in its own sacramental actions and assemblies. But sacramentality is pervasive in Christian experience and not restricted to the seven special moments. The liturgy (especially that of the Eucharist) is the peak or summit of Christian life in that everything should lead to it and everything should flow from it. That is to say, life for the Christian community should be progressively transformed in the grace of Christ, in lifestyle, in relationships, and in community structures and values by the repeated immersion of the community in the Eucharistic moment.

A distinct but related aspect of the renewed theology of the sacraments after Vatican II is the rediscovery of the link that was seen so clearly in the early church between Christian sacraments and social justice. The very ceremonies and symbols of the sacraments are seen as presenting a radical challenge to many of the existing structures of the world. Under the influence of biblical renewal and patristic scholarship, there is a continual effort in contemporary Catholic sacramental theology to correct a former bias by constant reminders that the sacraments are not simply acts of Christ but also of the community, are not only channels of grace but also acts of faith, worship and very concrete love.

It is here that there lies, from my point of view, the biggest contribution Roman Catholic church can give from her sacramental perspective to the unity of the Church: namely, the emphasis on sacraments not only as acts of Christ repeatedly celebrated but as acts of a community which is responsible for making happen truly and again in the midst of the world the same acts of Christ in different contexts, cultures and even different religious denominations. After all, the centre of the Catholic sacramental conception, as of any other ritual of symbol in Christian tradition, is love, agapic love, incarnated love that must be expressed in a sacramental praxis.

Each one of the churches has a rich contribution to give on this particular issue. The Roman Catholic Church, with its great pastoral emphasis on the celebration of sacraments as acts of Christ and the community of the followers of Christ and with the doctrine of the "real presence" contributes to the Christian churches in order to help them to celebrate rituals that not only are not empty but are the very true and concrete expressions of a love and service that should transform the world.

From the Sacramentality of the Church to the Sacramentality of the World

An Exploration of the Theology of Alexander Schmemann and Louis-Marie Chauvet

Ivana Noble

In this contribution I will explore the relationship between the church and the world in the sacramental theology of Alexander Schmemann and Louis-Marie Chauvet. My interest focusses on the question of how their notions of sacramentality influence an ongoing conversion towards participation in God and unity among Christians.

Alexander Schmemann (1921-1983)[1] was a Russian Orthodox theologian who lived most of his life abroad, first in Paris

---

[1] Alexander Schmemann was born in Estonia to a family of Russian emigrés. The family moved to France in his early childhood, where he studied, was ordained and started teaching theology at St Sergius Orthodox Seminary. There he was strongly influenced by the so-called "Eucharistic ecclesiology" of Nicholas Afanassieff. In 1951 he moved to New York, to St Vladimir's Orthodox Seminary, where he served as dean till his death. In his time St Vladimir's became the centre of a liturgical and Eucharistic revival which Schmemann saw as analogous to the Roman Catholic "return to sources" and "liturgical movement" as he had encountered them in France. Jean Daniélou and Louis Bouyer had a lasting influence on him. Schmemann took an active part in establishing the autocephalous Orthodox Church in America, whilst at the same time collaborating with "Radio Liberty," broadcasting religious programmes to Russia. Apart from theology, Schmemann was interested in contemporary Russian and French literature and philosophy, and was well acquainted with them. Among his main works are: *Introduction to Liturgical Theology* (London and Portland, 1966), *The World as Sacrament* (London, 1966), *For the Life of the World: Sacraments and Orthodoxy* (New York, 1998), *The Eucharist: Sacrament of the Kingdom of God* (Crestwood, 1987).

and then, from 1951 until his death, in New York, where for more than twenty years he was dean of St Vladimir's Orthodox Seminary.

Louis-Marie Chauvet (b. 1942)[2] is a Roman Catholic theologian, Professor of sacramental theology at the Institut Catholique in Paris. Both he and Schmemann can be viewed as revival figures for sacramental theology, criticising faulty practices and those theologies which had separated sacraments from their liturgical celebration and thus reduced sacramentality to a supernatural – other-worldly – reality. For both, the relation between the church and the world is given by God. For both, the notion of sacramentality is central to that relationship. But how? What are its sources and aims? And what priorities in Christian life does it emphasize?

In order to address these questions, I will have to start with a brief examination of the relational and symbolic knowledge of God with which they operate before moving on to their notions of sacrament and sacramentality, in order, finally, to analyse how exactly the church and the world are interwoven in their understanding of sacramentality and what implications this has for their speaking of conversion. Although I find both approaches attractive, I will also offer a critique of their ideas. How do we appropriate Schmemann's beautiful holistic vision without absolutising liturgy, restricting tradition and ending up with political or ecclesial conservatism? How do we learn from

---

[2] Louis-Marie Chauvet was born in France. He was ordained as a priest in the Diocese of Lucon and since 1973 has taught at the Institut Catholique. Among his works translated into English are: *Symbol and Sacrament: A Sacramental Reinterpretation of Christian Existence*, transl. P. Madigan and M. Beaumont (Collegeville, MN, 1995), *The Sacraments: The Word of God at the Mercy of the Body* (Collegeville, MN, 2001). In French also: *Du symbolique au symbole: essai sur les sacrements, Les sacrements*. He has coedited and contributed to the following titles: *Liturgy and the Body* (with François Kabasele Lumbala), *Le Sacrement de mariage entre hier et demain, Le Sacrement du pardon entre hier et demain* (with Paul De Clerck), *Le guide du baptisme, Pour accompagner la prière des personnes malades* (with Jean-Marie Humeau), *Illness & Healing* (with Miklos Tomka).

Chauvet's emphasis on the corporality of faith without absolutising the institution of church and eliminating the space for individual dissent in limit situations? In the conclusion I will ask what both approaches contribute, where they may benefit from each other, and where they need to seek help from elsewhere, in order to foster conversion towards God and thus also towards deeper ecclesial and creaturely unity that is not destructive of the individual.

Schmemann's Holistic Vision

Schmemann's sacramental theology grows from a synthesis of the Greek Fathers. It affirms that God is completely different from all our images of him, that we creatures are incapable of grasping God in his essence, but that at the same time it is truly possible to communicate with God and to participate in the communion of the Holy Trinity.[3] To understand this, we have to examine Schmemann's notion of theological knowledge, which holds together not only this "existential synthesis" of the apophatic and the cataphatic ways but also knowledge of God and *theosis*,[4] knowledge of God and the celebration of our participation in God. Liturgy is, for him, a vital source of theology. He shows that in liturgy we experience the unity of God's plan for creation, which is prior to and overcomes the fall, the power of sin and death. Celebrating liturgy, the church is led to become a sign of conversion for the world, an image of the world's destiny. Schmemann's holistic vision holds together the world, the church and the kingdom. We can, however, ask in what sense this vision is "sacramental" and what implications it has for the unity of the church?

---

[3] Schmemann's theology is influenced not only by the insights of Maximos the Confessor but also by the Cappadocians. Thus, in places it resembles Gregory of Nyssa's controversy with radical Arianism. See Gregory of Nyssa, *Contra Eunomium libri I et II*, ed. W. Jager, GNO II (Leiden, 1960) and I. Noble, "The Apophatic Way in Gregory of Nyssa," in: P. Pokorný and J. Roskovec, (eds), *Philosophical Hermeneutics and Biblical Exegesis* (Tübingen, 2002), pp. 323-39.

[4] See Schmemann, *For the Life of the World*, p. 140.

The Roots and Nature of Theological Knowledge

Although Schmemann lived most of his life in the West,[5] what he means by "knowledge" is something different from post-Enlightenment Western philosophy or theology. He emphasizes that our knowledge of God starts with the intuition of the divine mystery. This first intuitive knowledge, then, can be expressed only by means of symbols. They allow the revelation of the divine other precisely *as* the "other;" they can speak of "the visibility of the invisible *as* invisible, the knowledge of the unknowable *as* unknowable, the presence of the future *as* future."[6] In other words, it belongs to their nature not to allow for reduction, not to try to substitute relational knowledge for explanation, for something smaller, more similar to us creatures and to our creaturely way of thinking. Schmemann stands in line here with other Orthodox theologians, such as Lossky, Meyndorff or Zizoulas,[7] in his opposition to the reduction of knowledge to its discursive part and its isolation from mystery. He states that

> theology is not only related to the *"mysterion"* but has in it its source, the condition of its very possibility. Theology as proper words and knowledge *about* God is the result of the knowledge *of* God – and in Him of all reality.[8]

Thus, according to Schmemann, theological knowledge grows in relationship with God but also includes knowledge of the world and of ourselves. It is not clear here, however, whether the relationship to God is sufficient for the knowledge of the "whole of reality" or whether it leads us to recognize the need of knowing the world in relation to the sum of accessible

---

[5] See J. Meyndorff, "A Life Worth Living," in: T. Fisch (ed.), *Liturgy and Tradition: Theological Reflections of Alexander Schmemann* (Crestwood, 1992), pp. 143-54.

[6] Schmemann, *For the Life of the World*, p. 141.

[7] See, e.g., V. Lossky, *The Mystical Theology of the Eastern Church* (London, 1957); J. Meyndorff, *Byzantine Theology: Historical Trends and Doctrinal Themes* (New York, 1979); J.D. Zizoulas, *Being as Communion: Studies in Personhood and the Church* (Crestwood, 1997).

[8] Schmemann, *For the Life of the World*, p. 141.

human knowledge as well and to know ourselves in relation to all the dimensions of our being. Schmemann is vulnerable to the criticism that his views allow claims that holy people are, by reason of their relationship with God, experts in politics, medicine or psychology.

His holistic vision is rooted in liturgy. The symbols which make theological knowledge possible are taken from there. In the context of the liturgical celebration they reveal the levels of the mystery of God, which in our first intuition remained hidden. The one who does not participate in liturgy cannot do theology, because only in liturgy does the mystery become *epiphany*.[9] In liturgy all our existence is included into the "all embracing vision of life."[10] Liturgy does not create a new reality – it celebrates what theology has known as reality. Conversion and the mission of the church in the world, then, grow from the mutual relationship between knowing and celebrating.[11] Schmemann complains that the second aspect has been largely lost among contemporary Christians and this has contributed to the one-sidedness of theological knowledge:

> Feast means *joy*. Yet, if there is something that we – the serious adult and frustrated Christians of the twentieth century – look at with suspicion, it is certainly joy. How can one be joyful when so many people suffer? When so many things need to be done? How can one indulge in festivals and celebrations when people expect from us "serious" answers to their problems?

---

[9] Schmemann stresses that believers need to learn to understand this revelation in which they participate. See A. Schmemann, *Liturgy and Life: Christian Development through Liturgical Experience* (New York, 1993), pp. 13-14; and Schmemann, *The Eucharist*, p. 34.

[10] See A. Schmemann, "Liturgy and Theology," in: T. Fisch (ed.). *Liturgy and Tradition*, pp. 51-52.

[11] Schmemann interprets the relation between theology and liturgy on the base of the Latin connection between *lex orandi* and *lex credendi*. See Schmemann, *Liturgy and Life*, p. 22; see also B.T. Morrill, *Anamnesis as Dangerous Memory: Political and Liturgical Theology in Dialogue* (Collegeville, 2000), pp. 83, 90.

Consciously or subconsciously Christians have accepted the whole ethos of our joyless and business-minded culture.[12]

The joy which one experiences in liturgy is not a satisfaction with the world as it is, ignoring pain and suffering. It is a joy from experiencing that God has come to this world and that God fulfills his promises. This joy is eschatological. Its loss also takes away the eschatological hope which Christians are to bring to the world. The one-sidedness caused by alienation from the dynamics between knowledge and celebration impacts on the move from an experience of God's presence in the world to being confronted with God's absence.

Created and Instituted Sacramentality

Schmemann's holistic vision of theological knowledge is sacramental: it is included with the symbolic unity between the world and Christ that we celebrate in the sacraments and that reveals God's plans for creation. It rests on a strong understanding of the symbol and the symbolic. Losing the depth of the understanding of symbol leads, according to Schmemann, to a fragmentation of reality and the secularisation of theology. He emphasises that symbolic reality does not start with our categorising; it is not an extra layer added by our understanding to "what is here." Instead, Schmemann states:

> And the world is symbolical – "*signum rei sacrae*" – in virtue of its being created by God; to be "symbolical" belongs thus to its ontology, the symbol being not only the way to perceive and understand reality, a means of cognition but also a means of *participation*. It is then the "natural" symbolism of the world – one can almost say its "sacramentality" – that makes the sacrament *possible* and constitutes the key to its understanding and apprehension. If the Christian sacrament is *unique*, it is not in the sense of being a miraculous exception to the natural order of things created by God and "proclaiming His glory." Its absolute newness is not in its ontology as sacrament but in the specific "*res*" which it "symbolizes," i.e., reveals, manifests and communicates – which is Christ and His Kingdom. But even

---

[12] Schmemann, *For the Life of the World*, p. 53.

this absolute newness is to be understood in terms not of total discontinuity but in those of fulfilment. The *"mysterion"* of Christ reveals and fulfills the ultimate meaning and destiny of the world itself.[13]

The world is the first symbol and Schmemann would go as far as to say that we could speak of it even in terms of the first sacrament,[14] because it makes all other sacraments possible. God makes use of the elements of the world to reveal his mystery – and thus also to reveal that it is possible to encounter God in the world. Schmemann speaks of the continuity between the world and Christ, which is given by the world being created through *Logos* and by the eschatological fulfilment, when all things will be gathered in Christ (see John 1:1-5 and Eph. 1:10). It is the continuity of God's will for creation, which is the participation in the divine life. This continuity is, however, marked by the discontinuity caused by sin. Although Schmemann does not use the fall as an interpretative key for understanding the world,[15] he does not minimize its presence. In the continuity between the world and Christ given by creation we also recognise the discontinuity given by sin:

> "This world", by rejecting and condemning Christ, has condemned itself; No one, therefore, can enter the Kingdom without in a real sense dying to the world, i.e. rejecting it in its self-sufficiency, without putting all faith, hope and love in the "age to come", in the "day without evening" which will dawn at the end of time.[16]

---

[13] Schmemann, *For the Life of the World*, pp. 139-40.

[14] This is a recurring theme in Schmemann. One of his works is even called *The World as Sacrament* (cf. n. 1 above).

[15] Schmemann says that Christianity unites three fundamental truths: (i) the world is good; (ii) the world is fallen; (iii) the world is redeemed. See A. Schmemann, "Between Utopia and Escape" (lecture from 1981), http://www.schmemann.org/byhim/betweenUtopiaandescape. html, p. 7.

[16] A. Schmemann, "Ecclesiological Notes," *St. Vladimir's Theological Quarterly* 1 (1967): note 2.

We live in tension between participation in divine life and alienation from God. This tension is so strong that it destroys any possibility of continuing in a "natural life" without conversion, of being satisfied with the world as it is without striving for and eagerly expecting the kingdom of God. Can we also say that to live in our churches as they are, without desiring unity with God and with one another, without allowing the kingdom to break through into them too, is also to opt for self-sufficiency and alienation? I will return to this question in my conclusion.

Schmemann articulates the relation between the world, the church and the kingdom in the following way. The church is rooted in the world. It bears all the positives and the negatives of this rootedness. Its history is bound up with the history of the world. Schmemann recognizes that Orthodox theology traditionally places the beginning of the church in paradise and interprets its life as a manifestation of the Kingdom of God.[17] He holds together the cosmic and eschatological dimensions of the church, into which the tension between participation in divine life and alienation also enters. Like the world, the church is a symbolic, sacramental place, it is a passage to the new creation. "The church, as visible society and organisation, belongs to this world," says Schmemann. She is vulnerable and struggles with the same problems as the rest of the world, yet "she is 'instituted' to ... stand for the world," and to

> assume ... all the natural forms of human existence in the world ... in order to reveal and manifest the true meaning of creation as fulfilment in Christ, to announce to the world its end and the inauguration of the Kingdom.[18]

The world is created as sacramental, the church is instituted as sacramental. Schmemann distinguishes here the natural sacramentality of the world, given by creation, from the instituted

---

[17] See, e.g., P. Evdokimov, "La culture et l'eschatologie," *Semeur* 50 (1947): 363 and *L'Art de l'icôn. Théologie de la beauté* (Paris, 1970), p. 54; P.C. Phan, *Culture and Eschatology: The Iconographical Vision of Paul Evdokimov* (Bern, 1985), p. 59; compare Schmemann, *The World As Sacrament*, note 2.

[18] Schmemann, "Ecclesiological Notes," note 3.

sacramentality of the church. He speaks of the church as the "sacrament of the Kingdom" by means of which she "always becomes what she is, always fulfills herself as the One, Holy, Catholic and Apostolic Church, as the Body of Christ and the Temple of the Holy Spirit, as the new life of the new creation." Schmemann adds:

> The basic act of this fulfilment, and therefore the true "form" of the Church, is the Eucharist: the sacrament in which the Church performs the passage, the *passover*, from this world into the Kingdom, offers in Christ the whole creation to God, seeing it as "heaven and earth full of His glory", and partakes of Christ's immortal life at His table in His Kingdom.[19]

This addition is perhaps most striking when we take it into the situation of a divided church which is incapable of sharing the Eucharist. How, then, can she become what she is: one, holy and apostolic? Schmemann uses a beautiful cosmic symbolism, which includes every stone of the earth in this celebration, but gives only a partial answer to why it is in practice satisfactory for some to bring other Christians into the Eucharistic celebration more or less like the stones but not as fellow participants.[20] Schmemann conditions the sacramentality of the church – and also the overcoming of her divisions – on the preservation of the full and unaltered faith and traditions "once delivered unto

---

[19] Schmemann, "Ecclesiological Notes," note 3.

[20] And yet, in *For the Life of the World*, Schmemann writes: "The symbol of the world is fulfilled in Christ," people partake in it through conversion and faith, they share it, they "eat it" and are healed, are fed and live for ever in heavenly joy (p. 149). And in *The World as Sacrament* he adds: "Man must eat in order to live; He must take the world into his body and transform it into himself, into flesh and blood. He is indeed that which he eats, and the whole world is presented as one all-embracing banquet table for man. And this image of the banquet remains, throughout the whole Bible, the central image of life. It is the image of life at its creation and also the image of life at its end and fulfilment ... 'that you eat and drink at my table in my Kingdom'" (p. 10).

the saints."[21] In 1963, when he wrote his "Ecclesiological Notes," he was convinced that the Orthodox Church managed this best of all Christian churches. This position was step by step complemented by a critique of, especially, the Russian Orthodox Church.[22] His last work, *The Eucharist,* finished a month before his death in 1983, in which he returned to the theme of the Orthodox Church and the Orthodox crisis, affirms that a way forward has to be sought in dialogue with others, because we have many problems in common. Yet even here, in spite of all his criticism, Schmemann repeats that the Orthodox Church has carried the tradition more faithfully and continuously than any other church.[23] John Meyndorff points out that, however much Schmemann's work may be relevant to the ecumenical discussion, he himself moved, after a brief period of cooperation, out of the ecumenical movement and participated in more conservative Christian circles.[24]

Schmemann's desire to hold on to the "unaltered" tradition is admirable but also vulnerable. It lacks a good hermeneutics of tradition, which would help him to work better with the dynamic and pluralistic nature of the tradition.[25] Thus he becomes preoccupied with guarding the past, so that his ability to glimpse a new horizon or new possibilities for dealing with

---

[21] Schmemann, "Ecclesiological Notes," note 8.

[22] See e.g. Schmemann, *For the Life of the World* (written in 1973), where he sharply criticises the Russian Orthodox Church for alienating itself from its own tradition, for embracing Western scholastic forms of thought and separating theology from spirituality and liturgy. He points out that official Orthodox theological manuals from the sixteenth century are as far from the tradition of the Fathers as the Western ones are and that in Russia up to the 1840s theology was even taught in Latin (pp. 135-36).

[23] See Morrill, *Anamnesis as Dangerous Memory,* p. 76.

[24] See Meyndorff, "A Life Worth Living," p. 10.

[25] For Schmemann the concept of tradition is reserved primarily for the Church Fathers of the second and third centuries. These are contemporary in every period, he says, and are not to be adapted. We, however, are to adapt ourselves in order to be able to enter into their experience. See Schmemann, *For the Life of the World,* p. 146.

new problems in new ways is minimised, if not absent. This is true not only in the area of liturgy, where Schmemann criticises all attempts to make it more accessible to the people of today,[26] but also in the social and political expressions of Christian faith. This is perhaps most visible in Schmemann's relation to liberation theology, which he, even in his last work, criticises for building not on faith but on "ideology and utopian escapism," for replacing a "Christian vision of the world" with issues related to economics, politics and psychology.[27] Yet this position seems to be in contrast with Schmemann's sacramental understanding of the world, with the possibilities it opens for bonds between service to God and service to God's creatures. It seems that Schmemann's dynamic cosmological-eschatological view of sacramentality needs to be complemented by an equally dynamic notion of tradition.

Yet Schmemann's critique of Western "adaptation" of the tradition and its negative fruits should not be overlooked, because, in spite of the weaknesses of his own position, he uncovers with precision why our theology first "secularised" the world and then realised the absence of God.

Real and Unreal Presence

The first target of Schmemann's critique is the Western teaching on the "real presence" of Christ in the sacrament. Although it attempts to emphasise important truths, namely that God can truly be encountered, that God does give himself to us, it also rests on doubt in as far as it holds that God can be encountered, that God does give himself to us but only somewhere and only under certain conditions. This teaching also implies some kind of presence which is *"not* real." Reality is ontologically divided into the higher and the lower.[28] This problem started when sacraments were divorced from the context of liturgical celebration. The medieval treatise *De sacramentis* started to define the sacrament based on its *essence* and thus distinguished it from

---

[26] See e.g. Schmemann, *For the Life of the World*, p. 147.

[27] See Schmemann, *The Eucharist*, pp. 9-10.

[28] See Schmemann, *For the Life of the World*, pp. 138-39.

the "non-sacrament." The *signum* belonging to its essence, then, received an ontologically different status.[29]

Schmemann sees this as a betrayal of the older tradition and its symbolic understanding of all reality as one, because all reality was created and participated in the divine mystery.[30] This, then, has fatal consequences, for symbol is dispensable and symbolic reality is seen as opposed to the "real" reality, at most as a creation of human mind, if not as an obstacle to the "real".[31]

Schmemann lists three reasons why the usage of symbol was weakened in the West: (i) symbol was identified with the means of knowledge; (ii) knowledge was reduced to discursive knowledge; (iii) the "symbolical" mediation of sacramental reality was substituted by a "realistic" mediation. To this last point Schmemann says that, as the sacrament was defined as *verum*, i.e. real, a difference arose between the "reality" of the sacrament and "symbol," which was seen as unable to express the reality of the sacrament adequately. The Lateran Council of 1059 condemned the teaching of Berenger of Tours because he held that the body and blood of Christ in the Eucharist are not real but symbolic. This condemnation resulted, according to Schmemann, in the Council Fathers, instead of criticizing Berenger for not having a good theology of symbol, stating that the presence of Christ in the Eucharist is real because it is not symbolic. They therefore perverted the more original notion that held that the presence is real precisely because it is symbolic.[32]

---

[29] Cf. Thomas Aquinas, *Summa Theologica* IIIA, questions 60-65.

[30] See Schmemann, *For the Life of the World*, pp. 138-39.

[31] Cf. Tillich's effort to renew symbolic understanding in theology, e.g. P. Tillich, *Dynamics of Faith* (New York, 1958), p. 41, which, in spite of its return to a participation theory, still operates with the mediation between the symbolic and the real. This is overcome by Ricoeur, for whom all language is symbolica and who recognizes a semantic as well as non-semantic quality in the symbol. See P. Ricoeur, *Interpretation Theory: Discourse and the Surplus of Meaning* (Fort Worth, 1976), pp. 45-46.

[32] See Schmemann, *For the Life of the World*, p. 143; cf. Denzinger-Schönmetzer, *Enchiridion Symbolorum, definitionum et declarationum de rebus fiei et morum* (1965), 690.

The weakening or redefining of symbol[33] gave way to a different type of theological knowledge, which, according to Schmemann: (i) abandoned participation and headed towards atomisation; (ii) emphasized the fall and the discontinuity between Christ and creation; (iii) accepted the fundamental opposition of matter and spirit, profane and sacred, natural and supernatural, all of which led to a gradual secularisation of theology.[34]

---

[33] Luther similarly opposes the real to the symbolic (spiritual). Against Zwingli, he opts for the real presence of Christ in the sacrament and ascribes the reality of it to the words of the scriptures. However, in doing so he does not weaken the links of the sacraments to the rest of creation. See M. Luther, *Sermon von dem Sakrament des Leibes und Blutes Christi wider die Schwarmgeifter* (1526), in *Dr. Martin Luthers Werke*, vol. 19 (Weimar, 1897), pp. 474-523; J.F. White, *The Sacraments in Protestant Practice and Faith* (Nashville, 1999), pp. 76-80; P. Filipi, *Hostina chudých: Kapitoly o Večeři Páni.* [Feast of the Poor: Essays on the Lord's Supper] (Prague, 1991), pp. 70-71, 78-82. Calvin opts for the symbolic presence, but his view of symbol, influenced by Zwingli, is spiritualised. In his *Institutes of Christian Religion* he defines sacrament as "externum esse symbolum, quo benevolentiae erga nos suae promissiones conscientiis nostris Dominus oimbecillitatem," (cf. J. Calvin, *Institutiae Christianae Religionis* (1559), *Corpus reformatorum*, XXX (Brunsvigae, 1864), IV.xiv.1. Symbol here is a pedagogical concept, something external, that does not have a real being, unless it is given from outside: by the Holy Spirit at the celebration of the Lord's Supper and by the faith and state of grace of the believer. For the nonbeliever and those who are evil the symbol does not become anything real. See J. Calvin, *Petit traticé de la saincte cene de nostre Seigneur Iesus Christ, Corpus reformatorum*, XXXIII (Brunsvigae, 1886), pp. 426-59; *Catechismus sive christianae religionis institutio communibus renatae in evangelio geneviensis ecclesiae suffragiis recepta* (1538), *Corpus reformatorum*, XXXIII, pp. 312-62, esp. "De sacramentis" (p. 358), "De baptismo" (p. 359) a "De sancta coena" (p. 359); see also White, *The Sacraments in Protestant Practice and Faith*, pp. 78-80.

[34] In *The World as Sacrament*, p. 14, Schmemann says that Feuerbach's reduction of religion to anthropology, which inspired Marx, grows from "the same fundamental opposition of the spiritual to the material ... for centuries the only accepted, the only understandable moulds and categories of religious thought and experience. And Feuerbach, for all his nihilism, was in fact a natural heir to Christian

Western scholasticism, which prevailed in theology for centuries, brought a new focus, an analysis of causal relations and a conviction that what is real can be also conceptually grasped and legally controlled.[35] Schmemann laments the fact that in the history of theology this shift was often praised as progress towards scientific theology and the growth of a more precise theological method.[36]

Causality,[37] combined with the previously mentioned three features of the new type of theological knowledge, gave rise to a new absolute starting point and a new system derived from it.[38] The concept of "supernatural being," which became a dominant feature of this system, weakened the ontological status of everything else. This led to division and the alienation of being, to the loss of life-giving links between the church, the world and the kingdom, to the loss of a holistic vision and to the sub-

---

'idealism' and 'spiritualism'." Cf. L. Feuerbach, *Podstata křest'anství* (Prague, 1954), pp. 73, 83.

[35] See Schmemann, "Ecclesiological Notes," esp. note 1.

[36] Schmemann, *For the Life of the World*, p. 137.

[37] Schmemann does not completely deny the role of causality in theological argumentation, but he does weaken it. According to him, causality, the link between a cause and effect, is inseparable in theology from the symbolism in which this link is rooted. Theological talk of revelation, of transfiguration, of a new creation in Christ, can, then, work with several layers of these statements at the same time. "New creation" is not a creation of something "new," but it reveals "continuity" between creation and Christ, continuity granted by the *Logos*, by the life and light that Christ is. What is new is symbolised, i.e. revealed, in the mystery of Christ and his kingdom, which "reveals and fulfills the ultimate meaning and destiny of the world itself." Moreover, the causality employed by theology is subjected to the task of communicating the divine mystery and the divine closeness at the same time and thus it should not be reduced to the identity thinking so typical of Western theology. See Schmemann, *For the Life of the World*, pp. 139-40, 143-44

[38] Until Vatican II it could be observed that the words of institution were seen as the absolutely new starting point. See Schmemann, *For the Life of the World*, p. 144.

sequent atomisation and secularisation of theology.[39] Schmemann remarks that when patristic theology held all the levels of Christian existence together, they shed light on one another, and kept the inner unity of theology.[40]

Thus Schmemann's critique comes back to its initial point, that we will be unable to grasp what the sacramentality of the church means if we fail to renew its roots in the sacramentality of the world, and its fulfilment in the Kingdom of God. This renewal can have fascinating implications for an understanding of Christian unity as well as for responses to problematic ethical issues, such as taking action in situations of political or economic injustice or even in issues like the sacramental status of gay relationships. I will try to sketch these possibilities in the conclusion, while recognising that Schmemann would have very little sympathy with them. Schmemann proposes that for this renewal we need to return to the frame of mind of the Church Fathers of the second and third centuries. There seems here to be an implicit belief that the non-Orthodox would find that more difficult. When we examine Louis-Marie Chauvet's position, we will see an alternative (Western) approach to this renewal, trying to see the possibilities coming from within the tradition of scholastic theology and combining them with insights from twentieth-century philosophy.

Sacramentality in Chauvet

The Roman Catholic theologian Louis-Marie Chauvet examines sacramentality in its celebratory, liturgical and ecclesial contexts.[41] There is no primordial sacramentality given to the world by creation – which then would be fulfilled by Christ, the

---

[39] See Schmemann, *For the Life of the World*, p. 115.

[40] Schmemann, For the Life of the World, p. 144: "It was the source of theology – knowledge *about* God in His relation to the world, the Church, and the Kingdom – because it was knowledge *of* God and, in Him, of all reality."

[41] See also I. Dolejšová (Noble), "The Symbolic Nature of Christian Existence according to Ricoeur and Chauvet," *Communio Viatorum* 1 (2001): 39-59.

church and her sacraments of the kingdom. Chauvet starts from the opposite end. Sacraments represent the language of the church expressing what she believes and celebrates. As in Schmemann, for Chauvet liturgy is "a theological locus of first importance," because it "shows us, not by mode of reasoning but by mode of symbolic action" how Christian existence is born and rooted, namely, "that no one becomes a Christian except by being taken into the common 'womb' of the church" and that it is not "a question of Christians uniting to form the church, but of the church forming Christians."[42] In his understanding sacraments are, more explicitly than in Schmemann, linked to the Scriptures and to ethics[43] and examined in terms of the structures of our being and understanding.[44] On this basis Chauvet draws the sacramental dimension of our communication with God and with one another.

Chauvet finds inspiration in a Heideggerian critique of metaphysics, and his rehabilitation of the symbol starts with criticisms of causality, a concept preferred by the scholastics for explaining the relationship between God and the world, which strengthened the idea of knowledge at the expense of excluding symbolic "non-knowledge."[45] Schmemann's critique of the weakened status of everything other than supranatural reality

---

[42] Chauvet, *The Sacraments*, pp. 33-34.

[43] See Chauvet, *The Sacraments*, pp. 29-31.

[44] Chauvet, *The Sacraments*, p. 31: "If we widen the perspective, we see that the relation between Scriptures, Sacrament, and Ethics is superimposed on a probably fundamental anthropological structure which we have named 'knowledge,' 'gratitude,' and 'action.' For the human subject cannot live as subject without at once thinking the world ... singing the world ... and acting in the world." "Thinking the world" consists of "the logic of theoretical reason at work especially in philosophy and science," "singing the world" is, then, "the aesthetic value of poetry, music, the feast, whether religious or not" and, finally, "acting in the world" is seen in terms of "ethics ... constituting the essential human mode of action," which is given in contrast with "technique," seen, in spite of its indispensability, as an inadequate candidate for this constitutive role. See Chauvet, *The Sacraments*, p. 31.

[45] See Chauvet, *Symbol and Sacrament*, p. 7.

finds a partial analogy in Chauvet's understanding of symbol and sacrament. Yet Chauvet pays attention to different things. Instead of opposing the "second rate" reality attributed to the world, as Schmemann does, Chauvet examines the dialectics between the real presence and real absence in the sacrament. He brings a critique of instrumental and subjectivist sacramentality, which, according to him, deform the relationship between God and the world. He attempts to overcome Western Catholic/Protestant polarities: faith/belonging; grace/acting; Scripture/sacrament; Christ/church.[46] We may, however, ask what exactly his alternative to Schmemann's holistic vision is and what potential it has for conversion towards church unity.

Critique of Instrumental and Subjectivist Sacramentality

Chauvet's position is a response to what he sees as two defective models of sacramentality. The first one can be called instrumental, viewing sacraments as "instruments" of sanctification for believers, or "objectivist," stressing the *ex opere operato* dimension. The second model is a reaction to the first one – subjectivity replaces objectivity. Chauvet sees the first as more Catholic and the second as more Protestant, but he is aware that followers of both are found across church boundaries.[47] He demonstrates that both models end up in individualism and instrumentalism, even if of a different kind. Michael Kirwan sums it up as follows: if we start with an "instrument" or a "channel" of grace, "the celebrating community ... fades into the background" and we end up with as much individualism as if we embraced the second model; if we start from the "subjective"

---

[46] Prokop Brož offered a different way of grouping the polarities at the discussion on theology and church at the meeting of the Protestant and the Catholic Theological Faculties in Prague on April 30, 2004. He spoke of: "sola fide – intellectus; sola gratia – natura; sola scriptura – traditio; sola Christus – ecclesia." I have altered the scheme according to Chauvet's areas of interest.

[47] See Chauvet, *Symbol and Sacrament*, pp. 410-13, 416-24. As a prime example of objectivist sacramentality Chauvet uses the *Catechism for Use in the Dioceses of France* (1947) and, as an example of subjectivist sacramentality, he cites Karl Barth.

human response which confuses "authenticity with human sincerity and runs the risk of elitism, rigorism, or anti-institutional hostility towards the Church" – we end up with as much instrumentalism as if we began with the first model.[48] In both cases sacraments are isolated from their celebratory, liturgical, and ecclesial contexts.

Vatican II represents, for Chauvet, a change towards recognising these dimensions. Its return to the biblical and patristic sources helped to recover the centrality of the paschal mystery. It stressed Christ as the source-sacrament of God's encounter with humanity. It rediscovered the vital role of the Spirit and the anamnetic-epicletic character of the sacraments and theologically rehabilitated the local celebrating church, the community of believers, as the foundation of all seven sacraments.[49] Thus, it corrected the objectivist model, which had pushed

> vertical theocentrism to its limits, deprived the rite of its properly human significance and opened the way for an anthropological recapture of the rite closed to its theological understanding.[50]

The correction offered by the Vatican II, however, left opposing interpretations "unreconciled" and thus the scholastic and Tridentine current viewing sacraments as "means" and the newer current treating sacraments as "expressive signs" continue to be opposed to each other.[51] Alongside this, the anthropological reaction to the "vertical theocentrism" remained more vulnerable to the second defective model, the subjectivist, not because it left the church out of the picture but either because it wanted to "reintroduce the lived human experience into the sacraments" and did not have appropriate tools for doing so or because it dismissed the *efficacy* of sacraments as "magic" and

---

[48] See M. Kirwan, "The Word of God and the Idea of Sacrament: A Catholic Theological Perspective," ms., pp. 4-5.

[49] See e.g. *Gaudium et Spes* 22; *Lumen Gentium* 5, 16.

[50] A. Vergote, *Interprétation du language religieux* (Paris, 1974), p. 201, cited in Chauvet, *Symbol and Sacrament*, p. 412.

[51] See Chauvet, *Symbol and Sacrament*, pp. 415-16.

reduced communication with God to ethics. As a way forward, Chauvet proposes a symbolic mediation, which would be able to conceive of sacraments as "revealers" and "operators" simultaneously.[52] To do this, he needs to clear the ground first by means of a more general critique of metaphysics, which then will open up a space for his symbolic theology.

Chauvet is dissatisfied with Western metaphysics, in its various forms, because it has an underlying desire to explain being in its totality. Chauvet identifies this as onto-theology, and sees it as the biggest obstacle to the recovery of the symbolic understanding, which can by definition never be fully grasped by concepts.[53] Symbolic understanding presupposes what Heidegger calls revelation of being, which we have to understand precisely as revelation and not as something which we can own as "stock in trade."[54] Being is not an entity, a "being-ness." Rather, it is a non-thing; it "never ceases to hide within a difference which constitutes it."[55] Chauvet repeats, with Hei-

---

[52] See Chauvet, *Symbol and Sacrament*, pp. 416, 418-20.

[53] He is aware that the metaphysical tradition of the West cannot be reduced to one approach. So he speaks about a variety of diverse forms of the philosophical tradition inherited from the Greeks, which is called "metaphysics". At most, we can speak of a "family resemblance" of the unconscious logic underlying these approaches, namely that they aim at explaining the totality of being, which Chauvet identifies as onto-theology. He accepts that the best of these approaches were aware of their own conceptual limits, and did not think that we can describe being "as it is." Chauvet shows examples of this awareness of the limits, referring to Plotinus's notion of *oion* ("such as"), the *quasi* ("such as") of the Latin thinkers, or Thomas's *esse* ("being"), which also plays a critical role. See Chauvet, *Symbol and Sacrament*, p. 8.

[54] Chauvet recalls Marin Heidegger's critique of metaphysics as the "ongoing confusion between the entity and Being." See M. Heidegger, *Le retour au fondement de la métaphysique*, Q.1, 29 in Chauvet, *Symbol and Sacrament*, p. 47. See also Heidegger, *Le retour*, Q.1, 24 -25.

[55] See M. Heidegger, *Contribution to the Question about Being* (1955), in Chauvet, *Symbol and Sacrament*, p. 49.

degger, that we are thrown into Being.⁵⁶ From Emmanuel Levinas Chauvet takes the critique of the obsession with "identity" and a turn in attention, where the Other becomes constitutive for the subject and gives it its lost identity.⁵⁷

This critique of metaphysics provides Chauvet with new tools for sacramental theology. His initial points are remarkably similar to those of Schmemann, even if they are inspired by different sources. Sacramental theology, according to Chauvet, runs two risks, one of becoming narrow legalism, the other of being abstract speculation. Like every branch of theology, it must negotiate constantly between conceptual knowledge (without which it would no longer be theology but constructed discourse, i.e. "science" as the scholastics call it) and symbolic non-knowledge (without which it would no longer be respectful of the mystery of God). It must not forget to derive the concept from its living source: the symbols deployed by liturgical action.⁵⁸

Chauvet asks why the symbolic aspect, which is so necessary for sacramental theology, has been so often ignored:

The initial question of the present study may be formulated as follows: *How did it come about that, when attempting to comprehend*

---

⁵⁶ For Heidegger, to overcome metaphysics is finally to make metaphysics possible. Chauvet prefers to move into speaking about symbolic theology.

⁵⁷ Chauvet sees a doublesidedness in Levinas's approach, even if he partially accepts its emphasis on alterity, as summarised by Derrida: "None have struggled more vigorously than E. Levinas to liberate themselves from the Greek *logos* and to challenge the Greek tradition from the view point of the Jewish; that is to challenge Being (impersonal, anonymous, violent reducer of otherness to the totality of the same) with the Other (pure eruption and rupture bursting through the 'Face,' the unifying pretensions and the ultimately totalitarian essence of the Greek *logos*)." J. Derrida, "Violence et métaphysique," in: J. Derrida, *L'écriture et la différence* (Paris, 1967), p. 196; cited in Chauvet, *Symbol and Sacrament*, p. 46.

⁵⁸ L.-M.Chauvet, "The Liturgy in its Symbolic Space," in: L.-M. Chauvet and F.K. Lumbala (eds), *Liturgy and the Body*, Concilium (London/Maryknoll, 1995), pp. 36-37.

theologically the sacramental relation with God expressed most fully under the term "grace," the Scholastics (and here we will consider only Thomas Aquinas) singled out for privileged consideration the category of "cause"?[59]

In other words, why was their approach dominated by conceptual knowledge, the need to explain how God is related to his creation and, *vice versa*, at the expense of symbolic non-knowledge? Chauvet takes insights from the philosophy of language as well as from Freud's and Lacan's psychoanalysis and relates them to the symbolic communication of grace, which aims at restoring faith and its basic attitudes of gratitude and generosity, which lie at the heart of sacramental theology.[60] In the symbolic order to which Chauvet holds grace is an irreducible gift, out-

---

[59] Chauvet, *Symbol and Sacrament*, p. 7 (emphasis his). In his later book Chauvet also responds to this question (*The Sacraments*, p. 95): "... the sacramental mystery is simultaneously a revealer and an agent of Christian identity .... Furthemore, the symbol, like grace, is outside the value system. For these two reasons, the symbolic route seems to us to supply an approach much more akin to the sacraments than that of instrumentality employed by the Scholastics of the twelfth century, and still dominant in our day. This appears so plainly evident to us that one has to wonder how it is possible that the theologians in the past did not explore this avenue. The answer is clear enough: if they did not do it, it was certainly not for lack of philosophical and theological acumen. When one remembers the awesome intellectual work accomplished in the twelfth and thirteen centuries, in logic as well as in grammar, in physics as well as in metaphysics, there is only one possible answer: because they were part of a cultural age other than ours, the thinkers of those centuries could not ask certain questions that we ask today."

[60] Chauvet, *Symbol and Sacrament*, pp. 139-40: "[T]he communication of grace is to be understood, not according to the 'metaphysical' scheme of cause and effect, but according to the symbolic scheme of communication through language, communication supremely effective because it is through language that the subject comes forth in its relations to other subjects within a common "world" of meaning. It is precisely *a new relation of places between subjects*, a relationship of filial and brotherly and sisterly alliance, that the sacramental "expression" aims at instituting or restoring in faith."

side of our value system. Grace comes first, it is "always preceding and necessitated by nothing," it is not justified, it is not reducible to any "value," whether conceptual, physical or moral. A way to grace is also a way towards Heideggerian Being, which is spoken of in terms of a fundamental openness,

> an attitude of listening and welcome toward something *ungraspable* by which we are already grasped ... a gracious attitude of *"letting be"* and *"allowing oneself to be spoken"* which requires to renounce all ambition for mastery.[61]

Chauvet is aware that the metaphysical conceptualisation of grace is one of the forms of controlling it. The communication of grace – needed for restoring faith – has to restore symbolic language, which allows the subject to be open to others or, even more strongly, helps the subject to realise that it has its being in relation to others, that these relations are constitutive of it.[62]

Corporeality of Faith

Chauvet agrees with Schmemann that symbol is the key to sacrament, yet his understanding of symbol differs. For Schmemann the world is symbolic – and therefore sacramental – because it is created by God and thus to be symbolic belongs to its ontology.[63] Chauvet speaks about the *"arch-sacramentality* of the faith," which is symbolic – and therefore sacramental – in its constitution and which is corporeal and as such enables a subject to participate in it.[64] As was said earlier, it is not the faith of an individual Christian which comes first but the faith of the church which forms Christians.[65] The "arch-sacramentality"

---

[61] Chauvet, *Symbol and Sacrament*, p. 446.

[62] See Chauvet, *Symbol and Sacrament*, pp.139-40.

[63] See Schmemann, *For the Life of the World*, pp. 139-40.

[64] Chauvet links the corporeality of faith to the Trinity – as corporeality in God: "And theology that integrates fully, and *in principle*, the sacramentality of faith requires a consent to corporeality, a consent so complete that it tries to *think about God according to corporeality"* (*Symbol and Sacrament*, pp. 154-55).

[65] See Chauvet, *The Sacraments*, pp. 33-34.

and what we may call "arch-symbolicity" is born here. Before examining more closely the nature and implications of the corporeality of faith, let us pause and look at what else Chauvet says about symbol.

First, he is vulnerable to the criticism that the Western approach distinguished between symbol and reality. He says that symbol represents the real, not in a "real" but a "symbolical" way. In other words, it does not carry in itself the material reality (not even the material "value") of what it symbolises.[66] "What characterizes the symbol is not the material value in quantity or quality but its *relation* with the whole to which it belongs."[67] The ymbol cannot be isolated from that whole without being destroyed.

In this Chauvet deviates from the scholastics. He even says that

> it is impossible to transpose a symbolic element from one cultural or religious system into another or from one context (liturgical, for example) into another without causing it to produce effects completely different from those it had in its original system or its initial context.[68]

This raises difficult ecumenical questions. For example, could the Roman Catholic Church actually lift the Fourth Eucharistic Prayer out of its original (Greek and Orthodox) context and expect it to work in the Western Catholic context? Can Protestants have icons in their churches and expect people to understand their meaning? These questions come even before a more complicated one, i.e. whether, and under what circumstances, we can share the Eucharist with one another. Is a

---

[66] See Chauvet, *The Sacraments*, p. 72; Chauvet uses the following examples: one does not need a vast pool to symbolize the submersion into death with Christ in baptism; one does not need a large stone from the Berlin wall to symbolize Communist dictatorship.

[67] Chauvet, *The Sacraments*, p. 71.

[68] Chauvet, *The Sacraments*, p. 71; Chauvet uses the example of a gesture, which can be an effective symbol in an African liturgy but not in a Western one, or a posture that may be meaningful for celebrating liturgy with children but would not work with adults.

deep sharing of our symbols at all possible? For all the elements of the original context will never be present. But we could equally ask whether we can celebrate a liturgy today that was composed in the fourth century, given that we no longer live in that context. Or should we try to restore that context so as to be able to share in the symbol, which seems to be what Schmemann proposes?

Yet Chauvet's position is not lacking in a desire for communication and it is not exclusivist. In his work the net of relations in which the symbol has crystallised over time is carried in the symbol, and belongs to the process of "identification" or "recognition" of the symbol. He states:

> Such is without a doubt one of the major functions of the symbol: it allows all persons to *situate themselves as subjects* in their relation with other subjects or with the world of these other subjects ... or with their own worlds.[69]

But the recognition or identification of the symbol is possible "only inasmuch as the subjects are under the agency of the *Other*," binding subjects among themselves, subjecting them to a common "symbolic order" and allowing them to form a *community*. "Symbol is a mediator of identity only by being a *creator of community*."[70]

Not all reality is symbolic. Chauvet, like Tillich, distinguishes between sign and symbol[71] and yet "the symbol ... is in some way the *original language* of human beings."[72] Signs are

---

[69] Chauvet, *The Sacraments*, p. 73.

[70] Chauvet, *The Sacraments*, p. 74. Chauvet mentions the following features of the community: "language, tradition, ancestors, law, God (for the believer), Jesus or Mohammed (for Christians and Muslims), ideology (Marxist, for instance), and so on." Yet he does not ask whether all of them are a result of "being under the agency of the *Other*" or whether there is just one "*Other*" or several different ones.

[71] See Chauvet, *The Sacraments*, pp. 74-78; compare this to P. Tillich, *Dynamics of Faith*, and his "The Religious Symbol/Symbol and Knowledge," and "Biblical Religion and the Search for Ultimate Reality" in: Paul Tillich, *Main Works IV* (Berlin, 1987).

[72] Chauvet, *The Sacraments*, p. 77; here Chauvet moves from Til-

needed for scientific discourse, for, since signs do not participate in the reality they represent, they can aim at being as "objective" as possible. Signs transmit information. They are needed everywhere we need to know something. Yet signs are, even in those areas, complemented by the metaphorical or poetic presence of symbol, which is not "objective" in the sense of disengaged but participates in the reality it represents. Chauvet states that symbol is primary, and sign secondary, that *"language is in its essence primarily "poetic" or symbolic"* and that it is this symbolic or poetic language, the possibility to speak it, that makes humans human.[73] Symbol is corporeal – it creates a community. Symbolic language (including both knowledge and non-knowledge) enables us to express "the 'corporeality' of the faith"[74] and makes it possible. Language constitutes "a place" where we come into being.

What does Chauvet say about the corporeality or the *"archsacramentality* of the faith?"[75] It is symbolic, participatory; it enables the subject to recognise her or his identity within the wider whole, within the community, the church. Chauvet speaks of "the triple body which makes us into believers": first, the *social* body, the church with its network, interpretation of history, life and the universe; second, the *traditional* body, within which the church supports the whole of ritual, through references to the words and deeds of Christ attested by the apostolic witness of

---

lich's understanding to that of Ricoeur, to whom he refers in his footnotes. See P. Ricoeur, "Parole et symbole," *Revue des Sciences Religieuses* (1975): 142-61.

[73] Chauvet, *The Sacraments*, p. 78; here he refers to J. Lacan, *Ecrits* (Paris, 1966), p. 276. A similar statement can be found in B. Lonergan, who speaks of humans in terms of *zoon symbolikon*, "symbolic animals." See B. Lonergan, "First Lecture: Religious Experience," in: B. Lonergan, *A Third Collection* (Mahwah, 1985), p. 115.

[74] Chauvet, *Symbol and Sacrament*, p. 152.

[75] Chauvet (*Symbol and Sacrament*, pp. 154-55) links the corporeality of faith to the Trinity – as corporeality in God: "And theology that integrates fully, and *in principle*, the sacramentality of faith requires a consent to corporeality, a consent so complete that it tries to *think about God according to corporeality.*"

the Scriptures; third, the *cosmic* body of a universe received as a gift of the Creator, from which symbolic elements of water, bread and wine, oil are recognized as a "sacramental" mediation of God's acting in the Spirit.[76]

It is interesting that "the cosmic body" comes at the end here. It is not the continuity between the world and Christ to which we are invited, as we find in Schmemann,[77] the sacramental world as a condition for other sacraments, but rather a community, a body of interrelated subjects, which receives and recognises the world as a gift and takes "symbolic elements" of it to be transformed by the Spirit and to mediate God's actions sacramentally. Although the sacramental symbol carries in itself the whole of the world, Chauvet says, it does not carry it in a "real" way but "symbolically." It carries it in its language, in its structure of meaning, in its power to mediate new identity. We are symbolic beings, but, as such, we appropriate the world rather than participating in it. The primary materiality for the symbolic beings is their community – for Christians, the church, the celebrating assembly, which has given them identity. In this way faith is material but not in the sense of being rooted in the world, which would be symbolic as as a whole.

In Chauvet we find a weaker participation in the world but stronger participation in the church, "the church precedes the individual."[78] Chauvet is, like Schmemann, engaged in sacramental renewal, yet his position is formed against the background of the Catholic-Protestant debate and looks for ways to overcome the controversy and to express his Catholic view in a non-confrontational manner with the help of insights from contemporary philosophy and anthropology. His stress on the corporeality of faith is Catholic in the broadest sense of the word: it invites participation in the body of the church and stresses that there is no such thing as an individual faith. Having stated that, he opens some traditionally more Protestant themes and appropriates them for Catholicism, as was stated earlier. *Sola fide* has

---

[76] Chauvet, *Symbol and Sacrament*, p. 152.

[77] See Schmemann, *For the Life of the World*, pp. 139-40.

[78] Chauvet, *The Sacraments*, p. 31.

shifted from an individual to a corporeal faith; *sola gratia* is interpreted in terms of an irreducible gift, challenging our value systems; *sola scriptura* is widened and the Scripture is placed in the context of the celebrating community; *Solus Christus* is taken through the critique of temptations of immediacy – and translated as mediated through the church and opens space for what Chauvet calls respecting God's difference.[79] The theme of the immediate presence of Christ, whether in the world or in the sacrament, needs, according to Chauvet, perhaps the most attention, because it can give us false solutions and raise obstacles to being grateful and generous, which are the two key components of being Christian.

Real Presence and Real Absence

Chauvet emphasises the "materiality" of faith in contrast to what he calls "a nostalgia for an ideal and immediate presence to oneself, to others, and to God."[80] Faith, to be Christian faith, must leave a seal, a character, on one's body, the character testifying to a belonging to the Father, Son and the Holy Spirit, in the body of the Church, by means of participating in her tradition, receiving and offering the universe as a gift. In this light he interprets the story of the disciples going to Emmaus.[81] Here he starts with a key question: "How does one pass from non-faith to faith?"[82] In order to arrive at an answer, Chauvet analyses the structure of the turn-around, the transformation, that gradually takes place in the disciples in that story:

---

[79] See Chauvet, *The Sacraments*, pp. 39-40.

[80] Chauvet, *Symbol and Sacrament*, p. 154. In this Chauvet is a true son of Aquinas, who argued for a mediated presence of God over against Bonaventure's immediate presence. However, unlike Aquinas, Chauvet disregards the other position, without exploring its possibilities.

[81] Cf. Luke 24:13-35. Chauvet returns to this text in *The Sacraments* and sees it as key for understanding the structure of Christian identity. Here (cf. pp. 20-28) he complements it by the story of the baptism of the Ethiopian (Acts 8:26-40) and the first account of Saul's conversion (Acts 9:1-20).

[82] Chauvet, *Symbol and Sacrament*, p. 161.

In the first section of the story (vv.13-17, up until their first stopping on the road), the two disciples have in effect abandoned their mission; in turning away from Jerusalem, they are also in effect turning their backs on their previous experience with Jesus. They talk between themselves, each a sort of mirror-image of the other, tossing back and forth the same expression of a definite postmortem on the failed mission of theirs. Consequently, their eyes are "kept from recognising him"; their spirits, like their eyes, are shut. For that matter, everything is shut. They have allowed themselves to be sealed up together with the dead body of Jesus in the constricted place of his death, the sepulcher, whose mouth has been blocked with a huge stone. Their past is dead; in any case, it has no future.[83]

Chauvet points to a transition from a dualistic to a triangular relation, when, instead of speaking to each other in a closed circle, they open themselves to a stranger. He enters into a conversation with them, and lets them name their situation, lets them tell their story. He first appeals to their memory, then makes a link with the Scriptures: "remember ... slow of heart, all that the prophets have declared ... everything ... must be fulfilled" (Luke 24:25-27), and offers a rereading of all the Scriptures (cf. Luke 24:44-45). Chauvet says:

> Instead of holding forth with self-assured pronouncements *on* God, one must begin by listening to a word as the word *of* God. The reference to the *Scriptures as a third agency* plays a role that is of capital importance here. In allowing Jesus to open the Scriptures for them, the two disciples begin to enter into an understanding of the "real", different from what they previously thought evident.[84]

They urge the stranger to stay and, in his breaking bread, when his word becomes flesh, their eyes begin to open and they recognise the stranger in his radical strangeness. But their eyes open to an emptiness as he vanishes from their sight. But it is an emptiness full of presence. The disciples recognise the Risen

---

[83] Chauvet, *Symbol and Sacrament*, p. 167.

[84] Chauvet, *Symbol and Sacrament*, p. 168.

Lord and receive this recognition as a gift of good news and return it as a gift in terms of Christian witness. Chauvet emphasises that one is not possible without the other. He states: "In the last analysis, faith can exist only if it expresses itself in a life of *witness*."[85]

Chauvet seems to identify immediate presence with the real presence. Therefore he speaks of the symbolic presence not as unreal presence but as presence that carries in itself and reveals its opposing quality – real absence. Christ is not here, he has disappeared from our eyes to help us find him in our hearts, in our community. Yet Chauvet does not want to idealize the church. She is the "topos," the place where the sacramental is present, revealing the opposing qualities of the presence and absence of God:

> Those who reject the Church in order to find Christ by themselves misunderstand [Christ has departed] .... But those who live too comfortably in the Church also misunderstand it: they are then in danger of forgetting that the Church is not Christ and that if, in faith, it is recognized as the privileged place of his presence, it is also, in this same faith, the most radical mediation of his absence .... The Church radicalizes the vacancy of the place of God.[86]

The blank space of God, then, Chauvet calls the "anti-name of God, the Spirit ... which, while fully of God's very self, works to subvert in us every idolatrous attempt at manipulating God (whether at the conceptual, ethical or ritual level) ...."[87]

Still, the church is where we are given a share in faith, where we learn gratitude and generosity. For Chauvet, a Christian life and a Christian identity is unthinkable without the church. His strong concept of the church and weaker concept of the world would run the risk of restricting God's action for

---

[85] Chauvet, *Symbol and Sacrament*, p. 164.

[86] Chauvet, *Symbol and Sacrament*, pp. 177-78. He also points out that the church's mediation of Christ is a mediation of God's *kenosis*. See *Symbol and Sacrament*, p. 509.

[87] Chauvet, *Symbol and Sacrament*, p. 517.

Christians to the church and not being able to see God operating outside. But that is not Chauvet's position. As Christians we are engaged in a church, whether the Roman Catholic Church or another. We are not disengaged and thus cannot imagine the world from a neutral point of view, from a different point of view than that of the witnesses of the Lord. In this position we have to search for openness. Chauvet finds such an openness in sketching a theology of "the pastoral interview."[88] While in *Symbol and Sacrament* Chauvet stresses our epicletic bond with the Spirit, in *The Sacraments* he adds that the Spirit also blows where it wishes. He does not go back to the immediate presence of God, but states:

> it is important to constantly remember that the reign of God is wider than the church as institution and that the Holy Spirit is bound neither by sacraments nor – still less – by the discipline devised for their preparation, as indispensable as it may be. All this puts pastoral ministers on the spot concerning their own conversion. For in this domain, as in all other sectors of the mission, what counts above all is an inner attitude, a *spiritual potential*: that through which the Holy Spirit enables pastoral ministers to discern and welcome that part of the reign that comes to them and can come to them through persons who may be relatively distant from the ecclesial institution. The Spirit's subtlety is not on the side of rigorism; it is rather on this practical sixth sense, so precious in pastoral care, a sense to which the medieval theologians assigned the first place among the cardinal virtues and which they named "prudence."[89]

Conclusion

The initial question of this paper was how Schmemann's and Chauvet's notions of sacramentality could strengthen a conversion that would be personal as well as communal and would see the unity of the churches as a part of the journey towards unity with God. What is the potential of their sacramental theo-

---

[88] See Chauvet, *The Sacraments*, pp. 192-200.
[89] Chauvet, *The Sacraments*, p. 200.

logy for strengthening these areas? After having examined their theological positions, I will return to these questions, first evaluating their approaches and looking for areas where they can benefit from each other, and which are worthy of further investigation.

For both Schmemann and Chauvet conversion is communal first, before it can become personal, and both emphasize its non-individualistic nature. Schmemann emphasises that the church celebrating liturgy is a sign of conversion for the world, an image of the world's destiny. This celebration revitalises the image of God in ourselves. Our personal knowledge of God and our participation in God, the two poles of *theosis*,[90] are rooted in it. Conversion has a relational character. Therefore, Schmemann, together with other Orthodox theologians, can claim that our knowledge of God and participation in God unite us with God, that both of these aspects of *theosis* are personal but not individualistic. The process of becoming united with God also involves joining with one another. Or should we also say that if we want to be united with God, we have to be united with one another? Schmemann leaves this implication open.

For Chauvet, conversion is primarily communal because its possibility is rooted in the celebrating church, which gives life to Christians.[91] The first gift one receives there – or as Chauvet says, the arch-sacrament, the source of all sacraments[92] – is the gift of faith. It is possible for him to speak of the arch-sacramentality of faith, because faith is corporeal: it has a body, the church. Chauvet speaks of this body in a triple way, as a social, traditional and cosmic body.[93]

The first gift, as Chauvet puts it, the arch-sacrament of faith, makes conversion something sacramental as well. We find this in both Chauvet and Schmemann, although for different rea-

---

[90] See Schmemann, *For the Life of the World*, p. 140.
[91] See Chauvet, *The Sacraments*, pp. 33-34.
[92] See Chauvet, *Symbol and Sacrament*, pp. 154-55.
[93] See Chauvet, *Symbol and Sacrament*, p. 52.

sons. For both liturgy and personal piety do not stand in opposition; the latter flows from the former.

Schmemann says that in liturgy the whole of our existence is taken up into the "all embracing vision of life."[94] And in this vision we are brought to recognise the goodness of God in creation, in the incarnation and in sanctification, the goodness of God, whose intention for us is to participate in divine life. Schmemann speaks of the arch-sacramentality of the world, for in creating the world through *Logos* God has started communicating this intention to us.[95] The sacramentality of conversion follows directly from this, as in conversion we return to and are embraced by God's intention. In Schmemann's holistic vision, the world, the church and the Kingdom do not stand opposed to one another but find their salvific relation. This brings about conversion and gives meaning to it. Schmemann yet again emphasises that conversion, as well as a mission of the church in the world, grows from the mutual relationship between knowing and celebrating.[96]

What is interesting is that Schmemann operates both with the sacramentality of the world, given by creation, and with the sacramentality of the church, instituted by Christ and fulfilled by the Holy Spirit. He does not use the Fall as the key for understanding the world or sin for understanding conversion. He starts with the goodness of God being present in creation and in each person and emphasises the continuity of the goodness of God operating in the world, announcing the end of its turning away from God, of the discontinuity brought about by sin.[97] The church is the place of conversion in the first place, as the church celebrates the transformation of this world into the Kingdom. She is a passage into the Kingdom. Thus we cannot live in our churches without desiring unity with God and with one another, without allowing the Kingdom to break through to them. In the liturgical celebration every church renounces self-

---

[94] Schmemann, "Liturgy and Theology," pp. 51-52.
[95] See Schmemann, *For the Life of the World*, pp. 139-40.
[96] See Schmemann, *Liturgy and Life*, p. 22.
[97] See Schmemann, "Between Utopia and Escape," p. 7.

sufficiency – it is a celebration of relationship and self-sufficiency would be seen as an alienation from this relationship; it would be against Schmemann's participatory theology.

The Eucharist is the primary symbol of this relationship. In the Eucharist "the whole of creation is in Christ, by the power of the Holy Spirit, offered to God, and partakes of Christ's immortal life at His table in His Kingdom."[98] Yet in practice this partaking has different modes and is affected by the division of the church. In Schmemann's theology no one is completely outside of the Eucharistic celebration, outside of the church, for the whole of creation is included. Needless to say, this inclusion is something different from being able to receive communion. And if liturgy uniting us with God and with one another is so important, then not being able to share communion together is clearly highly problematic. The situation which permits this is sinful, and we, not only at the individual level but also at the communal level as churches, need to be converted.

Schmemann is convinced that the condition for *intercommunio* is the preservation of the full and unaltered faith and traditions, which for him – and this is ecumenically problematic – means in the Orthodox Church.[99] Although he frequently calls his own church to conversion, other churches seem for him to be further away from this condition. There is a further issue. We celebrate and recognise conversion. It seems that it is not something we can initiate. Our cooperation with God's grace is seen by Schmemann more in terms of living out what has been revealed to us in liturgy. So to speak about striving for church unity, or doing something about it, linking conversion more to human reality, may seem alien to Schmemann's theology.[100] Unity is here since the beginning of the world, according to Schmemann. "How things are with God" and "how they are

---

[98] Schmemann, "Ecclesiological Notes," note 3.

[99] See Morrill, *Anamnesis as Dangerous Memory*, p. 76.

[100] This is also why he does not have much time for liberation theology or even movements trying to appropriate liturgy for contemporary people. He sees them as betrayals of theology. See, e.g., Schmemann, *For the Life of the World*, p. 147, and *The Eucharist*, pp. 9-10.

celebrated in liturgy" is such a strong precedent that it at times overshadows the sensitivity to how our fellow brothers and sisters experience them here and now, how they are affected by them here and now. And in this I agree with Morrill's criticism that Schmemann's *theologia gloriae*, however good it is, needs complementing by a *theologia crucis*, that his "theology from above" needs to be complemented by a "theology from below," which would help it to become truly incarnational, which is what Shmemann wants.[101]

For Chauvet, conversion is sacramental because it is an act of faith. He links it to liturgy, but he recognises more explicitly than Schmemann other sources of conversion apart from liturgy, such as the Scriptures or ethics.[102] Conversion is sacramental, because it is rooted in our communication with God and with each other, because, as such, it touches the structures of our being and understanding.[103] Similarly to Schmemann, Chauvet emphasises that being and understanding are interwoven. Conversion is not a matter of explaining the world in its totality but one of seeing the world with the eyes of faith and living a life as God's witnesses. Symbols of faith, including the symbol of conversion, create a community where conversion comes into being.[104] Chauvet then expands this community and at the ultimate horizon it carries within itself the whole *kosmos*, all creation. Yet Chauvet makes the problematic distinction between the symbolic and the real, which Schmemann rejects. Chauvet employs more the language of appropriation than that of participation. This weakens our bonds with the world as it was created but strengthens our active work in the world.

Chauvet's theology develops the dialectics between the real presence and the real absence of God in the world and in the church. His notion of sacramentality allows talk of the privileged place of God's presence but also the most radical demonstration of the recognition that none of the things which testify

---

[101] See Morrill, *Anamnesis as Dangerous Memory*, p. 129.

[102] See Chauvet, *The Sacraments*, pp. 29-31.

[103] See Chauvet, *The Sacraments*, p. 31.

[104] See Chauvet, *Symbol and Sacrament*, p. 152.

to God are God. The church is not only the place of God; it also "radicalizes the vacancy of the place of God."[105] Conversion is required for both; both need the eyes of faith. The empty place of God is filled by the Spirit and it calls to conversion, it "subverts in us every idolatrous attempt at manipulating God";[106] it teaches us gratitude and generosity.

For us, these can be the keys to Christian unity. They are accompanied by a recognition that the reign of God is wider than any of our churches and call us to rediscover the inner attitude of openness to the Spirit, an openness rooted in our "body" – in the places we inhabit – and in faith. We must recognize that openness to the Spirit is one movement with the openness to the other and that our need of the Spirit is also bound up with the need of the other. Here Chauvet's theology, in particular Chauvet's pastoral interview,[107] can bring new life and movement to issues concerning which church has most faithfully kept the full and unaltered tradition, for here Schmemann's response is less then satisfactory.

Schmemann's strong point lies in his cosmology, in his inclusion of all creation in the celebration of our participation in divine life. His participatory theology, however, needs a stronger emphasis on history, and a better evaluation of human struggles for making this world and the church a better place in which to live. This can be achieved by a more consistent application of his own principles. To expand his understanding of tradition,[108] and to offer a better relation between liturgy and other sources of Christian conversion, he needs an inspiration from elsewhere, and Chauvet's approach may be of service.

---

[105] Chauvet, *Symbol and Sacrament*, pp. 177, 178, 509.

[106] Chauvet, *Symbol and Sacrament*, p. 517.

[107] See Chauvet, *The Sacraments*, pp. 192-200.

[108] In practice Schmemann often reduces tradition to the writings of the Church Fathers of the second and third centuries, of which he says that they are contemporary in any time and that it is not up to us to expand or appropriate them but rather to step into their experience. See Schmemann, *For the Life of the World*, p. 146.

Chauvet's strong point lies in his dialectics between the presence and the absence of God, which renew the place of the Spirit for conversion and for a Christian life as well as the recognition of the fact that we are the witnesses of God, that we are the church, the body, that now stands in the empty place of God. His theology can be expanded, when it comes to the relation of the world to the Spirit and it can benefit from the yet more radical reading of symbol in Schmemann, which does not presuppose the split between symbolic and "real" reality.

Both theologians are important when we deal with the corporeal and sacramental dimensions of conversion and yet application of their theology to practical issues concerning the lack of church unity – and often the lack of desire for it – still needs to be done.

Epilogue

Bernd Jochen Hilberath

"On the Way to *Koinonia* – Church Communion in Transition" was the theme of the 13th Academic Consultation of the *Societas Oecumenica*. In many respects this meeting stood as a sign of transition: for the first time a consultation of the *Societas* took place in a southeast European country. Since 1989 Europe has been continually finding itself in phases of transition, and possibly in a completely new one following the rejection of the European Union Constitution in France and the Netherlands, which renders the discernment of future paths at present impossible. In some Orthodox countries a phase of real tension has emerged with the revival of the Uniate churches. Now that a new pope, Benedict XVI, stands at the head of the Roman Catholic Church, many wait nervously for ecumenical signals from the Vatican. The churches of Europe find themselves both with internal tensions and in tense ecumenical relationships. Above all, however, they are called to accompany supportively and critically the phase of the transition of Europe itself into a united Europe. Since the churches are not ends in themselves, this orientation *ad extra* is to be warmly welcomed. European ecumenists have recognised that these changes can also mean a change in the perspective of how church community can be formed and lived out. Churches are on the way to communion (*koinonia*) and this is happening in an epochal phase of transition that offers dangers and opportunities. This also was something the Academic Consultation in Sibiu demonstrated.

What differences remain with respect to the position of the churches in their societies (nations)! What differences arise from their individual histories and from their own traditions! Without question, the churches could show how a united Europe, in which the valuable particularities of countries and peoples are not made uniform, could come into being and grow. But are they in a position to do so? Ideas as to what is necessary for a church community or for mutual recognition as authentic forms of the one church of Jesus Christ are still very divided. Hence, there are different evaluations of what individual churches have to leave behind on the journey. There were calls repeatedly in Sibiu for the conversion not only of individuals but also of churches, as the *Groupe des Dombes* so strikingly put it. But how strongly is the readiness for conversion already in place? It cannot be overlooked that in the relationships of the churches to one another the same tendencies show themselves as can be noted in the political changes in Europe. The fall of the Wall in no way brought about the unification of the previously divided states; even in Germany the unity has not been achieved in every respect. Rather, the desire for self-affirmation through insisting on their own traditions and history has arisen. Old scores are settled. Instead of unity, we see a plurality that certainly has not made – and, moreover, does not clearly make – the idea of an approaching unity self-evident or, at any rate, anything more than an economic union.

Is economic union the best-case scenario? But can we then speak of at least an ecumenical union? European Christians seem a long way from that, too. For they too display ample tendencies to seek and affirm their identities through distinction from others. So, to be Catholic would mean not to be Protestant and to be Protestant would mean, more than anything else, not to be Roman Catholic, etc. The churches are still seeking a way between an identity-robbing uniformity and a pluriformity which no longer enables unity. Unity in reconciled difference – this formula of the ecumenical movement still has to pass the reality test.

Europe is growing together step by step and will, it is to be hoped, continue further down this road. Is such a step-by-step journey to the goal imaginable with respect to the churches as well? For some churches it is indeed so, but others appear to have an all or nothing approach to unity, so there is no possibility of a gradual coming together. Can this gulf be bridged?

It is no accident that for the next Consultation, which will be held in Prague in 2006, the following theme was chosen: "The Ecumenism of Life as Challenge for Academic Theology." The ecumenical movement can progress only if the living together of Christians from different churches progresses where they live. Ecumenical theology, which has achieved so much in the past decades, and the ecumenical contacts of church leaderships stand in service to the people of God, who wish again to be one. Christians at the bases are, however, not the object of ecumenical action but the subjects of faith. Theology understands itself as reflection on the practice of faith. It pays attention, then, to the faith of people, especially to the *sensus fidelium*. For some time the key term in the ecumenical world has been "the ecumenism of life." If this means that church community arises from and in the specific living together of people, then theology and the church leaderships, in their own ways, have to attend to what is going on in this ecumenism of life, which theologies are implicity or explicity directing it. This does not entail a capitulation to the factual, which could be something feared by those who in principle mistrust people or for whom the inductive method of theology cannot be trusted. It is rather much more about the mutual relation of life (praxis) and reflection (theology), so that the insights of faith and theology which are gained there are also received by the church leaderships, so that the ecumenical movement gains commitment. Does the church community show itself to be in transition in the ecumenism of life? And may we hope that this is a transition to mutual recognition? Or will – as in political Europe – the consensus already achieved be terminated and what was commonly recognised be placed in question?

The *Charta Oecumenica* stood at the heart of the consultation. By means of a concrete example the state of ecumenical efforts was to be tested and the profile of future tasks outlined. This *Charta* can above all be described as a document of the ecumenism of life. Of course, the question arises as to how such movements can be more fruitfully allied with specialised theological ecumenism. Theology does not exist for its own sake, but ecumenical movements at the base or among church leaderships do not emerge without theology. With reference to Kant, one could say: theological ecumenism without the ecumenism of life is empty; ecumenism of life without ecumenical theology is blind.

The consultation in Sibiu confirmed the experience that direct contacts and meeting face to face cannot be replaced by the reading of papers. To the reception of challenging texts belongs the mutual reception of people. This can accurately be termed hospitality. It was given in Sibiu. When will it also occur as Eucharistic hospitality, which would already be a decisive step on the road to definitive *koinonia*?

Appendix

CHARTA OECUMENICA

Guidelines for the Growing Cooperation among the Churches in Europe

"Glory be to the Father, and to the Son, and to the Holy Spirit"

As the Conference of European Churches (CEC) and the Council of European Bishops' Conferences (CCEE)* we are, in the spirit of the Messages from the two European Ecumenical Assemblies of Basel (1989) and Graz (1997), firmly resolved to preserve and develop the fellowship that has grown up among us. We give thanks to the Triune God for guiding our steps towards an ever deeper fellowship through the Holy Spirit.

Various forms of ecumenical co-operation have already proved themselves. Christ's prayer is: "… that they may all be one. As you, Father, are in me and I am in you, may they also be in us, so that the world may believe that you have sent me" (John 17:21). If we are to be faithful to this prayer, we cannot be content with the present situation. Instead, aware of our guilt and ready to repent, we must strive to overcome the divisions still existing among us, so that together we may credibly proclaim the message of the Gospel among all people.

Listening together to God's word in Holy Scripture, challenged to confess our common faith and to act together in accordance with the perceived truth, let us bear witness to the love and hope which are for all people.

Europe – from the Atlantic to the Urals, from the North Cape to the Mediterranean – is today more pluralist in culture than ever before. With the Gospel, we want to stand up for the dignity of the human person created in God's image and, as churches together, contribute towards reconciling peoples and cultures.

In this spirit, we adopt this charter as a common commitment to dialogue and co-operation. It describes fundamental ecumenical responsibilities, from which follow a number of guidelines and commitments. It is designed to promote an ecumenical culture of dialogue and co-operation at all levels of church life, and to provide agreed criteria for this. However, it has no magisterial or dogmatic character, nor is it legally binding under church law. Its authority will derive from the voluntary commitments of the European churches and ecumenical organisations. Building on this basic text, they can formulate their own local addenda, designed to meet their own specific challenges and resulting commitments.

---

* To the Conference of European Churches (CEC) belong almost all Orthodox, Protestant, Anglican, Old-Catholic and independent churches in Europe. In the Council of European Bishops' Conferences (CCEE) are represented all Roman Catholic Bishops' Conferences in Europe.

I.

WE BELIEVE IN
"ONE HOLY CATHOLIC AND APOSTOLIC CHURCH"

"(Make) every effort to maintain the unity of the Spirit in the bond of peace. There is one body and one Spirit, just as you were called to the one hope of your calling, one Lord, one faith, one baptism, one God and Father of all, who is above all and through all and in all" (Ephesians 4:3-6)

1. Called Together to Unity in Faith

With the Gospel of Jesus Christ, according to the witness of Holy Scripture and as expressed in the ecumenical Nicene-Constantinopolitan Creed of 381, we believe in the Triune God:

the Father, Son and Holy Spirit. Because we here confess "one, holy, catholic and apostolic church" our paramount ecumenical task is to show forth this unity, which is always a gift of God.

Fundamental differences in faith are still barriers to visible unity. There are different views of the church and its oneness, of the sacraments and ministries. We must not be satisfied with this situation. Jesus Christ revealed to us on the cross his love and the mystery of reconciliation; as his followers, we intend to do our utmost to overcome the problems and obstacles that still divide the churches.

We commit ourselves

- to follow the apostolic exhortation of the Letter to the Ephesians and persevere in seeking a common understanding of Christ's message of salvation in the Gospel;
- in the power of the Holy Spirit, to work towards the visible unity of the Church of Jesus Christ in the one faith, expressed in the mutual recognition of baptism and in eucharistic fellowship, as well as in common witness and service.

II.

ON THE WAY TOWARDS THE VISIBLE FELLOWSHIP OF THE CHURCHES IN EUROPE

"By this everyone will know that you are my disciples, if you have love for one another" (John 13:35)

2. Proclaiming the Gospel together

The most important task of the churches in Europe is the common proclamation of the Gospel, in both word and deed, for the salvation of all. The widespread lack of corporate and individual orientation and falling away from Christian values challenge Christians to testify to their faith, particularly in response to the quest for meaning which is being pursued in so many forms. This witness will require increased dedication to Christian education (e.g. catechism classes) and pastoral care in local congregations, with a sharing of experiences in these fields. It is equally important for the whole people of God together to communicate the Gospel in the public domain, which also means responsible commitments to social and political issues.

We commit ourselves
- to discuss our plans for evangelisation with other churches, entering into agreements with them and thus avoiding harmful competition and the risk of fresh divisions;
- to recognise that every person can freely choose his or her religious and church affiliation as a matter of conscience, which means not inducing anyone to convert through moral pressure or material incentive, but also not hindering anyone from entering into conversion of his or her own free will.

3. Moving towards one another

In the spirit of the Gospel, we must reappraise together the history of the Christian churches, which has been marked by many beneficial experiences but also by schisms, hostilities and even armed conflicts. Human guilt, lack of love and the frequent abuse of faith and the church for political interests have severely damaged the credibility of the Christian witness.

Ecumenism therefore begins for Christians with the renewal of our hearts and the willingness to repent and change our ways. The ecumenical movement has already helped to spread reconciliation.

It is important to acknowledge the spiritual riches of the different Christian traditions, to learn from one another and so to receive these gifts. For the ecumenical movement to flourish it is particularly necessary to integrate the experiences and expectations of young people and actively encourage their participation.

We commit ourselves

- to overcome the feeling of self-sufficiency within each church, and to eliminate prejudices; to seek mutual encounters and to be available to help one another;
- to promote ecumenical openness and co-operation in Christian education, and in theological training, continuing education and research.

4. Acting together

Various forms of shared activity are already ecumenical. Many Christians from different churches live side by side and interact in friendships, in their neighbourhoods, at work and in their families. Couples in interdenominational marriages especially should be supported in experiencing ecumenism in their daily lives.

We recommend that bilateral and multilateral ecumenical bodies be set up and maintained for co-operation at local, regional, national and international levels. At the European level it is necessary to strengthen co-operation between the Conference of European Churches and the Council of European Bishops' Conferences (CCEE) and to hold further European Ecumenical Assemblies.

In the event of conflicts between churches, efforts towards mediation and peace should be initiated and/or supported as needed.

We commit ourselves

- to act together at all levels of church life wherever conditions permit and there are no reasons of faith or overriding expediency mitigating against this;
- to defend the rights of minorities and to help reduce misunderstandings and prejudices between majority and minority churches in our countries.

5. Praying together

The ecumenical movement lives from our hearing God's word and letting the Holy Spirit work in us and through us. In the power of this grace, many different initiatives now seek, through services of prayer and worship, to deepen the spiritual fellowship among the churches and to pray for the visible unity of Christ's Church. A particularly painful sign of the divisions among many Christian churches is the lack of eucharistic fellowship.

In some churches reservations subsist regarding praying together in an ecumenical context. But we have many hymns and liturgical prayers in common, notably the Lord's Prayer, and ecumenical services have become a widespread practice: all of these are features of our Christian spirituality.

We commit ourselves

- to pray for one another and for Christian unity;
- to learn to know and appreciate the worship and other forms of spiritual life practised by other churches;
- to move towards the goal of eucharistic fellowship.

6. Continuing in dialogue

We belong together in Christ, and this is of fundamental significance in the face of our differing theological and ethical positions. Rather than seeing our diversity as a gift which enriches us, however, we have allowed differences of opinion on doctrine, ethics and church law to lead to separations between churches, with special historical circumstances and different cultural backgrounds often playing a crucial role.

In order to deepen ecumenical fellowship, endeavours to reach a consensus in faith must be continued at all cost. Only in this way can church communion be given a theological foundation. There is no alternative to dialogue.

We commit ourselves

- to continue in conscientious, intensive dialogue at different levels between our churches, and to examine the question of how official church bodies can receive and implement the findings gained in dialogue;
- in the event of controversies, particularly when divisions threaten in questions of faith and ethics, to seek dialogue and discuss the issues together in the light of the Gospel.

III.

OUR COMMON RESPONSIBILITY IN EUROPE

"Blessed are the peacemakers,
for they will be called children of God" (Matthew 5:9)

7. Participating in the building of Europe

Through the centuries Europe has developed a primarily Christian character in religious and cultural terms. However, Christians have failed to prevent suffering and destruction from being inflicted by Europeans, both within Europe and beyond. We confess our share of responsibility for this guilt and ask God and our fellow human beings for forgiveness.

Our faith helps us to learn from the past, and to make our Christian faith and love for our neighbours a source of hope for morality and ethics, for education and culture, and for political and economic life, in Europe and throughout the world.

The churches support an integration of the European continent. Without common values, unity cannot endure. We are convinced that the spiritual heritage of Christianity constitutes an empowering source of inspiration and enrichment for Europe. On the basis of our Christian faith, we work towards a humane, socially conscious Europe, in which human rights and the basic values of peace, justice, freedom, tolerance, participation and solidarity prevail. We likewise insist on the reverence for life, the value of marriage and the family, the preferential option for the poor, the readiness to forgive, and in all things compassion.

As churches and as international communities we have to counteract the danger of Europe developing into an integrated West and a disintegrated East, and also take account of the North-South divide within Europe. At the same time we must avoid Eurocentricity and heighten Europe's sense of responsibility for the whole of humanity, particularly for the poor all over the world.

We commit ourselves

- to seek agreement with one another on the substance and goals of our social responsibility, and to represent in concert, as far as possible, the concerns and visions of the churches vis-à-vis the secular European institutions;
- to defend basic values against infringements of every kind
- to resist any attempt to misuse religion and the church for ethnic or nationalist purposes.

8. Reconciling peoples and cultures

We consider the diversity of our regional, national, cultural and religious traditions to be enriching for Europe. In view of numerous conflicts, the churches are called upon to serve together the cause of reconciliation among peoples and cultures. We know that peace among the churches is an important prerequisite for this.

Our common endeavours are devoted to evaluating, and helping to resolve, political and social issues in the spirit of the Gospel. Because we value the person and dignity of every individual as made in the image of God, we defend the absolutely equal value of all human beings.

As churches we intend to join forces in promoting the process of democratisation in Europe. We commit ourselves to work for structures of peace, based on the non-violent resolution of conflicts. We condemn any form of violence against the human person, particularly against women and children.

Reconciliation involves promoting social justice within and among all peoples; above all, this means closing the gap between rich and poor and overcoming unemployment. Together we will do our part towards giving migrants, refugees and asylum-seekers a humane reception in Europe.

We commit ourselves

- to counteract any form of nationalism which leads to the oppression of other peoples and national minorities and to engage ourselves for non-violent resolutions;
- to strengthen the position and equal rights of women in all areas of life, and to foster partnership in church and society between women and men.

9. Safeguarding the creation

Believing in the love of the Creator God, we give thanks for the gift of creation and the great value and beauty of nature. However, we are appalled to see natural resources being exploited without regard for their intrinsic value or consideration of their limits, and without regard for the well-being of future generations.

Together we want to help create sustainable living conditions for the whole of creation. It is our responsibility before God to put into effect common criteria for distinguishing between what human beings are scientifically and technologically capable of doing and what, ethically speaking, they should not do.

We recommend the introduction in European churches of an Ecumenical Day of Prayer for the Preservation of Creation.

We commit ourselves

- to strive to adopt a lifestyle free of economic pressures and consumerism and a quality of life informed by accountability and sustainability;
- to support church environmental organisations and ecumenical networks in their efforts for the safeguarding of creation.

10. Strengthening community with Judaism

We are bound up in a unique community with the people Israel, the people of the Covenant which God has never terminated. Our faith teaches us that our Jewish sisters and brothers "are beloved, for the sake of their ancestors; for the gifts and the calling of God are irrevocable" (Rom 11.28-29). And "to them belong the adoption, the glory, the covenants, the giving of the law, the worship and the promises; to them belong the patriarchs, and from them, according to the flesh, comes the Messiah" (Rom 9.4-5).

We deplore and condemn all manifestations of anti-Semitism, all outbreaks of hatred and persecutions. We ask God for forgiveness for anti-Jewish attitudes among Christians, and we ask our Jewish sisters and brothers for reconciliation.

It is urgently necessary, in the worship and teaching, doctrine and life of our churches, to raise awareness of the deep bond existing between the Christian faith and Judaism, and to support Christian-Jewish co-operation.

We commit ourselves

- to oppose all forms of anti-Semitism and anti-Judaism in the church and in society;
- to seek and intensify dialogue with our Jewish sisters and brothers at all levels.

11. Cultivating relations with Islam

Muslims have lived in Europe for centuries. In some European countries they constitute strong minorities. While there have been plenty of good contacts and neighbourly relations between Muslims and Christians, and this remains the case, there are still strong reservations and prejudices on both sides. These are rooted in painful experiences throughout history and in the recent past.

We would like to intensify encounters between Christians and Muslims and enhance Christian-Islamic dialogue at all levels. We recommend, in particular, speaking with one another about our faith in one God, and clarifying ideas on human rights.

We commit ourselves

- to conduct ourselves towards Muslims with respect;
- to work together with Muslims on matters of common concern.

12. Encountering other religions and world views

The plurality of religious and non-confessional beliefs and ways of life has become a feature of European culture. Eastern religions and new religious communities are spreading and also attracting the interest of many Christians. In addition, growing numbers of people reject the Christian faith, are indifferent to it or have other philosophies of life.

We want to take seriously the critical questions of others, and try together to conduct fair discussions with them. Yet a distinction must be made between the communities with which dialogues and encounters are to be sought, and those which should be warned against from the Christian standpoint.

We are committed

- to recognise the freedom of religion and conscience of these individuals and communities and to defend their right to practise their faith or convictions, whether singly or in groups, privately or publicly, in the context of rights applicable to all;
- to be open to dialogue with all persons of good will, to pursue with them matters of common concern, and to bring a witness of our Christian faith to them.

Jesus Christ, the Lord of the one Church, is our greatest hope of reconciliation and peace.
In his name we intend to continue on our common path in Europe. We pray for God's guidance through the power of the Holy Spirit.

"May the God of hope fill us with all joy and peace in believing, so that we may abound in hope by the power of the Holy Spirit" (Rom 15.13)

As Presidents of the Conference of European Churches and the Council of European Bishops' Conferences, we commend this Charta Oecumenica as a Basic Text to all the churches and Bishops' Conferences in Europe, to be adopted and adapted in each of their local contexts.

With this commendation we hereby sign the Charta Oecumenica, on the occasion of the European Ecumenical Encounter, on the first Sunday after the common celebration of Easter in the year 2001.

Strasbourg, 22 April 2001

Metropolitan Jérémie	Cardinal Vlk
President	President
Conference of	Council of European
European Churches	Bishops' Conferences

(Text downloaded from:
http://www.cec-kek.org/English/ChartafinE.htm)

Index

Ad Gentes 91
Assyrian Church of the East 141
Augsburg Confession
(see *Confessio Augustana*)

Baptism 2, 3, 10, 12, 13, 29, 32, 50, 63, 66-70, 88-89, 91-92, 94, 99, 100, 102, 114, 117, 120, 121, 132, 138, 139, 141, 148, 177, 187, 191, 206
Benedict XVI 137, 201
Berenger of Tours 176

Called to Common Mission 72, 73, 80, 81
Catholicity 38, 83-94, 95-104, 119
CCEE 1, 17-21, 23-25, 29-35, 37-39, 41, 119, 147, 205, 206, 209
CEC 1, 17-21, 23-25, 28, 29-35, 37-39, 41, 118, 119, 147, 205, 206, 209
CEC-CEE Joint Committee 17, 18, 19, 21, 23, 24, 31, 32, 33, 37-39, 41
Chaldean Church 141
Charta Oecumenica . . . 1, 2, 3, 7-12, 14, 15, 17-21, 25, 26, 28-33, 37-42, 84, 106, 118-22, 142, 203
Chauvet, Louis-Marie 163, 166, 167, 179-95, 198-200
Church of Sweden 7, 9, 10, 11, 13, 14, 67, 76
Colombo Statement . . . 85, 86
Conference on World Mission and Evangelism 87
Confessio Augustana 76, 77, 78, 134, 135, 138
Congregation for the Doctrine of the Faith 24, 79, 96, 97, 104

Contexuality 3, 29, 80, 89-94
Conversion 1, 5, 25, 26, 28, 29, 33, 34, 60, 88, 89, 101, 102, 156, 165-200, 202
Differentiated Consensus 35, 36, 38, 39, 41, 42

Eastern Catholic Churches 131, 136, 137
Ecumenical Assemblies (Basel, Graz) 2, 19-21, 30
Ecumenical Dialogue on Moral Issues 37
EKD (German Protestant Churches) 44, 63, 74, 128, 129, 134. 136, 138
Experience of God
(Religious Experience) 45, 146, 148, 149, 154-58, 160, 170, 189
Ethnicity
and Ethnic Identity . 3, 4, 84, 86-88, 96, 105, 106, 117, 119-24
Eucharistic Hospitality . . . 12, 29, 32, 36, 44, 58, 67-69, 72, 81, 120, 129, 138, 141-42, 204
Europe 1-3, 7, 10, 17-23, 42, 65-67, 71, 74, 84, 95, 105, 110, 112-16, 118-25
Evangelical Lutheran Church in Denmark 11, 114

"Facing Unity" 74, 75
Faith and Order 18, 38, 40, 88, 91, 100, 107, 123-24
Farrell, Bishop Brian 130
Free Churches 29, 139
Freedom of Conscience 26, 33

Gift of Authority, The 38
Giordano, Don Aldo 34

Groupe des Dombes 26, 89, 202

Heidegger, Martin 180, 183-84, 186,
Holy Spirit 32, 48, 50, 52, 88, 98, 99, 100, 102, 140, 142, 151, 157, 173, 177, 191, 194, 196, 197
Hryniewicz, Waclaw . 20, 24, 39, 40

Inculturation 83, 85, 87, 89, 100
Indonesia 4, 5
Intercommunion (see Eucharistic hospitality)
International Missionary Council 87
Interreligious Dialogue 104, 150-53

Joint Declaration on Justification 3, 11, 130, 139, 140
Jørgensen, Revd. S. R. 11
Kasper, Cardinal W. 128, 137, 142
Koinonia 1, 37, 39, 75, 91, 93, 99, 100, 101, 104, 105, 114-15, 127, 142, 201

Lehmann, Cardinal K. ... 24
Leuenberg Fellowship and *Concordia* 8, 65, 69, 74, 77, 84, 106, 112, 116, 131, 135, 136, 138, 139
Levinas, E. 184
Life and Work ... 84, 106-08, 123
Lima Text 2, 88
Liturgy of Catechumens 8, 50-52, 54
Liturgy of the Faithful 8, 52-54

Lutheran-Anglican Dialogue 69-73
Lutheran-Baptist/Mennonite Dialogue 67-69
Lutheran-Methodist Dialogue 66-67
Lutheran-Orthodox Dialogue 74
Lutheran-Roman Catholic Dialogue 74-76
Lutheran World Federation (LWF) 76, 77, 82 85-86, 131
Lumen Gentium 91, 97, 132, 137, 182

Meissen 69, 70, 71, 139
Metaphysics, critique of in relation to Eucharist 180, 183, 184, 185
Ministry 70, 71, 73, 75, 77-78, 82, 83, 88, 92, 94, 100, 102, 121, 138
Missio Dei 97
Morrill, B. 169, 197, 198

Nairobi (5th General Assembly of WCC) 91, 101
Nationalism 83, 86, 87, 105-07, 109-12, 114-16, 120-23, 125
Nicene-Constantinopolitan Creed 22, 29, 53, 54, 102

Oldham, J.H. 106-11, 125
Ordnungen 109, 110
Orthodoxy 1, 3, 7, 8, 12, 20, 22-26, 28, 32, 37, 39-41, 43-61, 66, 74, 102, 105, 111, 118, 119, 122, 127, 131-33, 136-40, 143, 165-68, 172-74, 179, 187, 195, 197, 201

Pontifical Council for Promoting Christian Unity 38, 130, 199, 141
Porvoo 9, 10, 64, 71, 130

Postmodernity and the crisis of modernity 143, 145-47, 148, 153, 157, 159
Praying Together 27, 30, 31, 36
Proselytism 3, 20-23, 25, 27, 33, 35
Protestant Churches (in general) 1, 4, 7, 9, 11, 15, 25, 28-30, 32, 39-41, 63, 65, 69, 92, 109, 111-19, 125, 127-36, 140, 177, 180, 187, 190, 202

Rahner, K. 147, 153
Raiser, K. 139
Ratzinger, Cardinal J. (see Benedict XVI)
Real Presence .. 163, 175-77, 181, 191, 193, 198
Reception of Ecumenical Dialogues 17, 18 20-21, 30, 42, 44, 55, 56, 60, 129-30, 197
Riano Statement 87, 88
Roman Catholic Church 1, 3, 13, 24, 25, 35, 66, 74, 91, 96-99, 101, 118, 125, 131, 132, 140, 141, 151, 152, 163, 187, 194, 201

Sacraments and Sacramentality 3, 8, 12, 14, 64, 65, 68, 70, 74-77, 82, 92, 100-01, 104, 120, 132, 137, 138, 143, 145-46, 158, 160, 162-63, 165-200
Salvation 33, 51, 54, 55, 57, 59, 70, 77, 95, 99, 156
Same-Sex Relationships 13-15
Schmemann, Alexander 163, 165-79, 180, 181, 184, 186, 188, 190, 194-200
Schreiter, R. 95
Skærved, P. V. 11
Societas Oecumenica 1, 5, 105, 127, 138, 142, 201
Symbols 85, 87, 91, 160, 162, 163, 166, 168-73, 176-200

Theology 5, 48, 94, 95, 96, 104, 113-15, 117, 124, 132-33, 140, 158-62, 165-69, 172, 174-85, 194, 195, 197-200
Theosis 49, 50, 57, 167, 195
Tradition 2, 7, 8, 14, 15, 27, 31, 34, 38, 39, 44, 45, 47, 48, 54, 55, 59, 60, 67-76, 77, 84, 93-96, 100, 102, 105, 107, 111, 115-17, 127, 131, 136, 138, 140, 141, 146, 148-51, 154, 155, 163, 166, 173-76, 179, 191, 197, 199, 202

Unitatis Redintegratio ... 132, 138, 139
United Evangelical Lutheran Church of Germany (see VELKD)

VELKD 63-65, 67-69, 75, 76, 81, 134, 136
WARC (World Alliance of the Reformed Churches) 85
WCC 13, 27, 35, 85, 88, 90, 91, 92, 129

Contributors

Kajsa Ahlstrand is a Research Fellow for the Church of Sweden. She has done research in the areas of theology of religions, interfaith relations, and religion in late modernity. Presently she is conducting a study on religion, health and spirituality in a local community in Sweden.

Maria Clara Lucchetti Bingemer teaches systematic theology at the Pontifical Catholic University in Rio de Janeiro (Brazil). She is the author of many books and articles and is also engaged in the area of spiritual direction.

Martien E. Brinkman is Professor of Ecumenical Theology in the Faculty of Theology at the Vrije Universiteit of Amsterdam (the Netherlands). He was president of the *Societas Oecumenica* from 2000 till 2004.

Peter De Mey is Professor of Ecclesiology and Ecumenism in the Faculty of Theology of the Catholic University of Leuven (Belgium). He is the chair of the Leuven Centre for Ecumenical Research and the current secretary of the *Societas Oecumenica*.

Anton Houtepen is Professor of Ecumenical and Intercultural Theology emeritus in the Faculty of Theology at the University of Utrecht (Netherlands). From 1990-1994 he was the president of *Societas Oecumenica* and until 2004 the director of the Interuniversity Institute of Missiological and Ecumenical Research in Utrecht.

Ivana Noble, a priest in the Czechoslovak Hussite Church, teaches in the Protestant Theology Faculty of Charles University, Prague. She is co-founder and former director of the Institute of Ecumenical Studies in Prague and also teaches at the International Baptist Theological Seminary in Prague.

Tim Noble is head of the Contextual Missiology programme at the International Baptist Theological Seminary in Prague, Czech Republic, and has studied, lived and taught in the UK and Brazil, as well as the Czech Republic.

Dorin Oancea, an Orthodox priest, is dean of the Andrei Saguna Faculty of Theology in Sibiu (Romania) and is also Professor of Philosophy of Religions there. He has long been active in the ecumenical movement.

Johannes Oeldemann, Roman Catholic, is Director of the Johann-Adam-Moehler Institute for Ecumenics, Paderborn (Germany), and treasurer of the *Societas Oecumenica*.

Oliver Schuegraf is a minister of the Evangelical Lutheran Church in Bavaria. At present he works in Coventry (UK) as Coordinator of the Community of the Cross of Nails at the International Centre for Reconciliation of Coventry Cathedral and as Chaplain at Coventry University.

Eddy Van der Borght is Associate Professor of Systematic Theology in the Faculty of Theology at the Vrije Universiteit of Amsterdam (the Netherlands) and is vice-president of the International Reformed Theological Institute.

CURRENTS OF ENCOUNTER

GENERAL EDITORS: Jerald D. Gort, Henry Jansen, Lourens Minnema, Hendrik M. Vroom, Anton Wessels

VOLUMES PUBLISHED OR AT PRESS

1   J.D. Gort, et al., eds.   *Dialogue and Syncretism: An Interdisciplinary Approach* (copublished with Eerdmans)

2   Hendrik M. Vroom   *Religions and the Truth: Philosophical Reflections and Perspectives* (with Eerdmans)

3   Sutarman S. Partonadi   *Sadrach's Community and its Contextual Roots: A Nineteenth-Century Javanese Expression of Christianity*

4   J.D. Gort, et al., eds.   *On Sharing Religious Experience: Possibilities of Interfaith Mutuality* (with Eerdmans)

5   S. Wesley Ariarajah   *Hindus and Christians: A Century of Protestant Ecumenical Thought* (with Eerdmans)

6   Makoto Ozaki   *Introduction to the Philosophy of Tanabe, According to the English Translation of the Seventh Chapter of the* Demonstratio *of Christianity*

7   Karel Steenbrink   *Dutch Colonialism and Indonesian Islam: Contacts and Conflicts, 1596-1950*

8   A.A. An-Na'im et al., eds.   *Human Rights and Religious Values: An Uneasy Relationship?*

9   Rein Fernhout   *Canonical Texts: Bearers of Absolute Authority (Bible, Koran, Veda, Tipiṭaka). A Phenomenological Study*

10   Henry Jansen   *Relationality and the Concept of God*

11   Wessel Stoker   *Is the Quest for Meaning the Quest for God? The Religious Ascription of Meaning in Relation to the Secular Ascription of Meaning*

12   Hendrik M. Vroom and Jerald D. Gort, eds.   *Holy Scriptures in Judaism, Christianity and Islam: Hermeneutics, Values and Society*

13   Nelson O. Hayashida   *Dreams in the African Church: The Significance of Dreams and Visions among Zambian Baptists*

14   Hendrik Hart et al., eds.   *Walking the Tightrope of Faith: Philosophical Conversations about Reason and Religion*

15   Hisakazu Inagaki and J. Nelson Jennings   *Philosophical Theology and East-West Dialogue*

16	Christine Lienemann-Perrin *et al.*, eds.	*Reformed and Ecumenical: On Being Reformed in Ecumenical Encounters*
17	Jerald D. Gort *et al.*, eds.	*Religion, Conflict and Reconciliation: Multifaith Ideals and Realities*
18	M. Dhavamony	*Hindu-Christian Dialogue: Soundings and Perspectives*
19	Ronald A. Kuipers	*Critical Faith: Toward a Renewed Understanding of Religious Life and its Public Accountability*
20	Martien E. Brinkman	*The Tragedy of Human Freedom: The Failure and Promise of the Christian Concept of Freedom in Western Culture*
21	Mercy Amba Oduyoye and Hendrik Vroom, eds.	*One Gospel — Many Cultures: Case Studies and Reflections on Cross-Cultural Theology*
22	Inus Daneel *et al.*, eds.	*Fullness of Life for All: Challenges for Mission in Early 21st Century. Essays in Honour of Jerald D. Gort*
23	C. Lienemann-Perrin *et al.*	*Contextuality in Reformed Europe: The Mission of the Church in the Transformation of European Culture*
24	Ton van Prooijen	*Limping but Blessed: Jürgen Moltmann's Search for a Liberating Anthropology*
25	J.D. Gort *et al.*, eds.	*Religions View Religions: Explorations in Pursuit of Understanding*
26	Pim Valkenberg	*Sharing Lights on the Way to God: Muslim-Christian Dialogue in the Context of Abrahamic Partnership*
27	Connie Aarsbergen-Ligtvoet	*Isaiah Berlin: A Value Pluralist and Humanist View of Human Nature and the Meaning of Life*

Volumes in this series are available from Editions Rodopi, Tijnmuiden 7, 1046 AK Amsterdam, the Netherlands, or 295 North Michigan Avenue - Suite 1B, Kenilworth, NJ 07033, USA